IMAGES
of America

THE WEST GEORGIA TEXTILE HERITAGE TRAIL

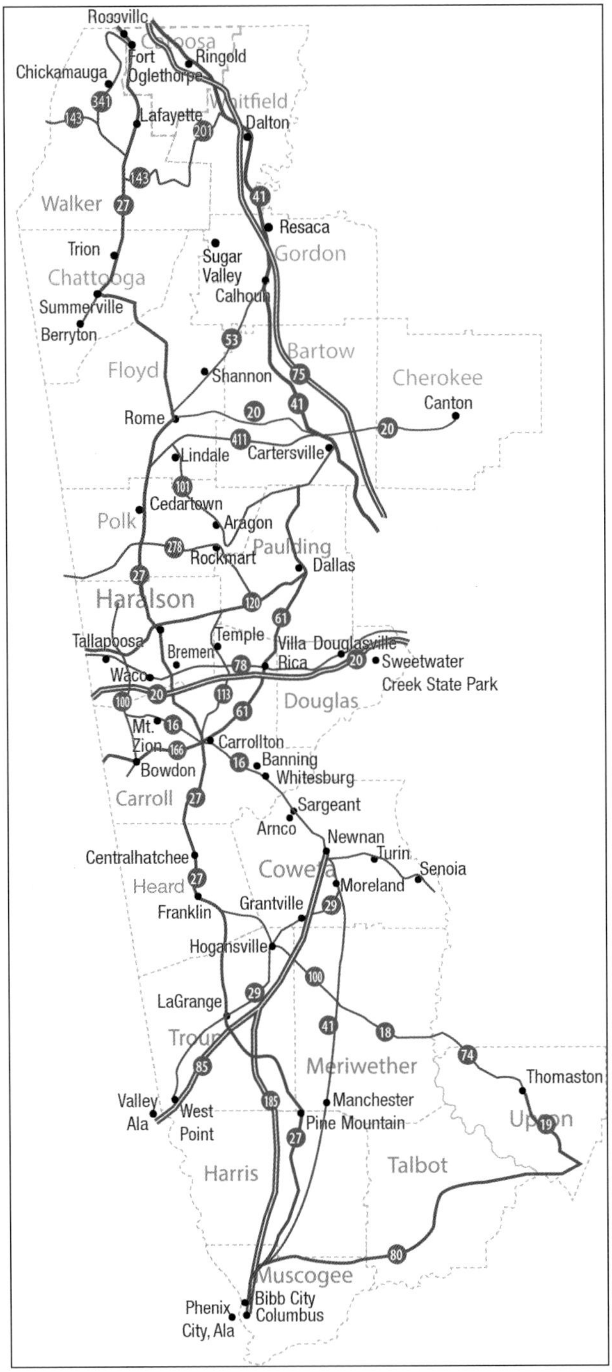

The West Georgia Textile Heritage Trail explores the rich heritage of the textile industry in west and northwest Georgia, from Columbus to Dalton. Following a broad swath along the US Highway 27 corridor, the trail highlights historic communities that played a vital role in the cotton, hosiery, apparel, chenille, carpet, and more recent textile industries. The trail is a heritage tourism initiative that promotes historic preservation and economic development while telling the significant stories that shaped the history and culture of the region. (Courtesy of the University of West Georgia Center for Public History.)

On the Cover: Women sew zippers in men's slacks at the Sewell Manufacturing Company plant in Temple, Georgia, in the summer of 1954. The region's apparel industry became a significant employer of women in Carroll and Haralson Counties in the mid- to late 20th century. This plant opened around 1950. (Courtesy Harold Brock family.)

IMAGES
of America

THE WEST GEORGIA TEXTILE HERITAGE TRAIL

The Center for Public History
at the University of West Georgia

ARCADIA
PUBLISHING

ISBN 978-1-4671-1520-9

Published by Arcadia Publishing
Charleston, South Carolina

Printed in the United States of America

Library of Congress Control Number: 2015944545

For all general information, please contact Arcadia Publishing:
Telephone 843-853-2070
Fax 843-853-0044
E-mail sales@arcadiapublishing.com
For customer service and orders:
Toll-Free 1-888-313-2665

Visit us on the Internet at www.arcadiapublishing.com

Contents

Acknowledgments 6

Introduction 7

1. The Southern Trail 11
2. The Central Trail 51
3. The Northern Trail 89

ACKNOWLEDGMENTS

This book was a collaborative project between faculty and students working on the West Georgia Textile Trail at the University of West Georgia. Ann E. McCleary and Keri P. Adams served as project directors and editors. McCleary, Adams, Jae Turner, Cecelia Stephens, Yanique Leonard, Chanell Lowery, Heather Rodriguez, and Mollie Dominy helped to research and write the captions. Kymberli Darling, Patrick J. Elias, Janae Hightower, and Rachel Opolka served as photography interns and contributed images. Debby Holcombe at UWG Publications and Printing prepared the maps. Dusty Dye and students Kamil McElwee, Lacey Lawrence, Dustin Klein, and Daniel Kellogg contributed to the publication as well.

Organizations and members who have contributed photographs include the Atlanta History Center, Bandy Heritage Center, Bartow History Museum, City of Bowdon, Bowdon Area Historical Society, City of Bremen, Cherokee County Historical Society, Chickamauga Public Library, Columbus State University, Coweta County Genealogical Society, Doug Roth Photography, Georgia Archives, Special Collections and Archives at Georgia State University, Gordon County Historical Society, Haralson County Historical Society, Heard County Historical Center and Museum, Hills & Dales Estate, Library of Congress, Newnan-Coweta Historical Society, Polk County Historical Society, Rockmart Historical Museum, Rome Area History Museum, Shaw Industries, Southeastern Quilt and Textile Museum, University of West Georgia Special Collections, Sanborn Library LLC, Thomaston-Upson Archives, Trion Public Library, Troup County Archives, City of Villa Rica, Watters District Council for Historic Preservation, Wayne State University, West Georgia Museum of Tallapoosa, and Whitfield-Murray Historical Society.

Individuals along the trail who have contributed to the project are Judy Alderman, Martha Allgood, W. Jeff Bishop, Ashley Callahan, Janet Cochran, Jennifer Detweiler, Elmira Eidson, Patricia Eidson, Douglas Flamming, John D. Fowler, Katherine Gallman, Trey Gaines, Deborah A. Goodson, Ima Gravitt, Susan Hamersky, Russ Harwell, Brad Hayes, Monica Haynes, Brian S. Hilliard, Allison Hudgins, Johnnie Huey, Ellen Johnston, Stefanie Joyner, Kathleen Mason, Melanie McClellan, Greg McCollum, Kaye Minshew, Sara Moore, Blynne Olivieri, Darwin B. Palmer, Terrell Parham Jr., Karen Payton, Gail Priest, Judy Rowell, Leon Shiver, Lydia Simpson, Ellen Tew, Carol Theune, Ellen Thompson, Teddy Williamson, Daniel Scott Wilson, Sharon Sewell, Dana Strack, Mignon Wessinger, Carlton Wood, Jane Powers Weldon, Robin Sewell Worley, and Kathy Young.

Funding for this project comes from the Callaway Foundation Inc. We appreciate the University of West Georgia Department of History and College of Arts and Humanities for their continued support of the Center for Public History.

Unless otherwise noted, all images are courtesy of the University of West Georgia Center for Public History.

Introduction

The textile industry has dominated the development of west and northwest Georgia, adding an industrial economy to an agricultural landscape. Few communities in this region remained untouched by the textile industry, from growing, ginning, and transporting cotton to manufacturing textile products. Production began in the early 19th century when the first mills were established in Columbus and continues through today with the carpet industry centered on Dalton. Over these two centuries, few lives and communities have been untouched by this industry, spanning from cotton to hosiery, chenille, apparel, carpet, and other textiles.

This book tells the story of the impact of the textile industry on the 19 counties in west and northwest Georgia that compose the West Georgia Textile Heritage Trail, a heritage tourism initiative created in 2011.

Textile production had its roots planted in Georgia soon after the American Revolution, when Eli Whitney, in collaboration with Catharine Green, invented the cotton gin in Chatham County in 1793. The cotton gin transformed cotton into a marketable commodity and became a familiar feature across the cotton fields of Georgia in the 19th century.

The manufacturing of cotton began in the northern states in 1790, when Slater Mill started spinning cotton into yarn in Rhode Island. The industry spread throughout the New England states over the next several decades. In 1814, Boston investors opened the first planned textile mill town of Lowell, Massachusetts, which introduced the power loom. Now, factories could process raw cotton into cloth in one factory. The creation of mill towns, with housing for workers, became popular in the north and spread into southern communities as well.

Georgians began to invest in building textile mills in the 1810s. These were small, water-powered cotton factories established along the fall line, a strip of land across the piedmont from Columbus to Augusta where rapids provided sufficient water power to operate the mills. In 1847, the Georgia legislature passed an act to encourage industrial development. Three years later, Georgia had 50 cotton and woolen mills producing coarse wool and cotton duck.

The west and northwest Georgia region participated in this antebellum boom in cotton manufacturing. Situated at the head of navigation for the powerful Chattahoochee River, Columbus quickly became a center of textile manufacturing. The first textile mill dates to 1838, and by 1850, Columbus boasted five textile mills. The Eagle Manufacturing Company was the largest of these. Established by New York–native William Young, the company operated 10,000 spindles and employed 500 people. Local entrepreneurs established smaller cotton mills along rivers in the region during the 1840s, including the Troup Factory near LaGrange, Bowen's Mill in Carroll County, New Manchester in Douglas County, and Trion in Chattooga County.

Georgia textile mills turned to military production during the Civil War. Columbus mills ranked among the top five producers for the Confederacy. Federal forces destroyed many of this region's manufacturing facilities, from the productive Columbus mills to the New Manchester mill. Trion avoided a similar fate when the owner reportedly told Gen. William T. Sherman that he was a "Union man" and only produced cloth for the Confederacy under duress.

Textile owners rebuilt soon after the Civil War. With great optimism, the owners of the largest Columbus mill reestablished their factory and named it the Eagle & Phenix Mills, incorporating the symbol of the phoenix rising from the ashes of war. Young added four more mills by 1876, increasing production four times over the antebellum years. A few new mills were constructed, such as the Wilcoxon Mill in Sargent in 1866. By 1880, Georgia boasted the largest number of spindles and looms among all southern states.

The greatest boom for cotton mill production in Georgia and this region occurred between 1880 and 1910, spurred by New South ideologies, financial opportunities, and new technology. *Atlanta Constitution* editor Henry Grady fervently pushed for a "Cotton Mill Campaign" in 1886, arguing that the South needed to rebuild the region economically and "bring the cotton factory to the cotton fields." In his vision of the New South, railroad lines would link cotton mills to markets in the South and the North. Northern investors and companies began to join southern industrialists to finance and build new mills, attracted by lower taxes, cheaper labor, and the absence of labor unions. The counties in this book boasted 48 cotton mills by 1910.

The new mills were large, multistory brick factories operated by efficient steam or electric power. This new technology allowed investors to construct mills in towns and cities along railroad lines, which sparked urban development and brought prosperity to many communities. These new factories produced cotton yarn, cloth, rope, and other products.

The Chattahoochee River Valley solidified its position as a cotton manufacturing center and symbolized this expansive growth in the New South period. By 1910, Columbus had nine mills, West Point had six, and LaGrange had five—the largest numbers among any towns in this book. With George Park Swift's Muscogee Mills and the Paragon Mills (established in 1888), Columbus was still one of the largest textile manufacturing centers in Georgia and the South. West Point and LaGrange were not far behind. Beginning in 1888, merchant Fuller E. Callaway Jr. established a series of nine mills known as the Callaway Mills that transformed LaGrange into a textile powerhouse.

In the early 20th century, some cotton mills began making tire cord and other textile products for the new automobile industry. These operations proved costly, leading owners to sell mills to national companies. In the 1920s, Goodyear Tire and Rubber Company bought mills in Cedartown and Cartersville and built a third in Rockmart, and U.S. Rubber purchased the Stark Mill in Hogansville in 1931.

Cotton manufacturers usually built mill villages to maximize their profits and manage their employees. Workers left nearby farms and settled into company mill villages looking for a better life. Mill houses provided workers with convenient access to the workplace while helping the company create a stable workforce and establish a measure of control over their workers. Rows of housing surrounding the mills featured several different plans. Many were duplexes housing two families, while others were single-family homes. Workers rented homes, with the size and location based on the type of job the employee had or the number of family members working at the mill. Employees bought food and supplies at high prices from the company store, attended the mill church with a preacher hired by the company, and sent their children to the mill school. The mills supported baseball teams, concert bands, scout troops, parades, yard improvement campaigns, libraries, barbecues, and other social events.

Within these towns, mill workers built communities. They shared music and stories on the front porches of their homes and enjoyed holidays and celebrations together. They married other mill workers and created extended family networks within the village. The villages became, in the expression of many workers, "like a family."

Cotton mills employed primarily white families, including adults and children. White men obtained high-paying jobs as supervisors and mechanics, while white women and children operated the machines. Sometimes, widows moved to mill villages and sent their children to work in the factories to support the family. Lewis Hine, a photographer and reformer who worked for the National Child Labor Committee, came to this region to document children in the mills in 1909 and 1913. His powerful photographs taken here and in other southern mills encouraged state and national efforts to end child labor. However, it was not until 1938 that Congress passed the Fair Labor Standards Act to prohibit the employment of children under 16 in manufacturing.

In the segregated South, African Americans had fewer employment opportunities and received lower pay for their work. Black men worked "on the yard," in the cotton house, or in janitorial positions, while their wives and daughters found employment as domestics in the homes of white families in the mill village. Companies sometimes designated separate areas for African Americans to live on the edge of the mill town, if they provided housing at all.

The textile industry began to diversify beyond cotton in the early decades of the 20th century, as hosiery production followed the cotton mills south by 1900. Hosiery mills were established throughout west and northwest Georgia, but they became more common in the 1920s. These mills produced seamless hosiery and socks made of cotton, silk, and rayon for men, women, and children. Similar to cotton mills, they hired primarily white men and women, but later mills did not build company towns. With the growing popularity of the automobile, employees could now drive to work from homes in the country or other towns.

Work in the cotton factories began to change in the early 20th century. New technology required fewer operators, and companies brought in engineers to conduct studies about how to make the work process more efficient. Increasingly, the mills required workers to operate more machines and increase production, an effort operators called the "stretch-out." The decline in textile production during the Great Depression led to mill closings, decreased production, and more layoffs. Although the New Deal's National Industrial Recovery Act of 1933 offered some relief, requiring companies to meet new guidelines for employee hours, wages, and benefits, some companies did not follow these regulations. Cotton mills became fertile ground for unrest.

The General Textile Strike of 1934, called on September 1, energized workers throughout the South. "Flying Squadrons" of organizers from the United Textile Workers traveled by car to mills to encourage workers to join the strike. Many mills in this region experienced some strike activity, including Columbus, Cedartown, Newnan, and LaGrange, where violence ensued. Deaths were reported in a few places, including Trion. Gov. Eugene Talmadge declared martial law and sent the National Guard to arrest striking workers and exterminate the protests. The first arrests occurred in Sargent and at the East Newnan Cotton Mills, where the largely female strikers were rounded up and sent to detention campus. The strike ultimately proved unsuccessful, leading many strikers to be blacklisted and evicted from their homes.

Two other major sectors of the textile economy gained strength by the 1930s: chenille and apparel. Catherine Evans Whitener began selling hand-tufted bedspreads in 1900 around Dalton. Her work formed part of the handicraft revival blossoming in the southern Appalachian region at the turn of the 20th century. She and other local women used tufted yarn to create patterns on plain cotton sheets. North Georgia women began to sell bedspreads to tourists traveling to Florida along US Highway 41, part of the Dixie Highway. As chenille attracted a national market, merchants began to sell products to department stores in Atlanta, New York, and other major cities. Several companies in northwest Georgia mechanized chenille production in the 1930s by moving the tufting process out of the home and into small factories.

The apparel industry also took off in the 1920s, primarily in Carroll and Haralson Counties. At the time, most of the apparel industry was centered in northern cities, especially New York. Brothers Robert, Roy, and Warren Sewell moved their small but growing clothing business from Atlanta to Bremen in 1928. They chose this community because it had access to railroad lines and a good supply of labor. In 1934, the company opened a manufacturing plant in Bowdon. The Sewell family launched the development of the apparel industry in western Georgia.

World War II brought new military contracts to the textile and apparel industries in Georgia, cultivating economic prosperity after the leaner Depression years. All of the mills contributed in some way to the war effort, and workers now enjoyed more steady employment. Regional textile companies made uniforms as well as military supplies, including parachutes.

The textile industry continued to evolve after World War II. One area of tremendous growth during this period was the carpet industry, which developed from tufted chenille spreads. Carpet factories began to use the newly adapted tufting machines to make small scatter rugs, and eventually larger, room-sized rugs and wall-to-wall carpet. By the 1950s, tufted carpets were far cheaper and more popular than the woven woolen rugs made in the northern states. With the introduction of nylon by Dupont in 1957, the Dalton carpet industry boomed in northwest Georgia.

The apparel industry also grew in the post–World War II years. Still centered in Bremen and Bowdon, the industry now included several companies owned by various members of the Sewell family as well as former employees. Manufacturing plants spread throughout Carroll and Haralson Counties and expanded the range of products beyond men's suits to include women's clothing, windbreakers, and leisure suits. While most apparel companies were locally owned, national manufacturer Cluett, Peabody & Co. produced Arrow brand shirts in Bremen, Buchanan, and Douglasville. Although the apparel companies did not build mill villages, Bremen and Bowdon became, in essence, company towns filled with workers, especially in the boom years of the 1940s through 1960s.

The cotton and apparel industries faced increasing competition from Asia and Europe by the 1950s and 1960s. Trade laws contributed to lower prices for imported textiles and apparel. To remain competitive, some regional textile companies installed new technology developed for cotton mills, such as robotic machinery to make their operations more efficient, but these changes eliminated jobs for many workers. Other companies chose not to invest in the new machinery and closed. Some mills sold out to larger regional or national firms. In 1968, Milliken and Company bought the Callaway Mills. Milliken joined the carpet boom and shifted production from cotton products to tufted carpet printing, using computerized ink-jet technology to create carpet and rug designs.

Several mill owners transitioned to new types of products. The owners of the Trion Mill, purchased by Mount Vernon Mills, installed new machines in 1971 to produce denim and tap into the growing popularity of jeans. The grandson of the founder of Mandeville Mills in Carrollton closed the old mill in 1953 and opened a new company to make cotton rope and twisted yarns for upholstery, automobile seat covers, and knitted outerwear. His son transformed the plant by the 1980s to produce a popular, internationally known synthetic climbing rope.

Labor unions continued to try to organize in this region after World War II, demanding better pay and work conditions. Unions proved successful in some companies, but many workers still remembered the consequences of the 1934 strike and remained wary. Some company owners made their opinions against unions known to the workers, threatening to close plants if workers unionized and offering to provide comparable benefits. Unions never became common in this region.

In 1964, the federal Civil Rights Act required all businesses and industries to integrate their workforce. Until this time, Georgia textile manufacturing had remained segregated. Some tension occurred as companies enforced the national policy. White employees learned to accept working alongside and eventually being supervised by African American employees. African American—and increasingly, Latino workers—now find employment in many of the surviving manufacturing plants.

The North American Free Trade Agreement (NAFTA), passed in 1994, brought more change to the textile industry. NAFTA facilitates free trade by removing tariffs and other trade barriers between the United States, Canada, and Mexico. Many companies could not compete with the cheaper labor and production in other countries and some began to outsource their production to Asia and Central and South America. Hosiery mills and most cotton companies closed.

Other sectors of the textile industry continue, although sometimes on a reduced scale of operations. Regional apparel companies have received government contracts to make military uniforms, which have allowed them to continue some operations here. Carpet companies have added engineered hardwood floors to their repertoire of products. Dalton has become the center of the carpet industry in the United States, although LaGrange boasts two companies as well.

Today, the landscape and culture of west and northwest Georgia illustrates the textile heritage of this region. Some companies are still in operation, often with a rich heritage to share. Closed textile mills and plants remain in many cities, towns, and rural communities, surrounded by rows of mill village housing. Some mills have been restored as loft apartments or businesses. As historic buildings have burned or been torn down, community leaders and preservation groups are taking action to preserve what remains. Local residents who remember this history are fighting to save it through museums and archives that share exhibits and records about the textile industry. People throughout this region still reminisce and reflect upon their work in the mills and plants that formed an important part of their community.

This book tells the story of the people, places, products, and machines that weave together the West Georgia Textile Heritage Trail. Explore this region, learn about the cultural and economic landscape of the textile industry, and hear the stories that shaped these communities and the people.

One

The Southern Trail

Columbus anchors the southern end of the West Georgia Textile Heritage Trail, which follows the Chattahoochee River and US Highway 27. During the mid-19th century, the power generated by the Chattahoochee River and its tributaries determined where textile mills could thrive. The falls of the Chattahoochee at Columbus drop 125 feet in two-and-a-half miles, generating the waterpower that positioned the city to become a leading manufacturing center in the South. By the early 20th century, electricity freed mills from the river's bank. The trail follows the historical development of the industry east to LaGrange, Hogansville, Manchester, and Thomaston.

Community leaders and investors pooled resources, which frequently included northern capital, as "mill fever" spread across the landscape in the late 19th century. Industrial development depended upon the strengths of particular leaders, such as the Callaways in LaGrange, the Laniers in West Point, and the Hightowers in Thomaston. The success of the mills also came from the hundreds of men, women, and children who operated the spindles and looms.

The history of these textile mills is also connected through the products they made. During the mid-19th century, mills such as the Troup Factory near LaGrange and the Eagle Mill in Columbus produced an array of cotton cloth, yarns, and threads, including osnaburgs, kerseys, and cassimeres. After the Civil War, the production of cotton duck, a canvas-like cloth, dominated production for use in ship sails, tents, and covered wagons. Duck gained new value as an industrial fabric for the booming new rubber tire business for automobiles in the early 20th century.

As the textile industry began to decline after World War II, most cotton mills closed or were converted to new types of production. The Callaway Mills produced terry cloth towels, industrial fabrics, and carpet when Milliken purchased the company in 1968. In Columbus, where most mills closed, preservation advocates have worked to preserve the historic industrial waterfront.

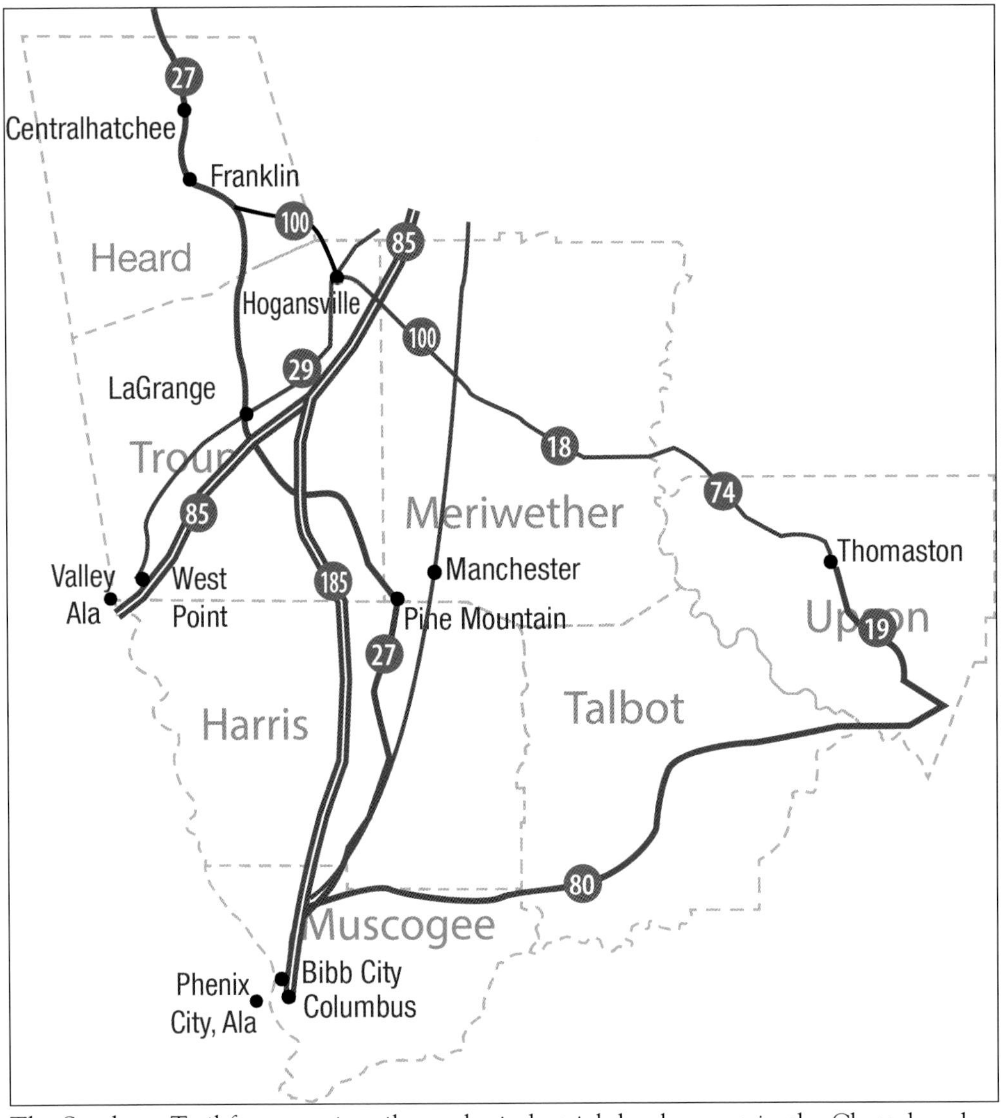

The Southern Trail focuses primarily on the industrial development in the Chattahoochee Valley but includes related mills that are just across the state line in Valley, Alabama, such as the Riverdale Cotton Mill and part of the Alabama-Georgia Manufacturing Company.

In 1848, Robertson, Leslie and Company converted a grist mill on Flat Shoals Creek near LaGrange into one of west Georgia's earliest textile mills. The Troup Factory produced osnaburgs by harnessing the creek's power with a waterwheel. A village of around 500 workers developed around the mill, which operated until 1902 when it moved to LaGrange as the Park Cotton Mills. (Courtesy Troup County Archives.)

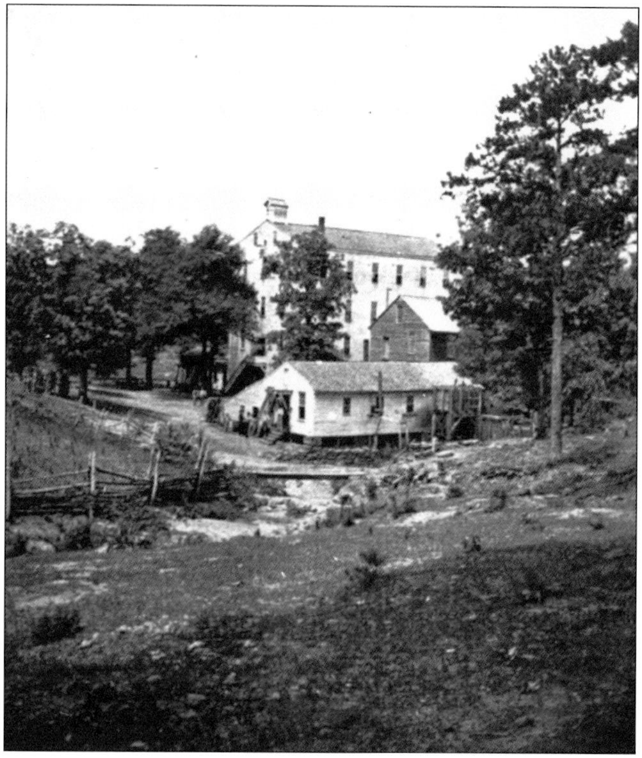

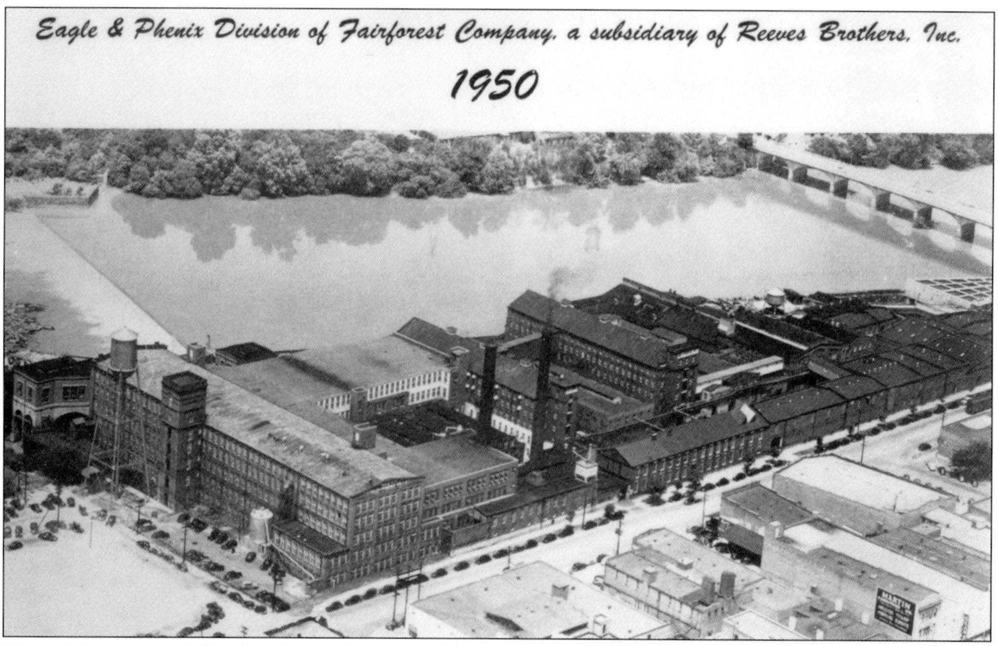

This 1950 view of the Eagle & Phenix Mill in Columbus shows the close relationship between the development of the textile industry and the Chattahoochee River. The rapidly falling course of the Chattahoochee generated power for large textile mills from West Point to Columbus. In 1851, William H. Young built the Eagle Mill along the most powerful stretch of falls at Columbus. (Courtesy Columbus State University.)

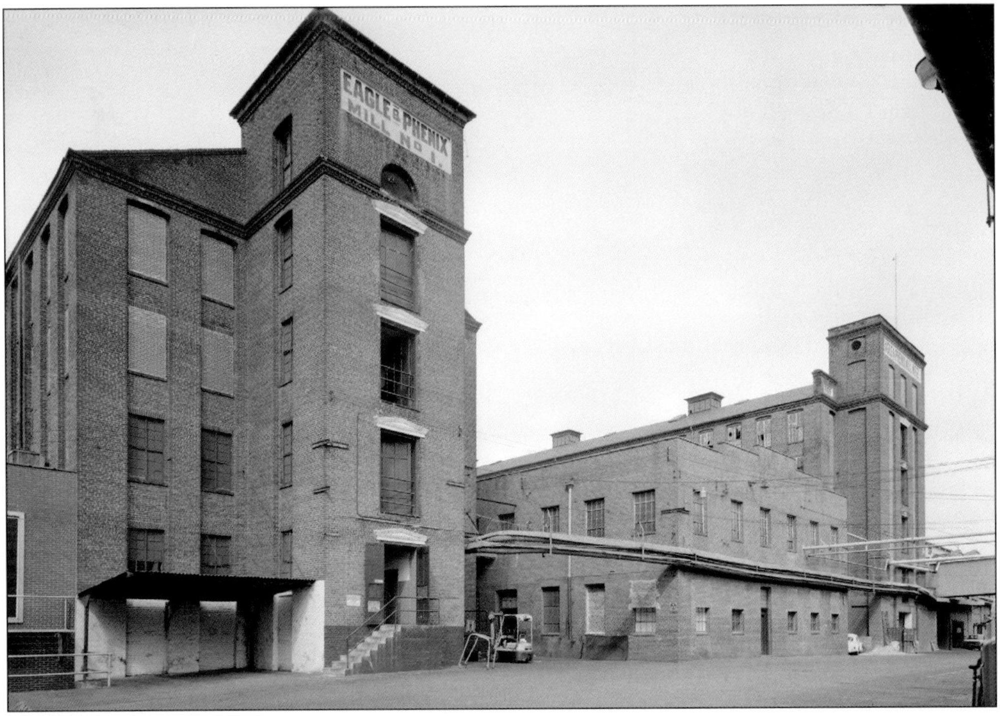

Federal troops burned Eagle Mill near the end of the Civil War in 1865. William H. Young and G. Gunby Jordan rebuilt and enlarged the mill in 1868, and symbolically renamed the operation Eagle & Phenix Mill. Within 10 years, the new operation produced 110 varieties of textile products and was widely recognized as the largest textile mill in the South. (Courtesy Library of Congress [LOC], HAER GA, 108-COLM, 17–6.)

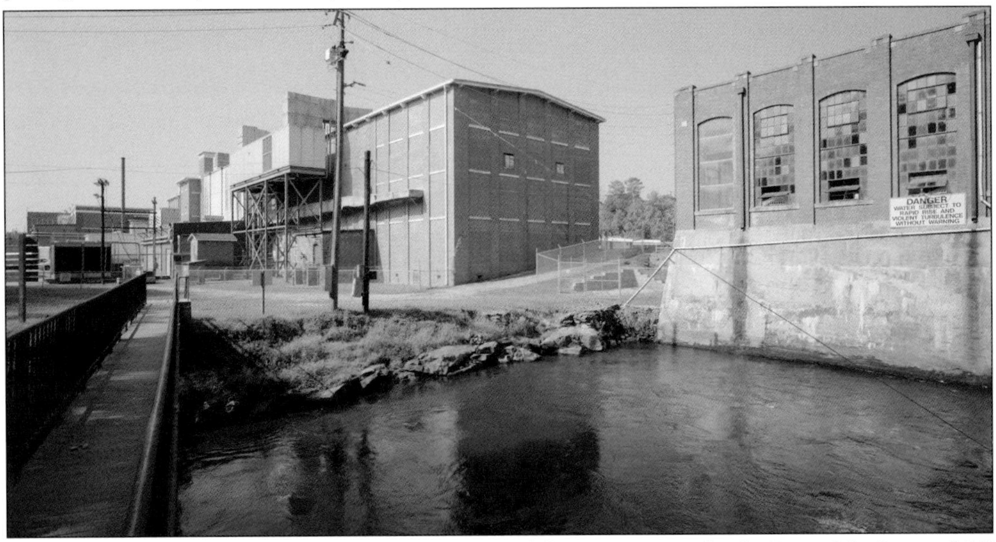

The Georgia-Alabama Manufacturing Company laid the cornerstone for the Riverdale Cotton Mill on the same day in 1866 that another group of West Point investors placed one for the Langdale Mill. Both mills drew power from the Chattahoochee River. The Georgia Power powerhouse sits adjacent to Riverdale Mill. The two companies merged into West Point Manufacturing Company in 1892. (Courtesy LOC, HAER AL-166–5.)

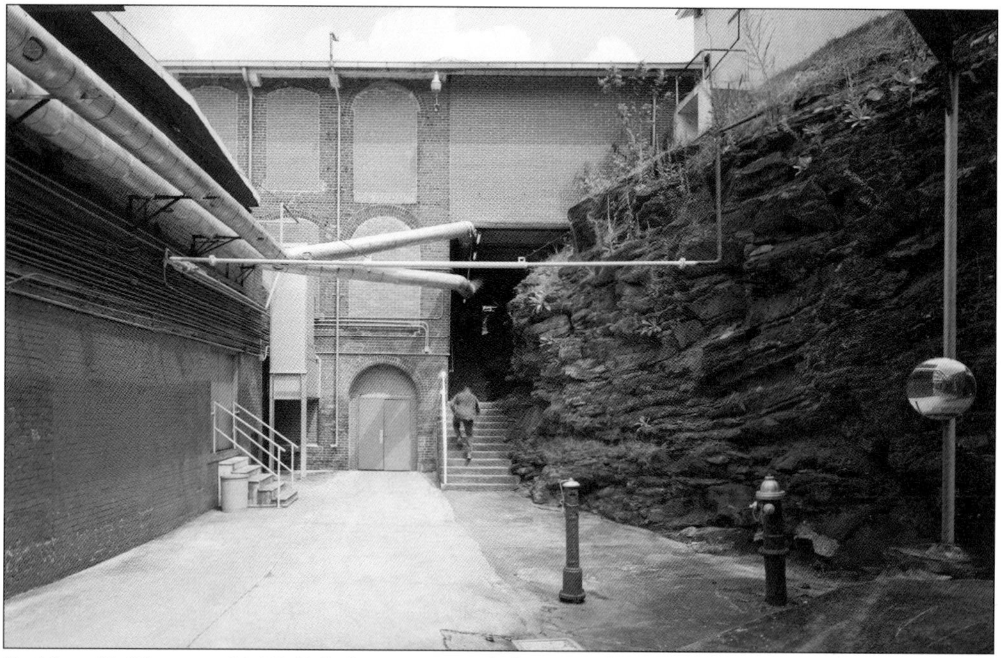

Builders J.J. Havis and M.F. Echols constructed the Riverdale Cotton Mill into a hillside along the Chattahoochee River. This passageway along an exposed rock ledge provided a shady and cool place for employees to informally socialize and escape the heat of the mill. (Courtesy LOC, HAER AL-166–6.)

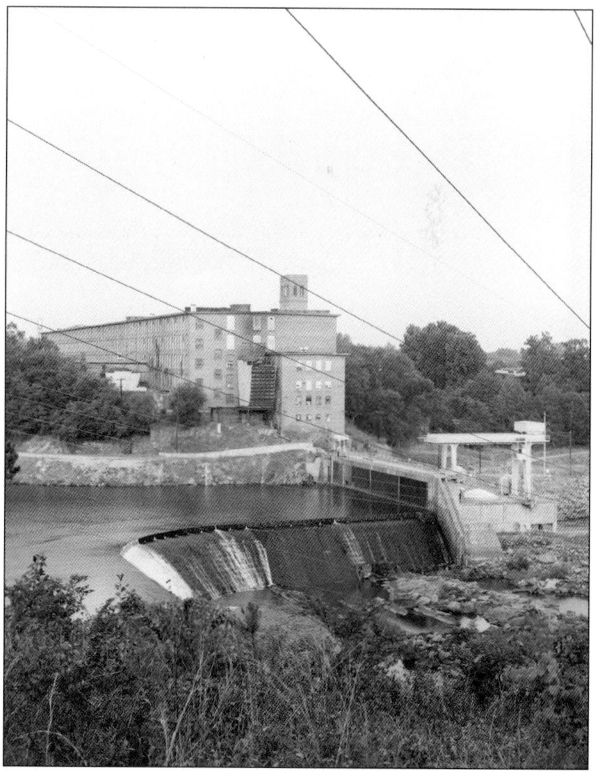

In 1897, Gunby Jordan of Eagle & Phenix Mill joined forces with the investors behind the new Bibb Company Mill to establish the Columbus Power Company and construct a new dam on the Chattahoochee River to generate electric power for their mills and the city. The Bibb Company, operating 25,000 spindles, built strategically close to the new dam to take power directly from it. The mill produced fine yarns using mule-spinning machines, which required skilled labor. In 1907, the Bibb Company began shifting production toward cotton duck to be used in tire manufacturing. (Courtesy LOC, HAER GA, 108-COLM, 27–14.)

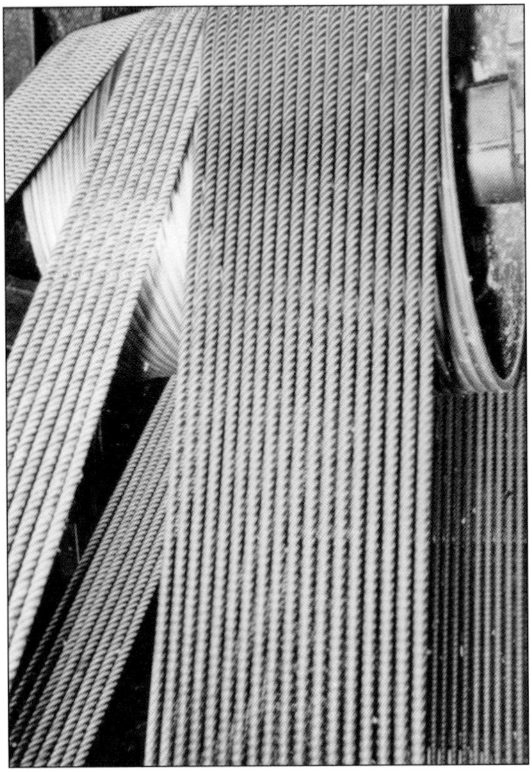

The Bibb Company harnessed the power of the Chattahoochee Falls with hydroelectric turbines and a rope drive system. The new dam generated far more electricity than the Bibb Company could use. This sparked a building boom of four new mills to take advantage of the electric power distributed by the Columbus Power Company: the Columbus Manufacturing Company, Perkins Hosiery Mill, Swift Spinning Mill, and Meritas Mills. (Courtesy LOC, HAER GA, 108-COLM, 27–20.)

With the new dam in place and generating hydroelectric power, the Eagle & Phenix Mill modernized around 1900 with Holyoke Hercules turbines housed in the lower wheelhouse and fed by the old raceway. In response to changing market demands with the advent of ready-made clothing sold in department stores, the company also upgraded to automatic Draper looms and a modernized product line. (Courtesy Columbus State University.)

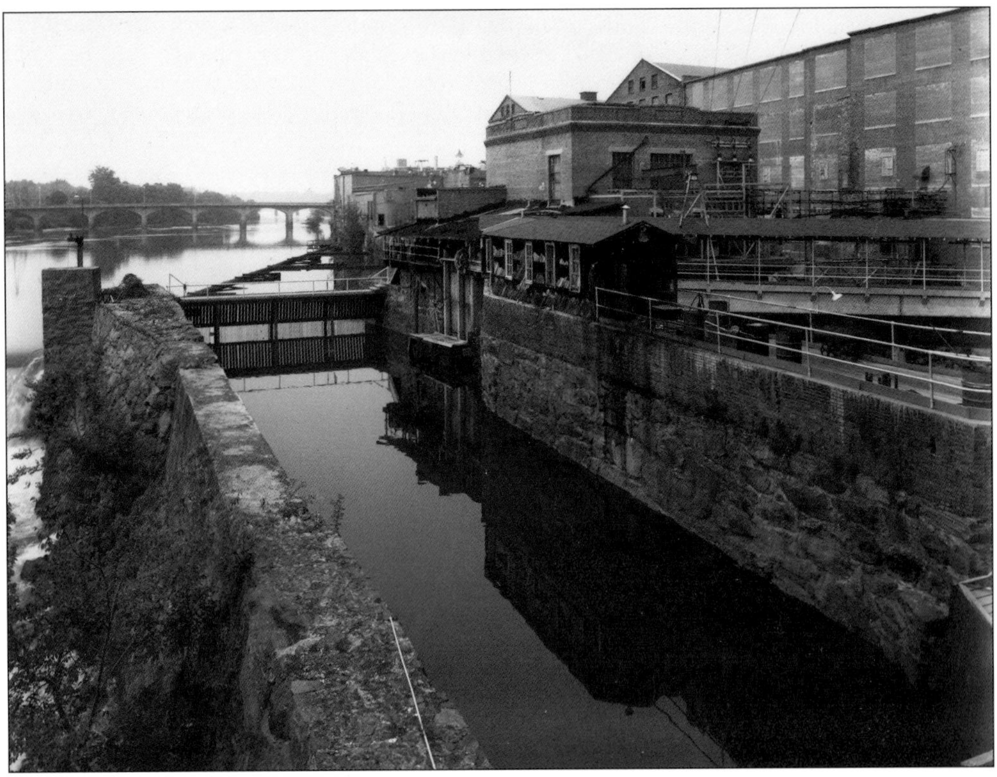

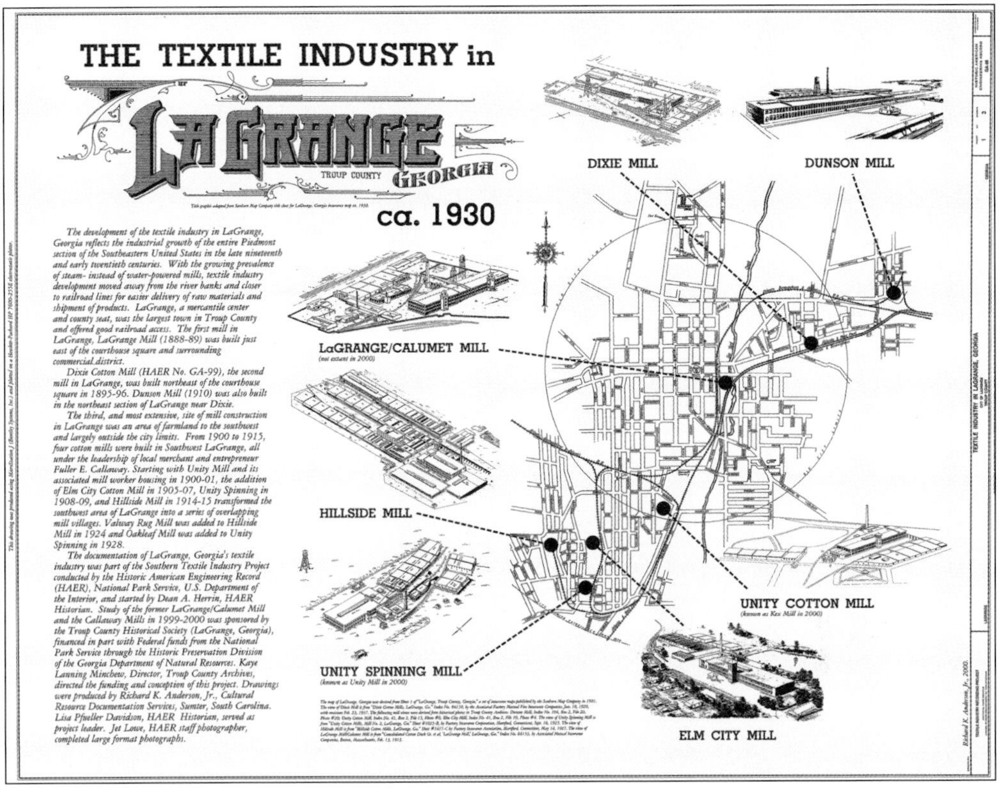

LaGrange residents including Fuller E. Callaway responded to mill fever with Dixie Mills. LaGrange soon became a successful textile center under Callaway's leadership. By 1930, LaGrange included seven mills: Dixie Mill, Dunson Mill, Unity Cotton Mill, Unity Spinning Mill, Elm City Mill, Hillside Mill, and LaGrange/Calumet Mill. The mill village of Southwest LaGrange was incorporated in 1917 around four of the mills and was made a part of the city of LaGrange three years later. (Courtesy LOC, HAER GA, 143–LAGR, 37.)

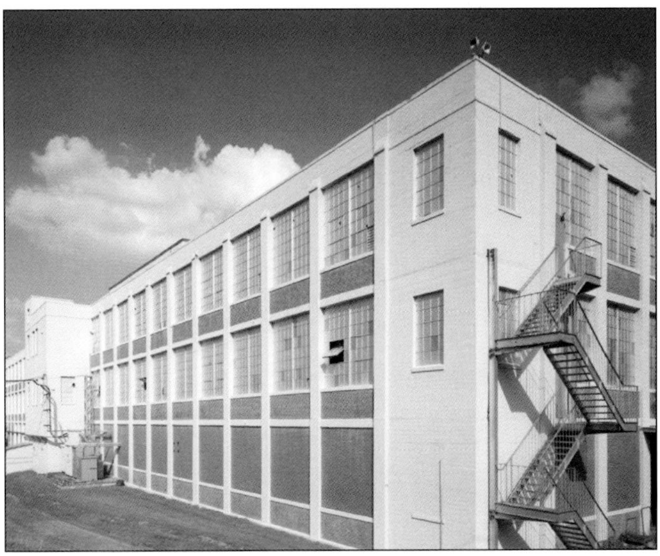

Lockwood, Greene and Company, which acquired Hogansville's textile mill in 1913, built the Hogansville Stark Mill in 1923–1924 to take advantage of cheaper labor costs in the South. Lockwood Greene Engineers, which had specialized in textile mill construction since the 1870s, created a cutting-edge production facility using the most up-to-date technology, including reinforced concrete construction and air conditioning. (Courtesy LOC, HAER GA, 143-HOVI, 6–3.)

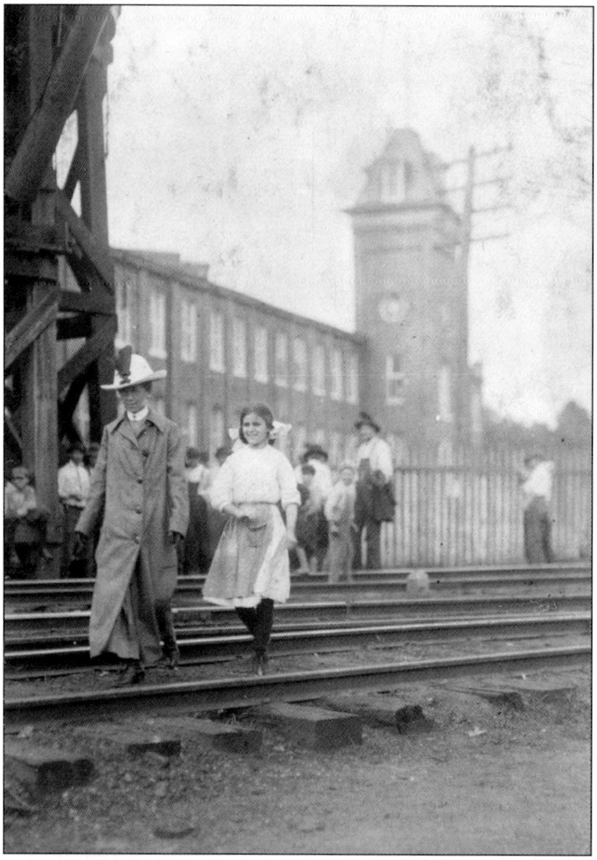

In 1897, Hogansville business leaders established the Hogansville Manufacturing Company with the help of northern investors. However, the town lost local control of the mill in 1905 when it was purchased by Consolidated Duck of Delaware. Duck is a canvas-like textile with many industrial applications including cord used in making rubber tires. The mill changed ownership a number of times. When the photograph below was taken in 1939, it was called Reid Mill and operated as part of Callaway Mills. Eventually, the mill was purchased by the U.S. Rubber Company, later Uniroyal; today, this mill operates as Industrial Specialty Fabrics. Throughout the 1900s, it was common practice for a mill to change names and owners several times, which can lead to a complicated industrial history of the South. (Left, courtesy LOC, LC-DIG-nclc-02810; below, Troup County Archives.)

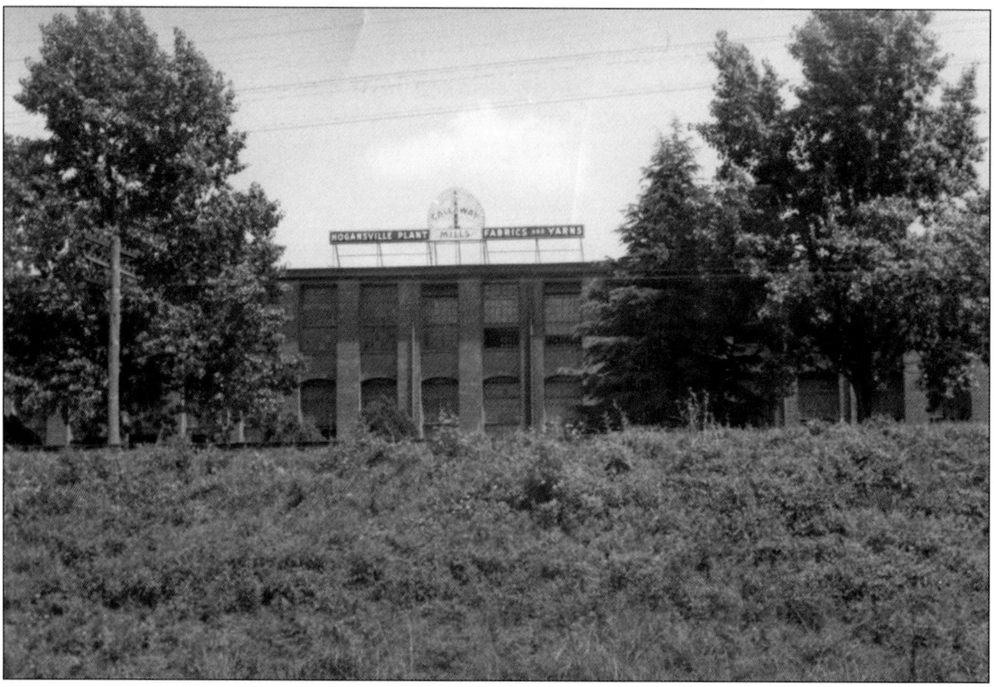

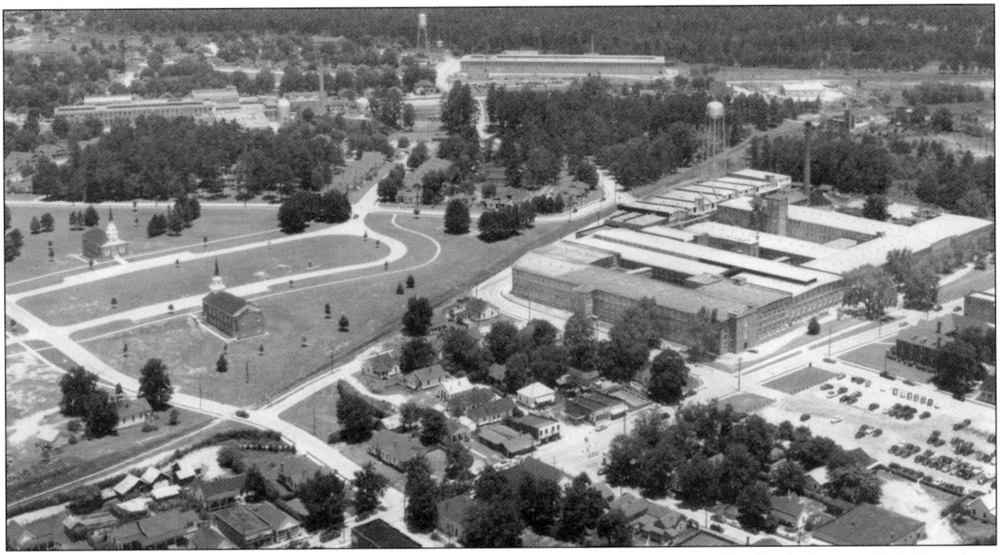

Robert Edgar Hightower led the way in establishing Thomaston Mills (right) in 1899. Peerless Mills (center) followed in 1919 and the Thomaston Bleachery was next in 1924. The three mills clustered around the East Thomaston mill village, which featured a large open green space. The Methodist and Baptist churches faced each other in the center of the village. The Village of East Thomaston was incorporated in 1900 with a governing body of three commissioners. By the late 1930s, the mill village included 624 houses. Hightower's son Harrison, like many second generation textile men, graduated from Georgia Tech's textile school in 1909 and took over management of the company during the 1930s. In 1942, Harrison Hightower led the state's textile mills in organizing the Textile Education Foundation in support of the industry. In appreciation, Georgia Tech named its new textile building for Hightower in 1949. (Courtesy Thomaston-Upson Archives.)

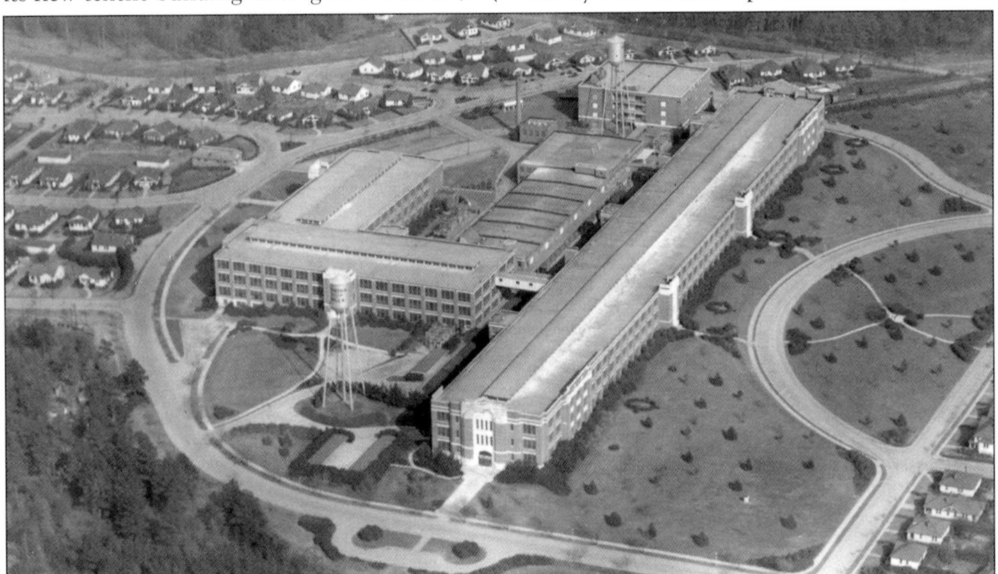

In 1925, the B.F. Goodrich Company teamed up with Thomaston Mills to build a new $2 million factory, named Martha Mills after Robert E. Hightower's wife, to manufacture industrial textiles including tire cord, cotton duck, and yarns. Martha Mills's Nylock conveyor belt made a significant impact in the mining industry. (Courtesy Thomaston-Upson Archives.)

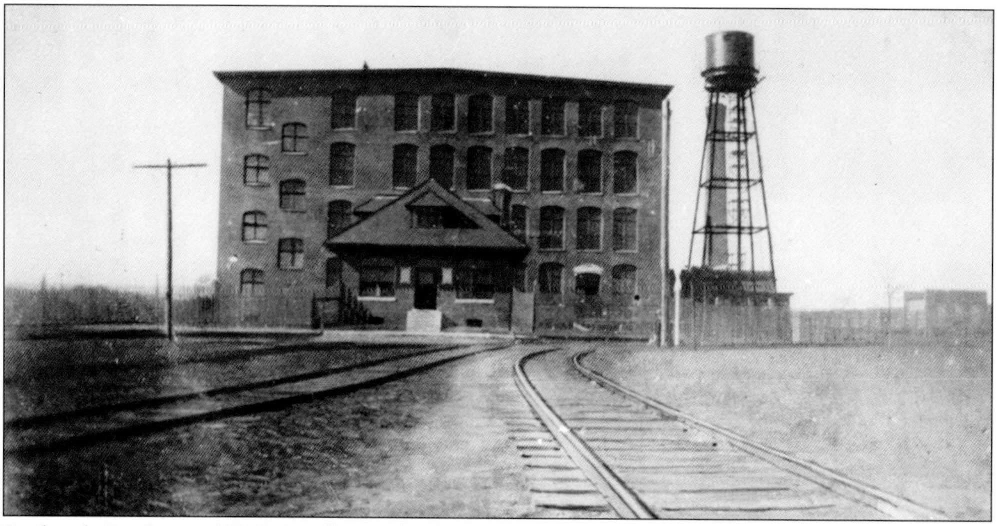

Frederick Gordon and W.C. Bradley took advantage of the new hydroelectric power provided by the Columbus Power Company to build the Columbus Manufacturing Company in 1900. In addition to power, the successful textile mill also needed easy access to the railroad to bring in raw cotton and send out textile products to distant markets. (Courtesy LOC, HAER, 108-COLM, 26–3.)

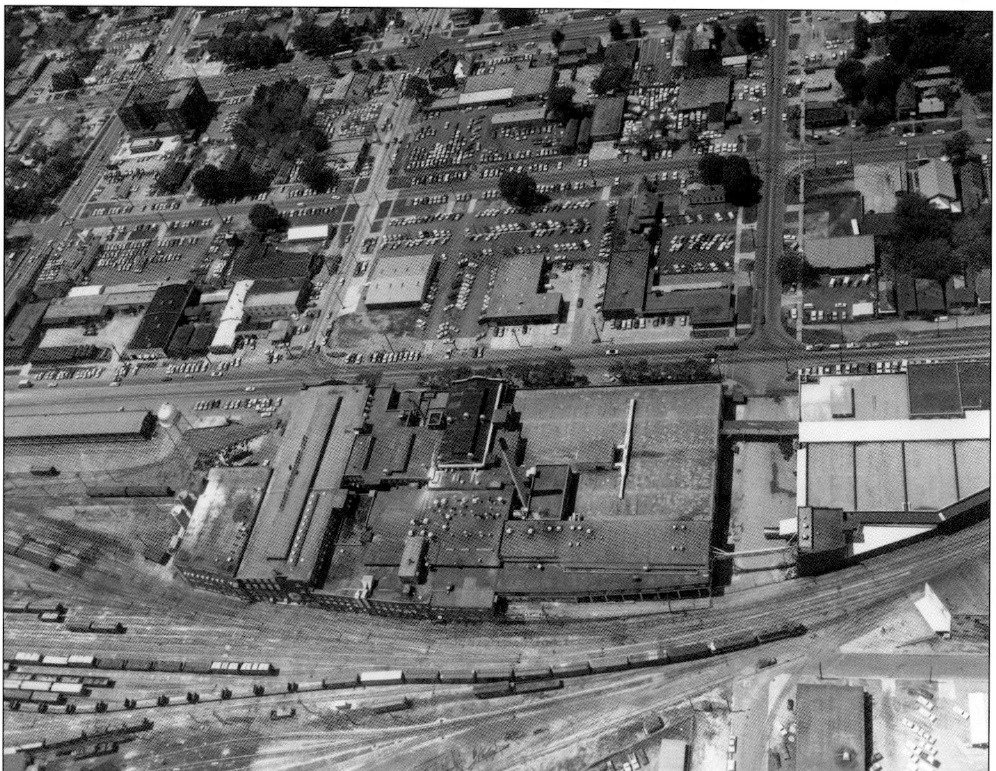

Edward W. Swift and A. Illges also seized the opportunity to use the power produced by the Columbus Power Company to build the Swift Spinning Mill in 1906. This aerial view emphasizes the importance of the railroad to textile manufacturing once it was freed from the banks of the Chattahoochee River. (Courtesy Columbus State University.)

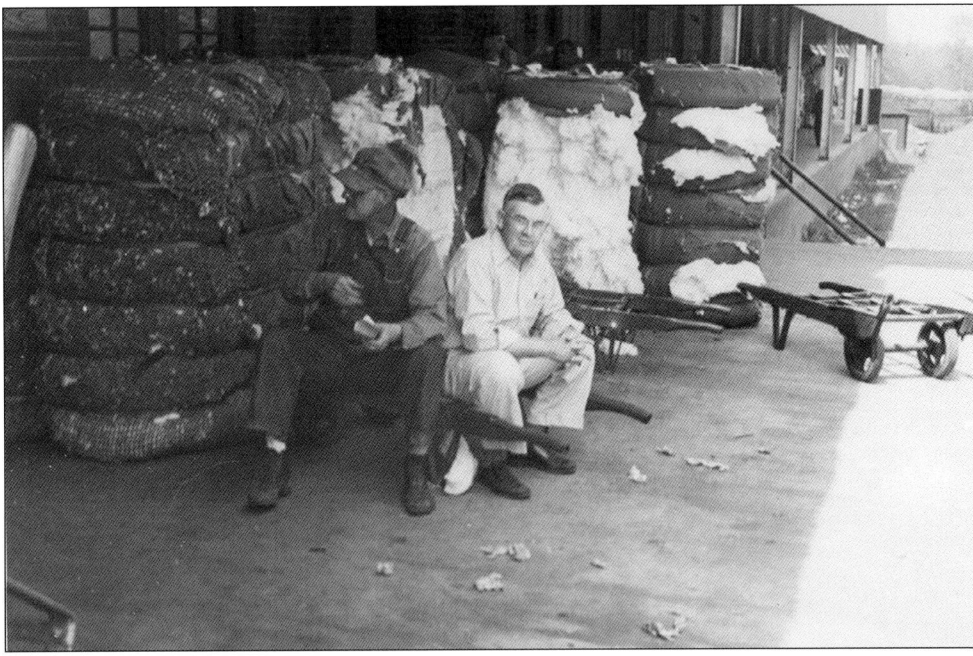

Cotton, manufacturing, and the railroad all come together on the loading dock of Hogansville's Stark Mill. A railroad conductor takes a break with C.W. Sims (right) with raw cotton in the background. Stark Mill is best known locally as Uniroyal, which operated the company through the 1980s and 1990s. Westech currently operates the Stark Mill. Images and histories of these mills can be discovered at the Troup County Archives and Museum on Main Street in downtown LaGrange. (Courtesy Troup County Archives.)

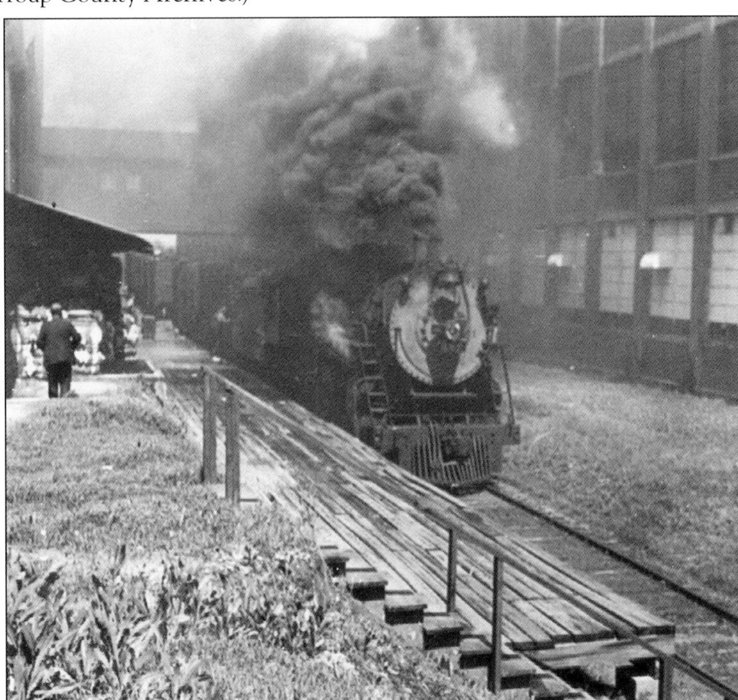

Engine No. 400 thunders by Hogansville's Stark Mill. Railroad access was vital to the success of any textile mill and played a key role in determining where mills sprang up once electricity freed manufacturing from the banks of fast flowing rivers and creeks. Notice the pervasive presence of cotton lint on the ground, which could easily be mistaken for a dusting of snow. (Courtesy Troup County Archives.)

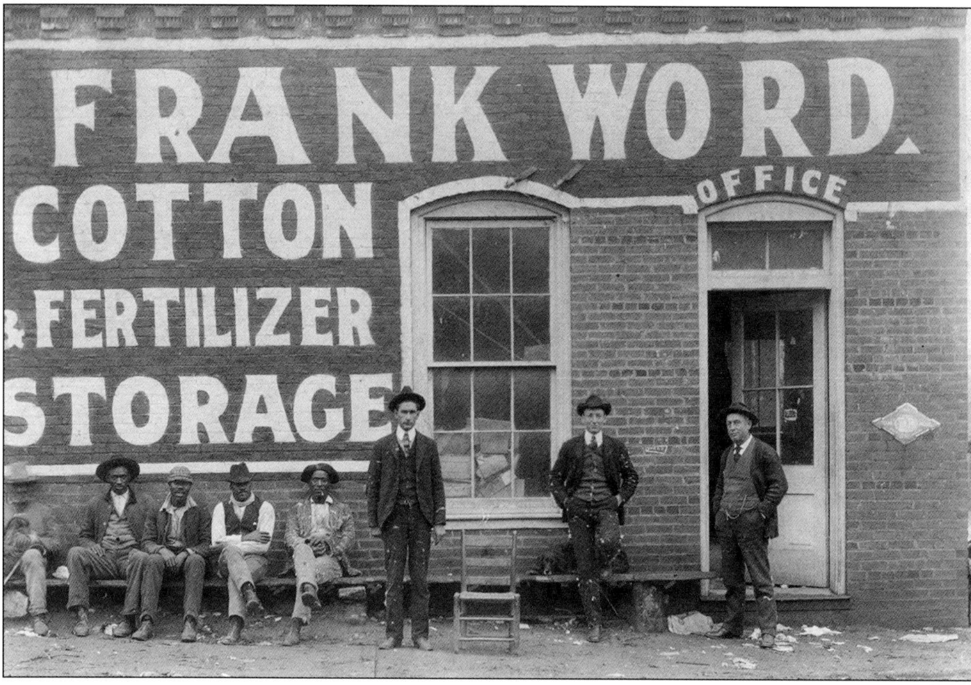

Frank Word's cotton warehouse in Hogansville connected local cotton farmers with the commercial world. The shift to tenant farming and sharecropping after the Civil War enhanced the social and economic power of rural merchants like Word. In addition to the warehouse, he participated in establishing the Hogansville Manufacturing Company and the Mutual Cotton Oil Company, all prominently located along the railroad. (Courtesy Troup County Archives.)

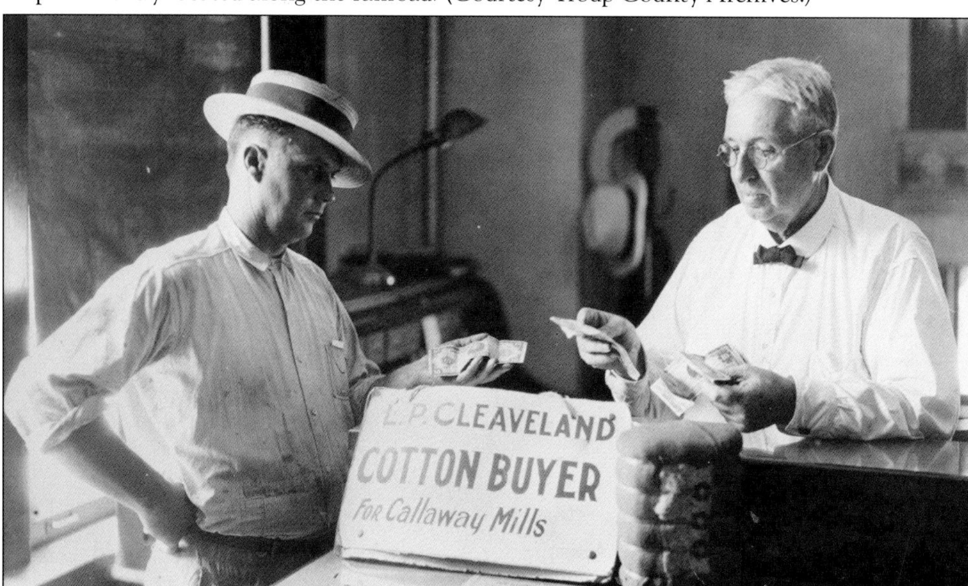

In LaGrange, the Troup Warehouse, located on Main Street, connected cotton buyers such as L.P. Cleaveland with farmers and their raw product. Warehouses did more than just store cotton; they often weighed the bales and graded the fiber as well. Cleaveland did this bit of business for Callaway Mills around 1927. (Courtesy Georgia Archives, Vanishing Georgia Collection, trp283.)

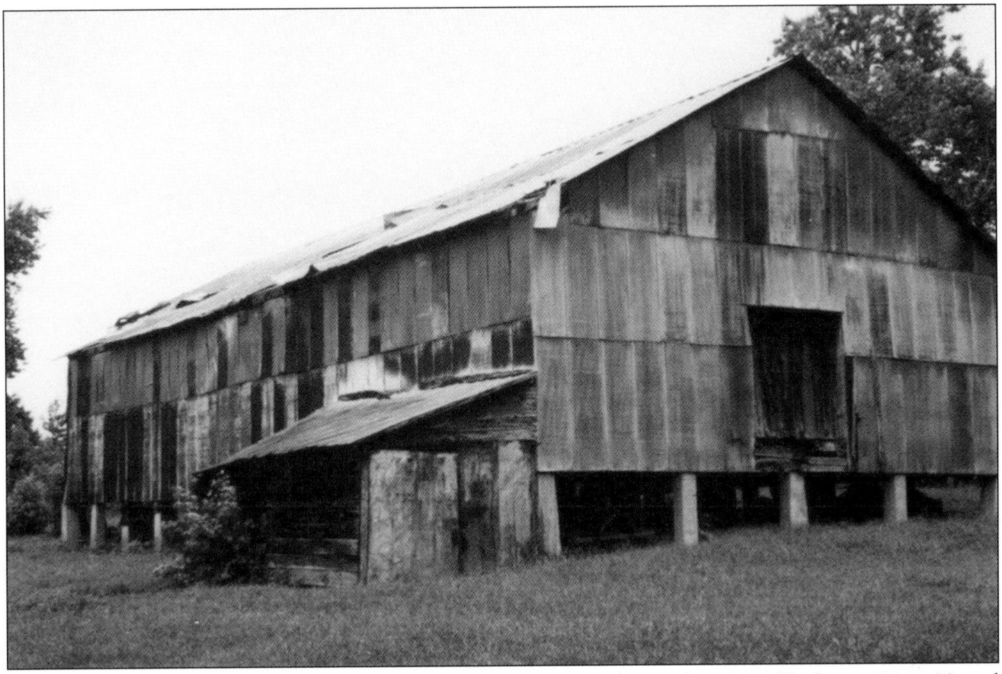

During cotton season, Frank Terrell operated Burns Gin, located on US Highway 27 in Heard County, preparing raw cotton for sale to textile mills. In 1900, thirty cotton gins dotted the Heard County landscape. With the decline of cotton farming in the area, Burns Gin stopped operating in the 1950s. (Courtesy Heard County Historical Center and Museum.)

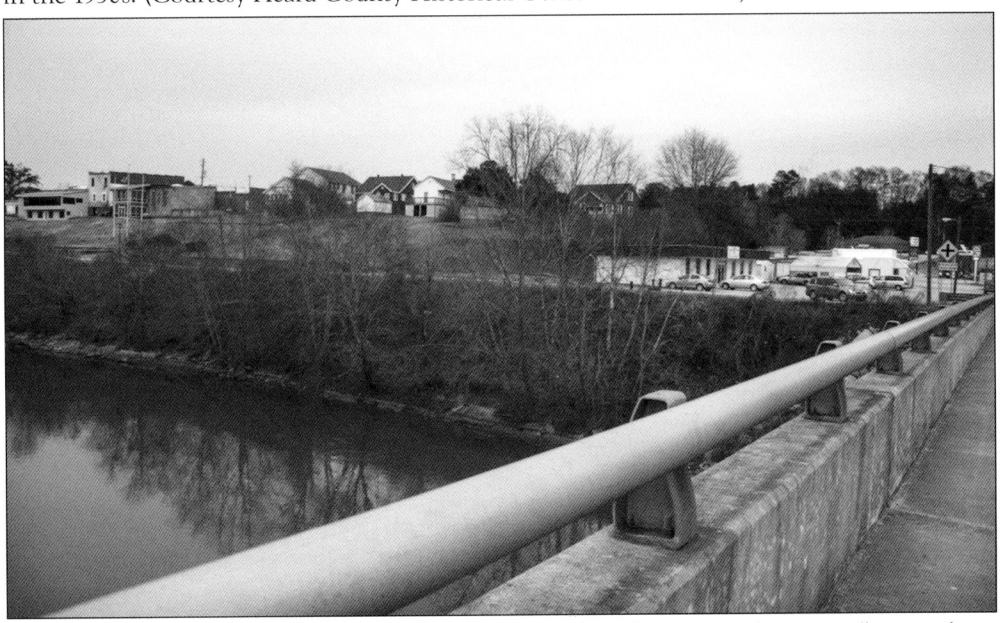

Even though Franklin sits on the bank of the Chattahoochee River, the water flows without sufficient power to sustain large textile mills as it does at West Point and Columbus. Without hydropower or railroads, Heard County failed to attract large textile mills. However, the Union Mills, located near Centralhatchee in 1863, appears to have been a small textile mill. (Photograph by Kymberli Darling.)

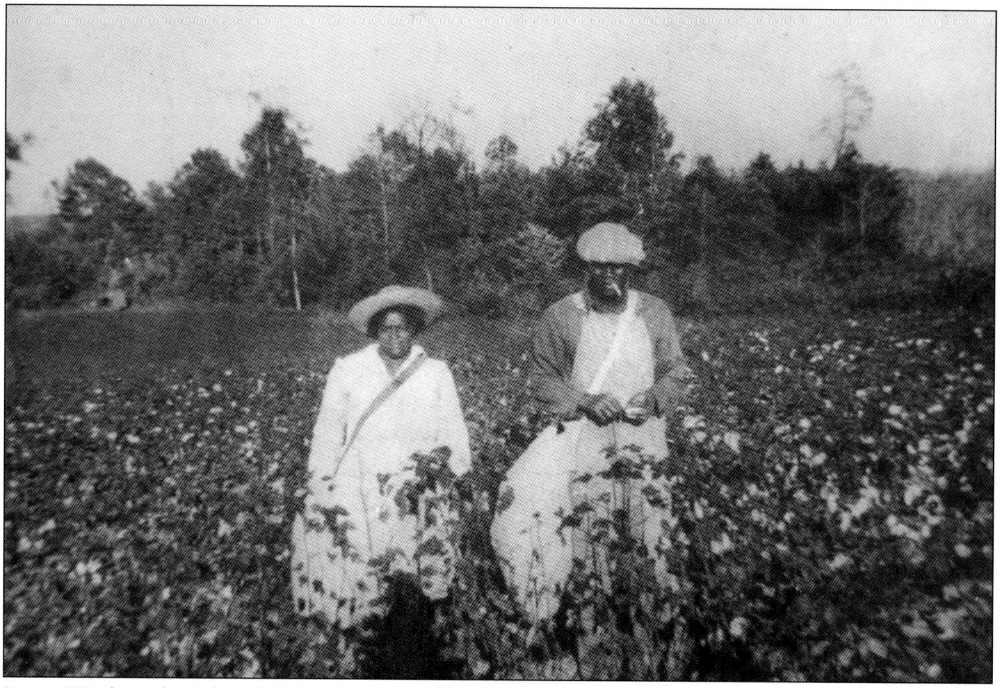

James Watkins (right) and Tobe Greene pick cotton on the David Crockett farm in Heard County in the 1950s. Farmworkers harvested cotton by hand before the raw product traveled through cotton gins and warehouses to reach the factory floor. Cotton production ties Heard County to the west Georgia textile story. (Courtesy Heard County Historical Center and Museum.)

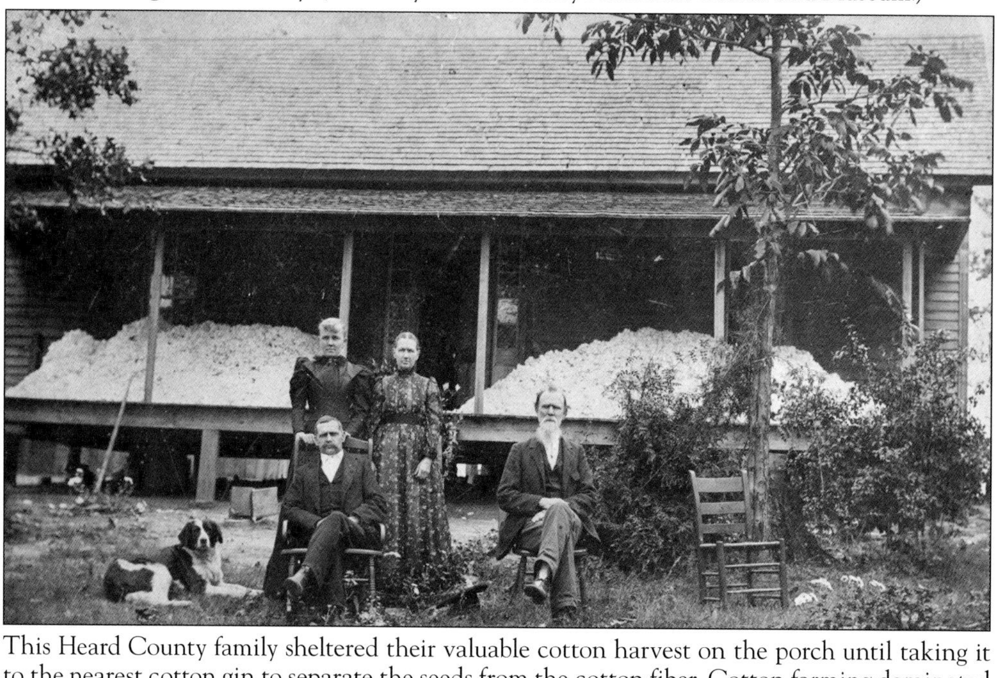

This Heard County family sheltered their valuable cotton harvest on the porch until taking it to the nearest cotton gin to separate the seeds from the cotton fiber. Cotton farming dominated the local economy through the late 19th and early 20th centuries. (Courtesy Georgia Archives, Vanishing Georgia Collection, hrd005.)

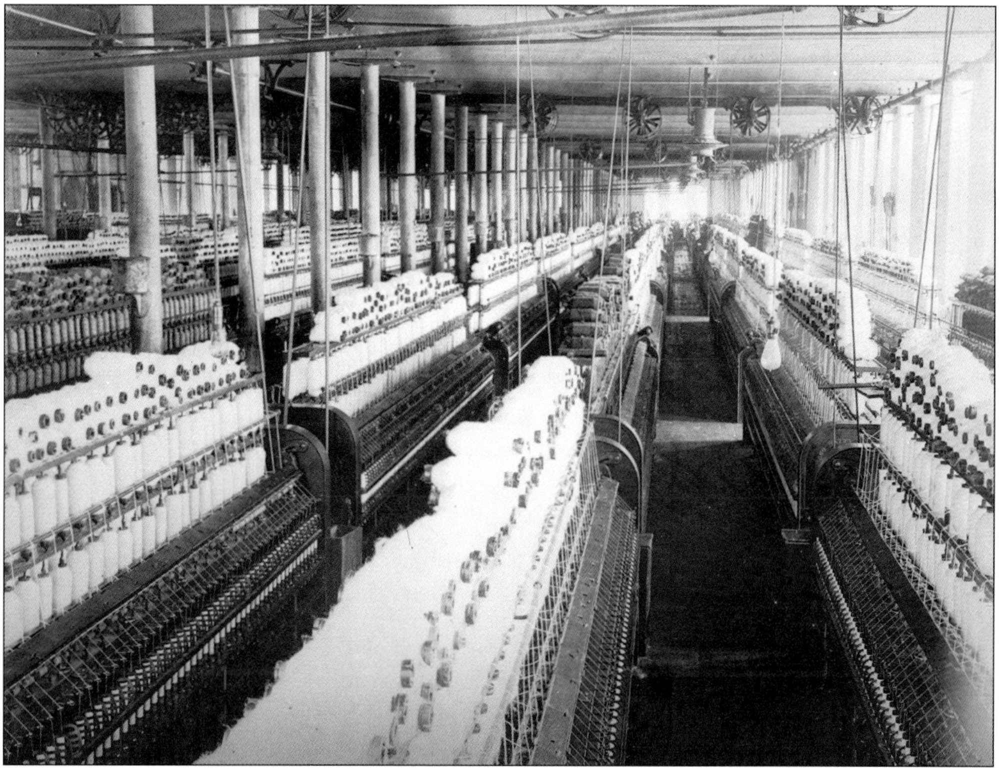

After the destruction of Columbus's Eagle Mill by federal troops near the end of the Civil War, the rebuilt and renamed Eagle & Phenix Mill resumed operations in 1871, with spinning located on the fourth floor. The mill produced an unusually large variety of products, including osnaburgs, stripes, solid colors, shirting, ticking, checks, ginghams, denims, woolen cassimeres, yarns, twine, and rope. (Courtesy LOC, HAER GA, 108-COLM, 17–12.)

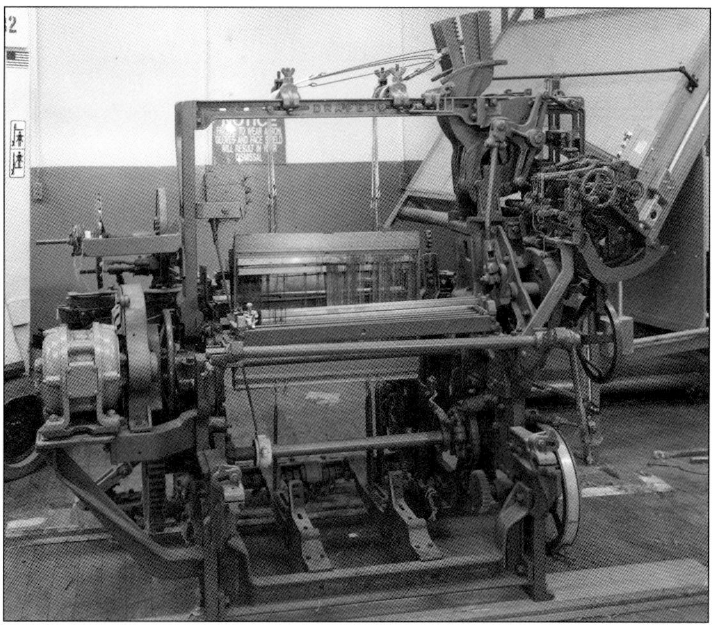

The West Point Manufacturing Company's Riverdale Cotton Mill bought this Draper darby chain loom around 1941. This design, which was patented in 1913, included an automatic spindle changer. Such mechanical innovations simplified even the most complex aspects of the manufacturing process, such as weaving, and opened up mill work to unskilled workers from nearby farms. (Courtesy LOC, HAER AL–177.)

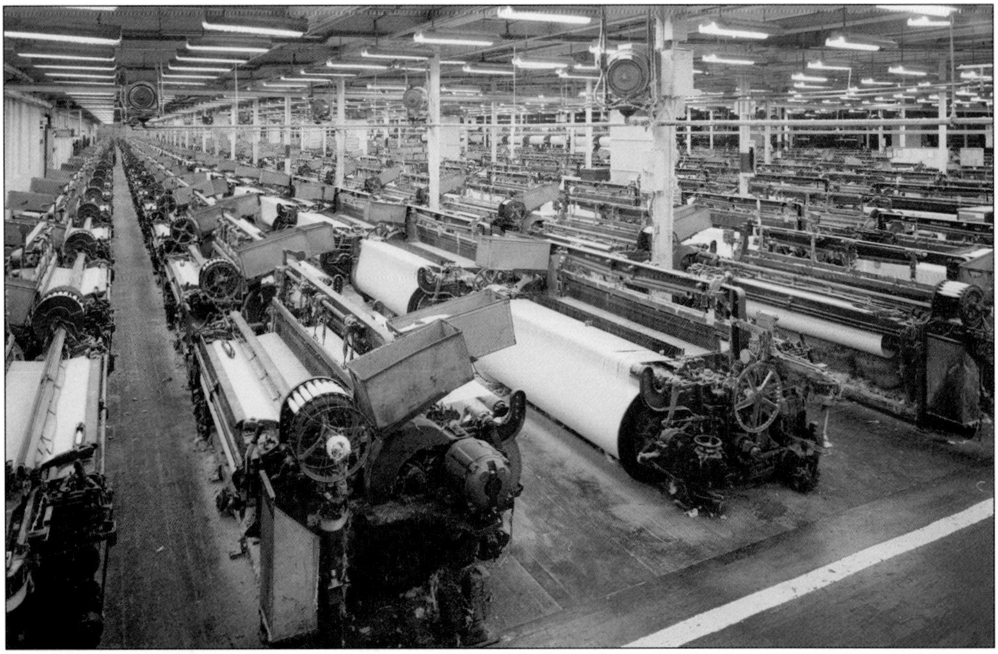

After 1907, the Bibb Manufacturing Company's Columbus mill responded to the growing demand for automobile tires by refocusing production on cotton duck used to add strength to rubber tires. The Bibb Company kept up with new technologies and shifted to the manufacture of tire cord in the 1920s. (Courtesy LOC, HAER GA, 108-COLM, 27–13.)

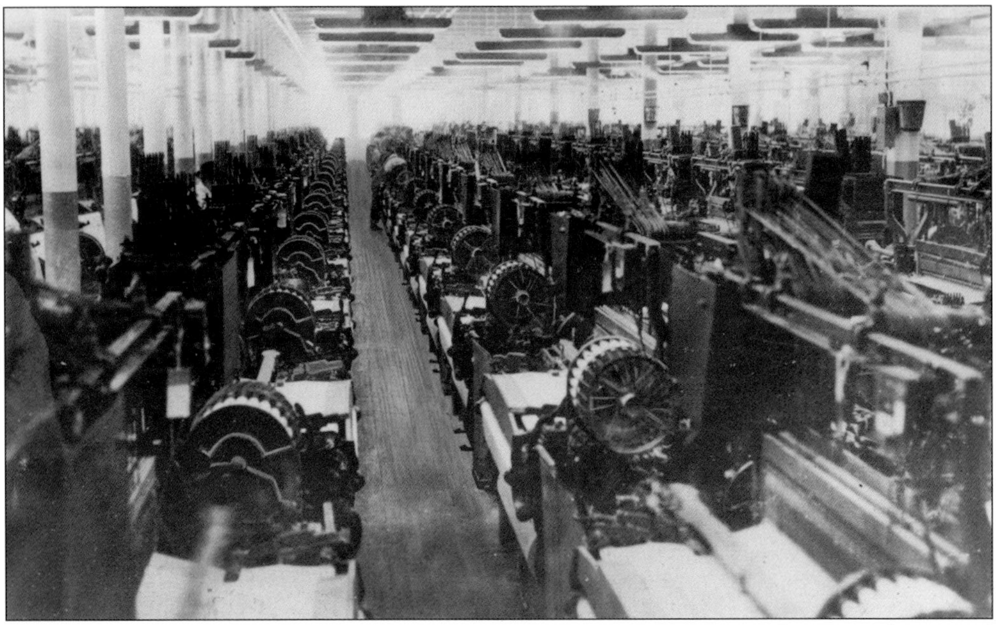

Thomaston Mills looms also produced tire cloth. In 1921, the *Macon Daily Telegraph* reported that the mill shipped 40 train carloads of tire fabric to B.F. Goodrich to compete with the more expensive "cord tires" on the market. This was particularly good news for the Thomaston Mills community, since the plant had been running only half-time in response to a weak market. (Courtesy Thomaston-Upson Archives.)

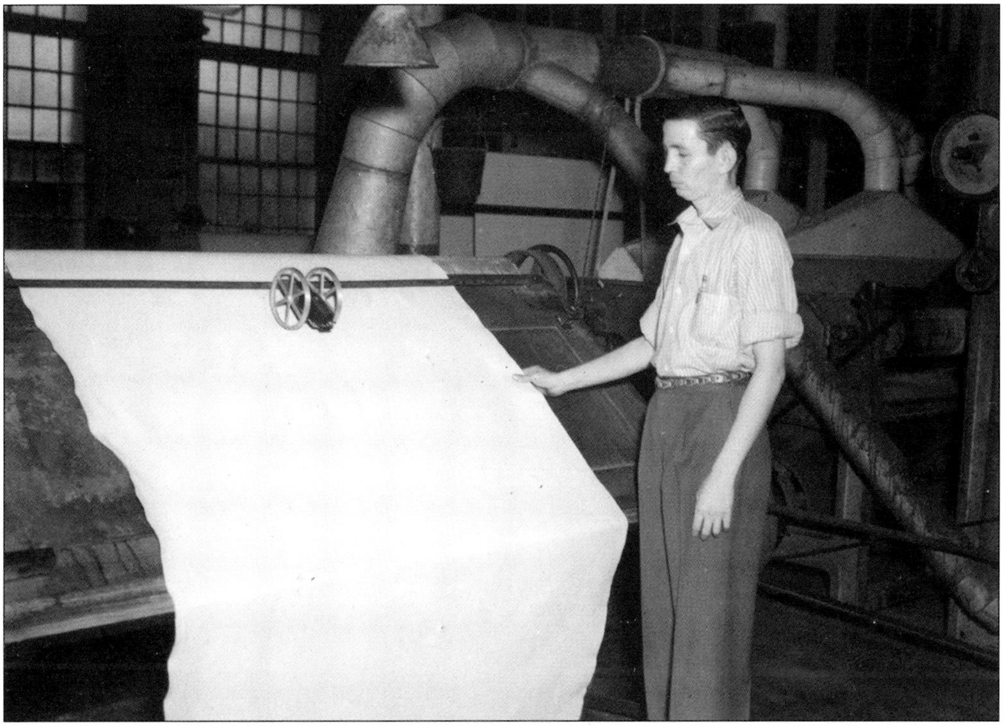

During World War II, U.S. Rubber expanded its operations to meet demand for tire fabric by buying and enlarging the old Hogansville Manufacturing Company. It was renamed Reid Mill, after a longtime supervisor, when this worker posed with the mill's product and machinery in 1943. Beginning in 1942, the mill was one of only two plants in the nation to produce woven asbestos pipe insulation for the US Navy. (Courtesy Troup County Archives.)

This 1939 product display from U.S. Rubber's Stark Mill follows cotton through the manufacturing process to produce cord used to reinforce rubber tires. Although U.S. Rubber expanded its operations in Hogansville during the war years, it also began selling homes to its workers in the village. (Courtesy Troup County Archives.)

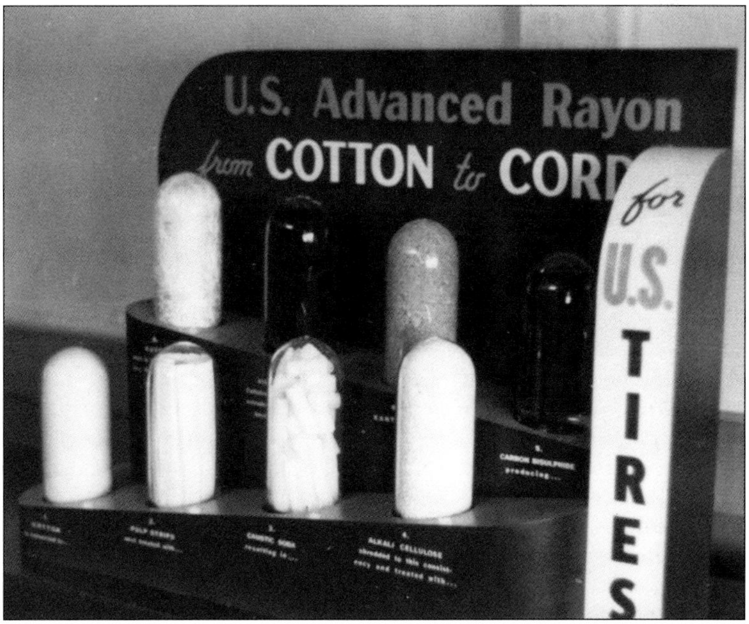

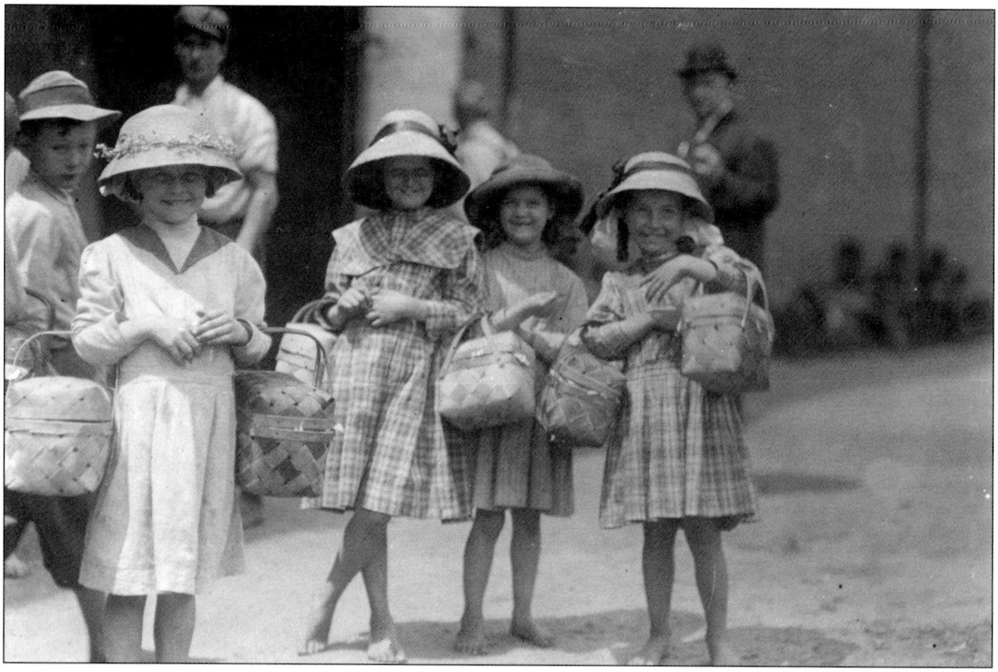

"Dinner toters" wait for the mill gates to open at noon in 1913 in Columbus. They delivered lunches to workers for 25¢ a week and often began learning how to tend the machines while operatives ate their meals. An unusually large number of small children worked in Columbus as dinner toters. In response, a local charity—the Head, Heart, and Hand Society—established a special school in 1895 for these children, with sessions that ran from 8:00 a.m. to 10:30 a.m. and 1:00 p.m. to 3:30 p.m., so they could do their jobs without missing classes. (Both, courtesy LOC; above, LC-DIG-nclc-02838; below, LC-DIG-nclc-02839.)

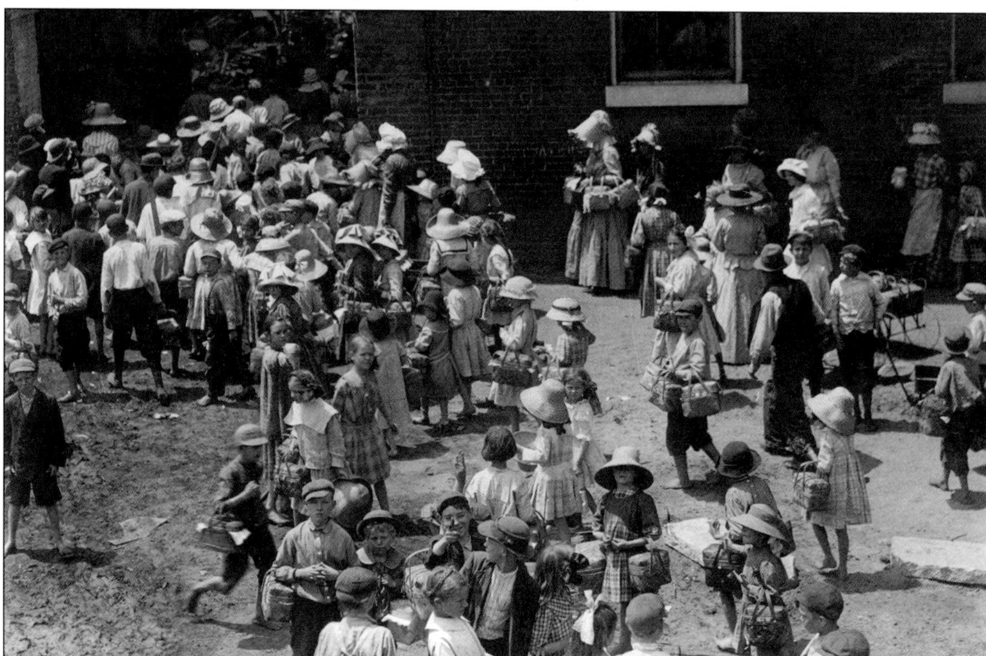

An Ordinary's Certificate allowed children to work in the mills if the parent provided proof that he or she was unable to work. Curtis Wynn was nine years old when this certificate was issued in 1912, which would have made him too young to work in the mill and the certificate illegally issued. (Courtesy LOC, LC-DIG-nclc-02830.)

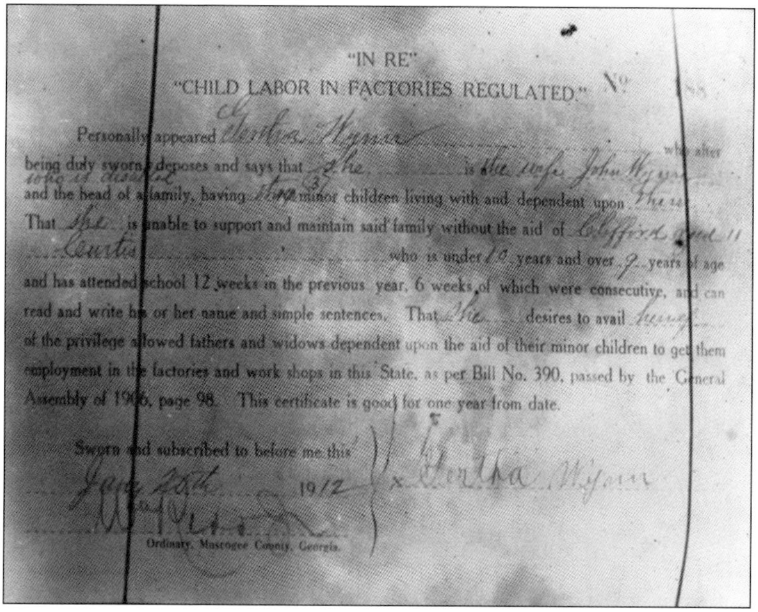

"IN RE"

"CHILD LABOR IN FACTORIES REGULATED." No. 188

Personally appeared Bertha Wynn who after being duly sworn deposes and says that she is the wife John Wynn who is disabled and the head of a family, having three minor children living with and dependent upon them. That she is unable to support and maintain said family without the aid of Clifford aged 11 Curtis who is under 10 years and over 9 years of age and has attended school 12 weeks in the previous year, 6 weeks of which were consecutive, and can read and write his or her name and simple sentences. That she desires to avail herself of the privilege allowed fathers and widows dependent upon the aid of their minor children to get them employment in the factories and work shops in this State, as per Bill No. 390, passed by the General Assembly of 1906, page 98. This certificate is good for one year from date.

Sworn and subscribed to before me this June 20th 1912 x Bertha Wynn

Ordinary, Muscogee County, Georgia.

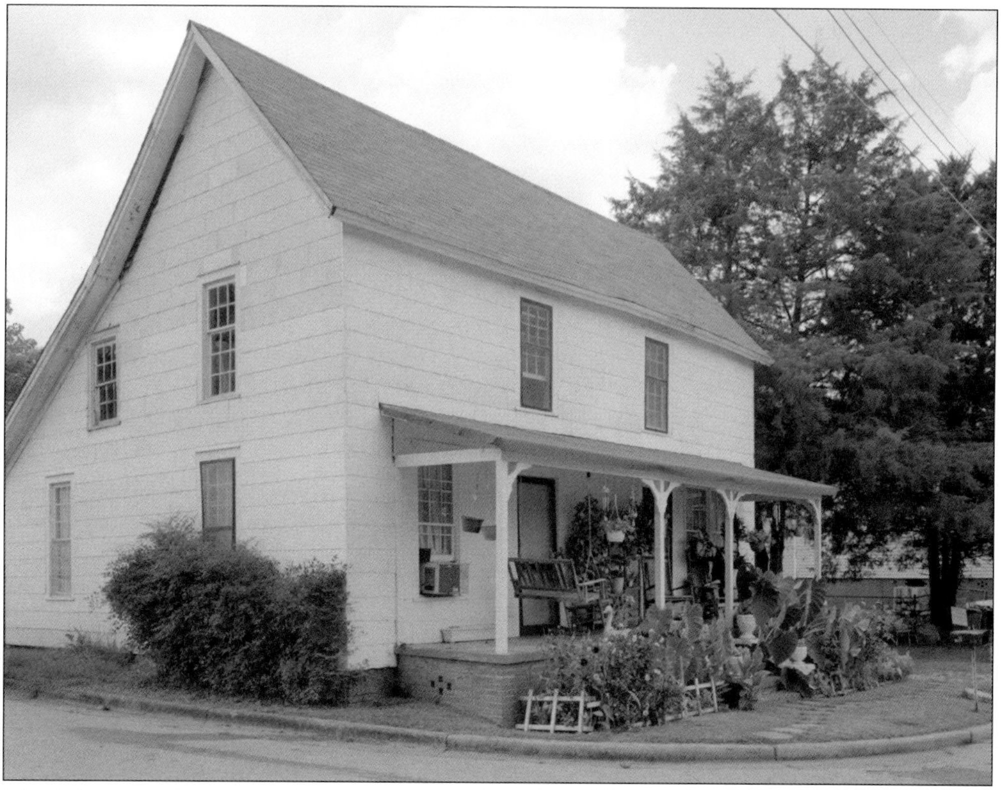

The influence of northern investors may explain the saltbox-style mill housing for Dixie Mill in LaGrange. The local newspaper reported that construction of houses for approximately 1,500 operatives had begun in September 1895. Although occasionally seen in southern textile mill villages, the saltbox, with its distinctive two-story profile, is rarely found in other southern towns. (Courtesy LOC, LC-DIG-nclc-02753.)

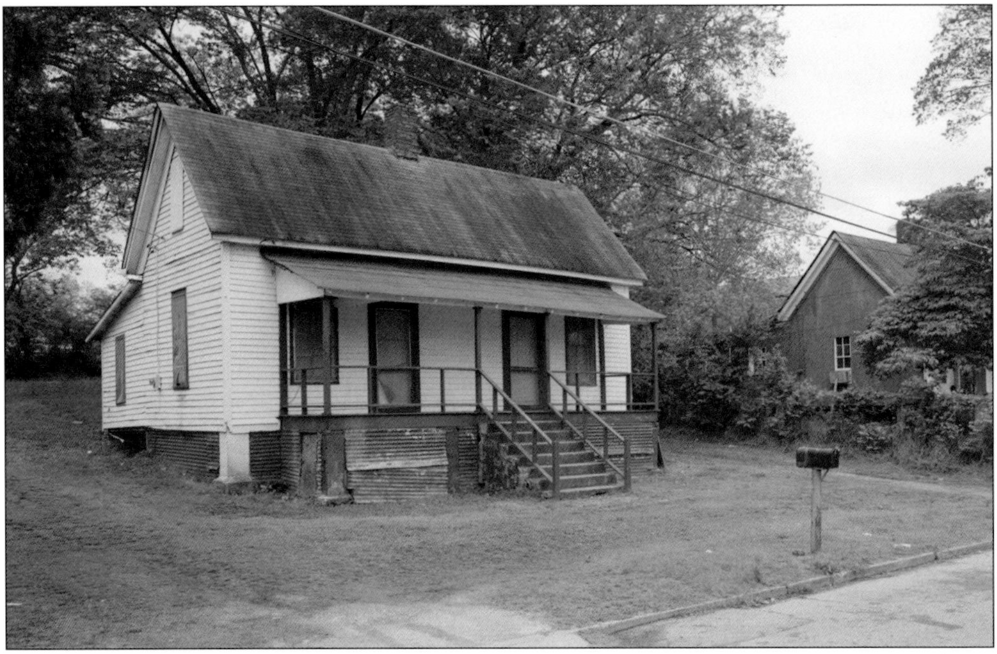

The one-story, side-gable, duplex-type house, like this one built around 1900 in LaGrange's Calumet Mill Village, may have seemed familiar to new mill workers. It looks very much the same as the common rural house type known as a saddlebag double pen, with two doors onto the porch and a chimney in the center of the house. (Courtesy LOC, HAER GA, 143-LAGR,44–1.)

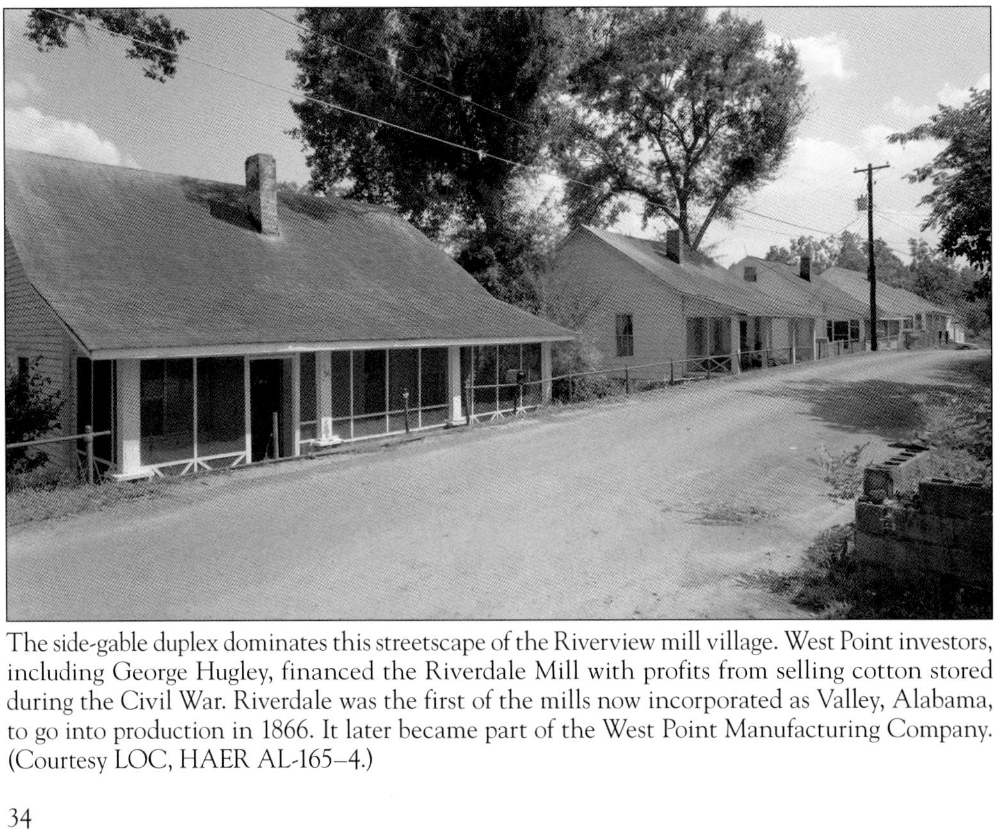

The side-gable duplex dominates this streetscape of the Riverview mill village. West Point investors, including George Hugley, financed the Riverdale Mill with profits from selling cotton stored during the Civil War. Riverdale was the first of the mills now incorporated as Valley, Alabama, to go into production in 1866. It later became part of the West Point Manufacturing Company. (Courtesy LOC, HAER AL-165–4.)

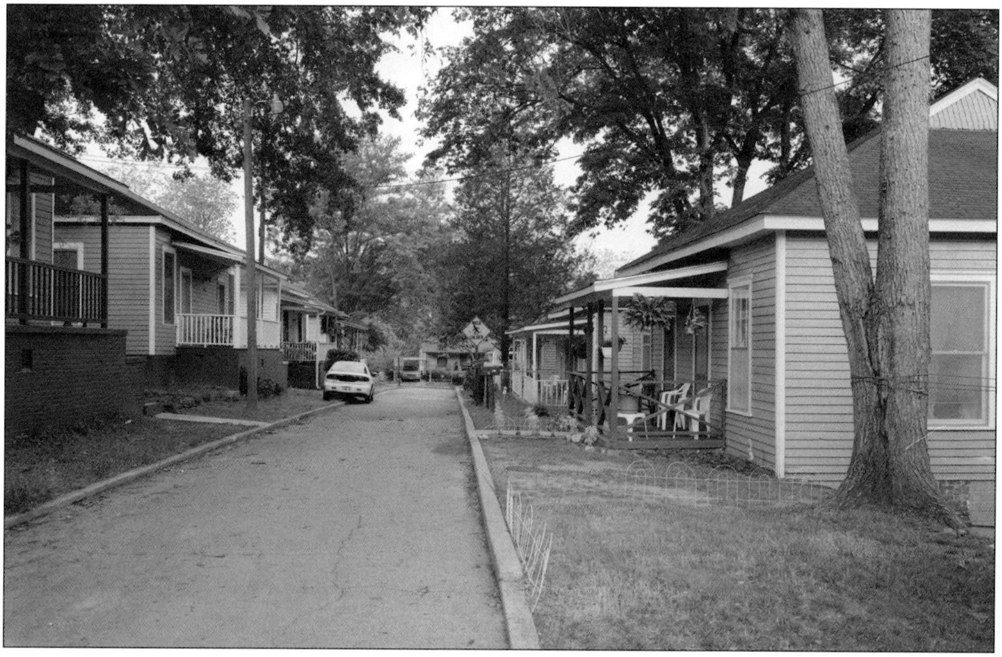

These identical duplexes with gable-on-hip roofs face each other in the LaGrange's Calumet Mill Village. Fuller E. Callaway established the Calumet Company in 1907 after clashing with other local textile leaders in LaGrange. The history of textile mills is filled with changing names resulting from corporate restructuring and changing ownership. (Courtesy LOC, HAER GA, 143-LAGR, 41–1.)

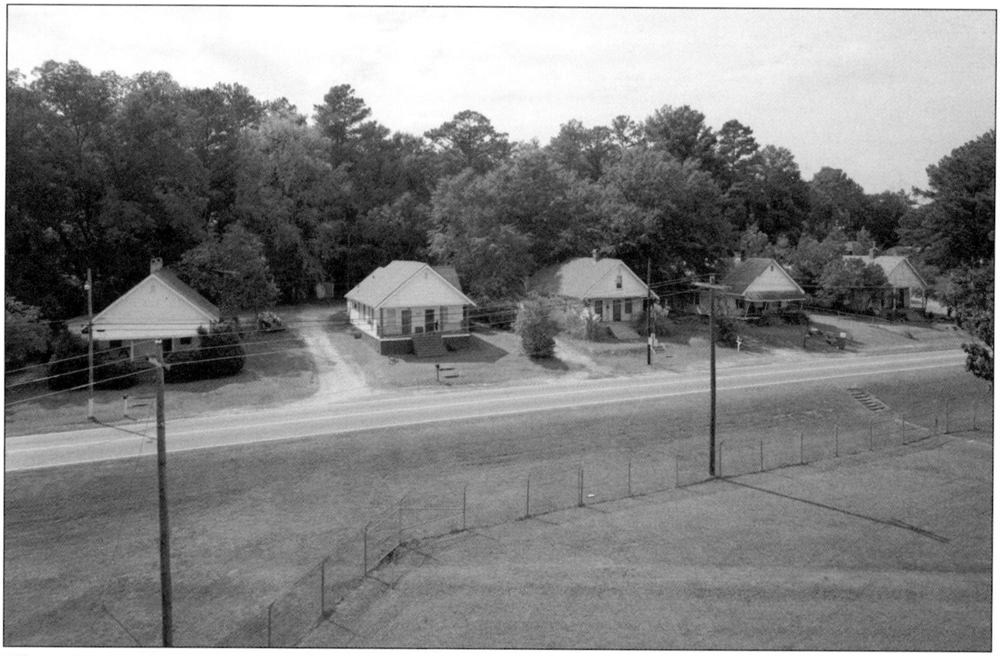

These hip roof cottages, seen from atop Hogansville's Stark Mill, are typical mill housing built in the early 20th century. This mill village first developed around the Hogansville Mill, established around 1895. The village grew as the mill changed ownership and names over the years, especially when Stark Mill was built in 1923. (Courtesy LOC, HAER GA, 143-HOVI, 2–1.)

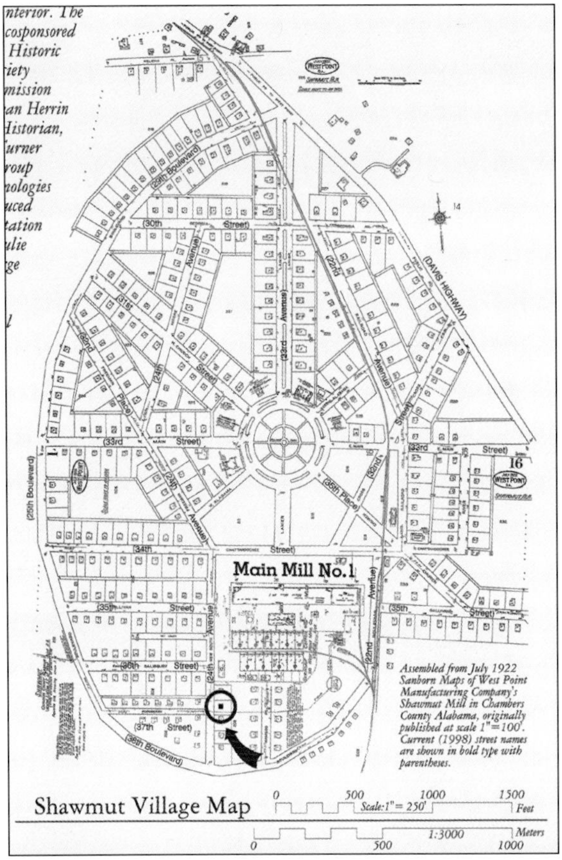

The West Point Manufacturing Company built the Shawmut mill and village in 1907 in response to the demand for cotton duck. Unlike the early mill villages of the 19th century, Shawmut was planned and laid out according to the ideals of the City Beautiful movement. The village radiates along eight streets from a circle situated in front of the mill building. Shawmut mill turned out its first shipment of cotton duck for the International Harvester Company in 1908. (Courtesy LOC, HAER AL-168–2.)

Fuller E. Callaway Sr. (1870–1928) led the way in the development of the textile industry in Troup County. He engaged Neel Reid, an architect from Atlanta, to design his home Hills & Dales in 1914. The Italian Renaissance Revival–style home complemented the existing antebellum gardens with four terraces separated by boxwoods that were established on the site by the Ferrell family. (Courtesy Hills & Dales Estate.)

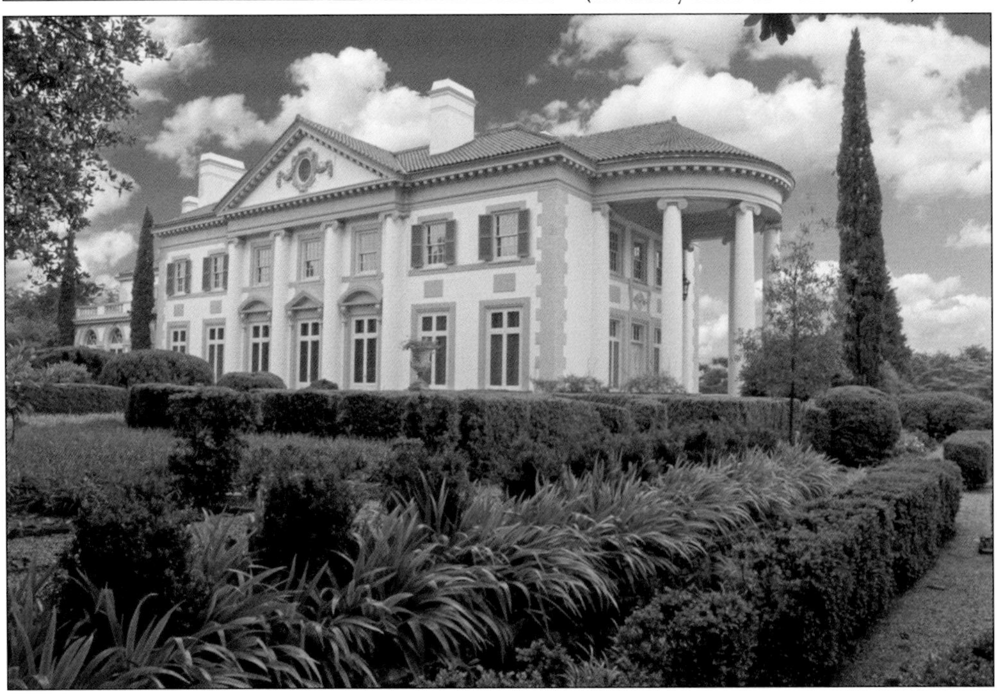

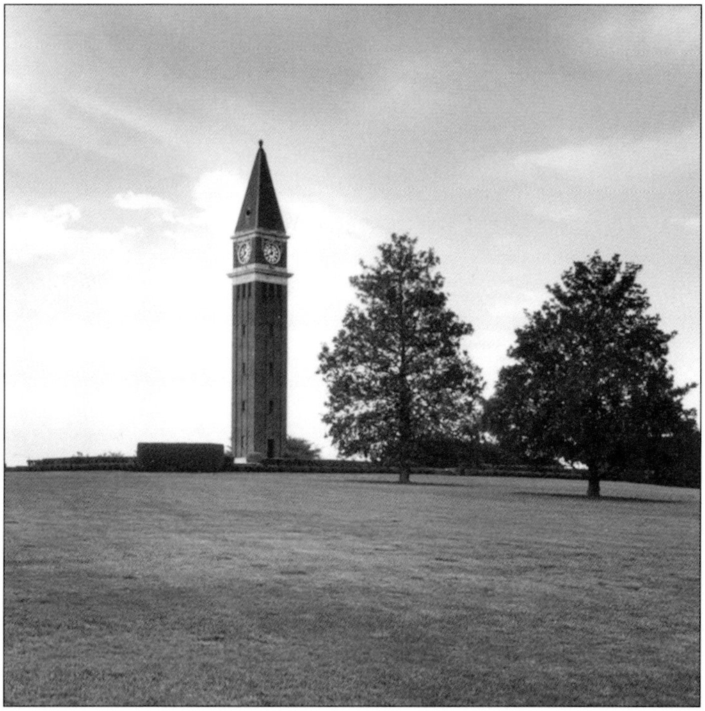

The Callaway Memorial Clock Tower, built after the death of Fuller E. Callaway Sr., is situated prominently on the highest point of Southwest LaGrange. Atlanta architectural firm Ivey and Crook, along with landscape architect Earle S. Draper, designed it in 1929. The Overseers Club, composed of Callaway Mills foremen, took the lead and gathered donations from the millworkers. (Courtesy Troup County Archives.)

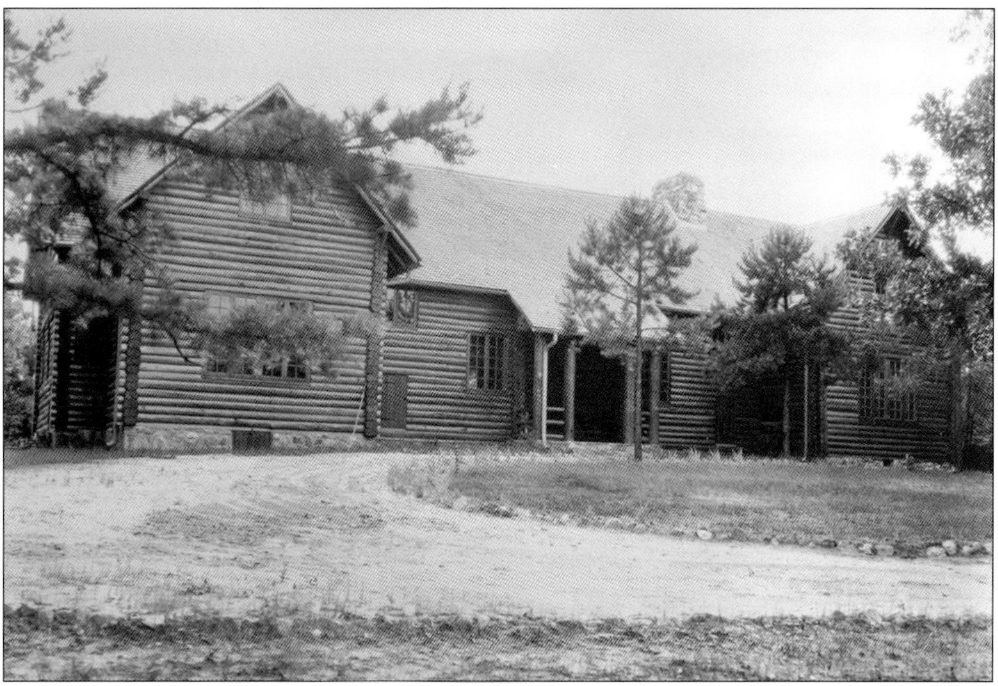

Cason Jewell Callaway (1894–1961) built this family retreat cabin at Blue Springs Farm in Harris County in 1930 after taking over Callaway Mills. In 1935, he turned mill operations over to his younger brother, Fuller E. Callaway Jr., and focused on agricultural innovations. In 1952, he and his wife, Virginia Hand Callaway, opened Callaway Gardens to the public. (Courtesy Georgia Archives, Vanishing Georgia Collection, trp168.)

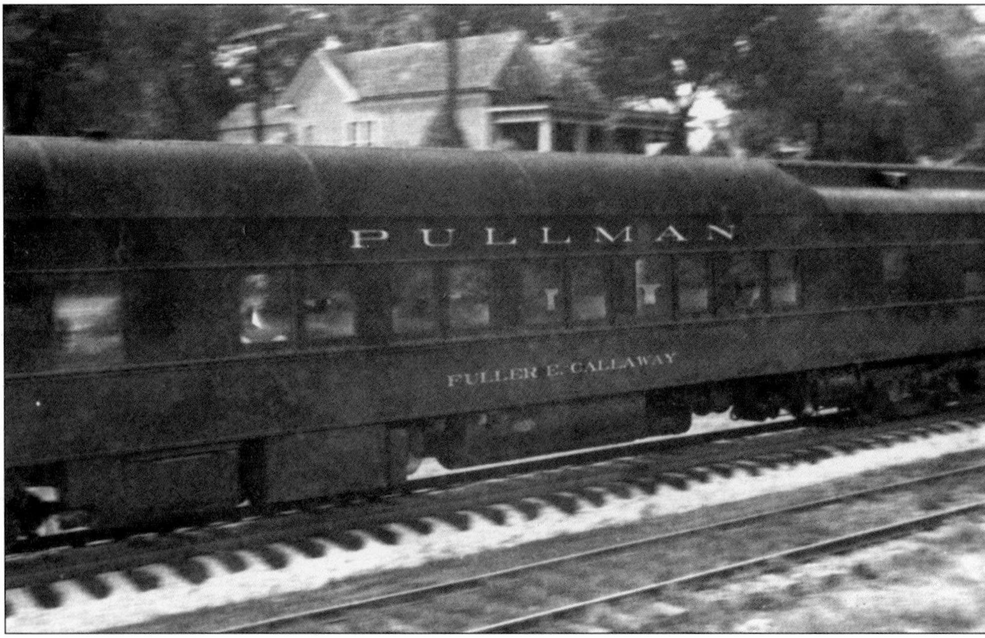

Engine No. 180 pulls the Fuller E. Callaway Pullman railcar through Hogansville in 1939. Callaway Mills owned the original Hogansville Manufacturing Company mill at the time. Railways provided the most efficient and comfortable travel for industrial leaders. The Pullman Company made private cars that could be coupled and uncoupled as needed. (Courtesy Troup County Archives.)

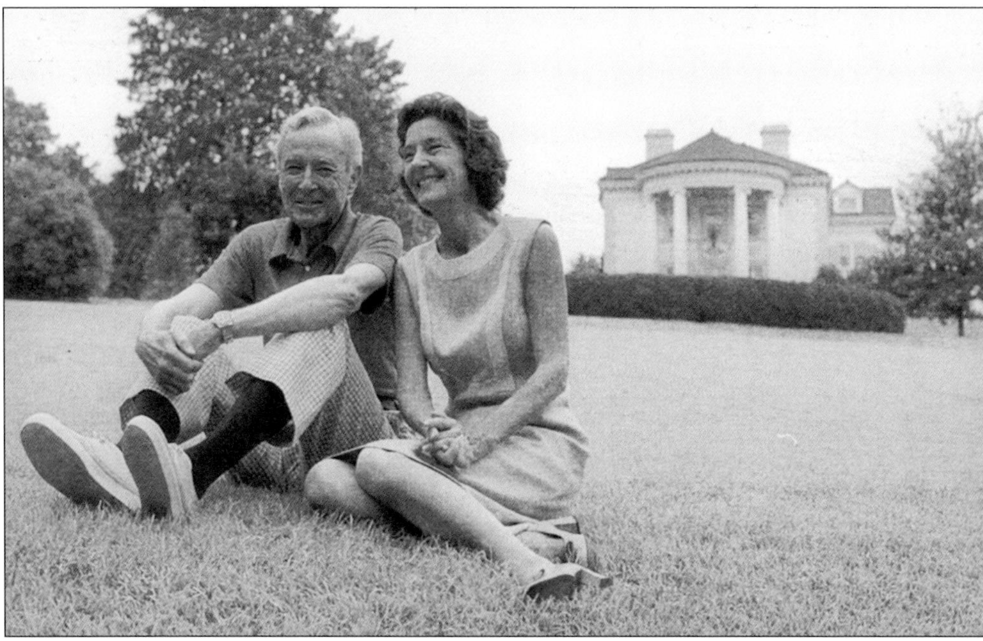

Fuller E. Callaway Jr. (1907–1992) began learning the textile industry as a coal stoker for his father's Elm City Cotton Mill when he was 14 years old. He became president of Callaway Mills in 1935. The Callaway Foundation Inc. and the Fuller E. Callaway Foundation, which Fuller and his wife, Alice, established, continue to support charitable initiatives in the west Georgia region. (Courtesy Troup County Archives.)

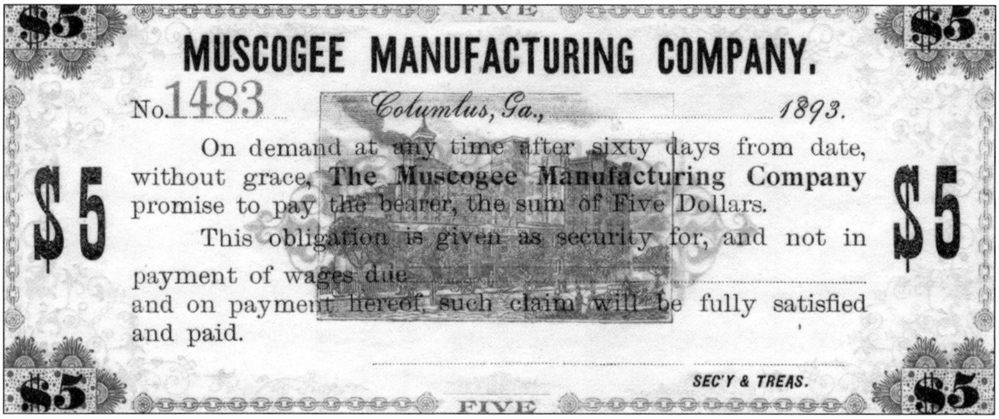

Textile mills paid employees in company tokens and scrip, which could be redeemed at the company store. These Upson County Waymanville Mill tokens (below), issued between 1840 and 1900, and Muscogee Mill 1893 paper scrip (above) share a common link to George Parker Swift (1814–1897). Swift, who started out as a merchant in Crawford County in 1832, later became an industrial leader in Upson County and invested in the Waymanville Mill, the Franklin Factory, and the Flint River Factory. He then moved to Columbus where he established Muscogee Mills in 1870 on the falls of the Chattahoochee River. (Below, courtesy Thomaston-Upson Archives.)

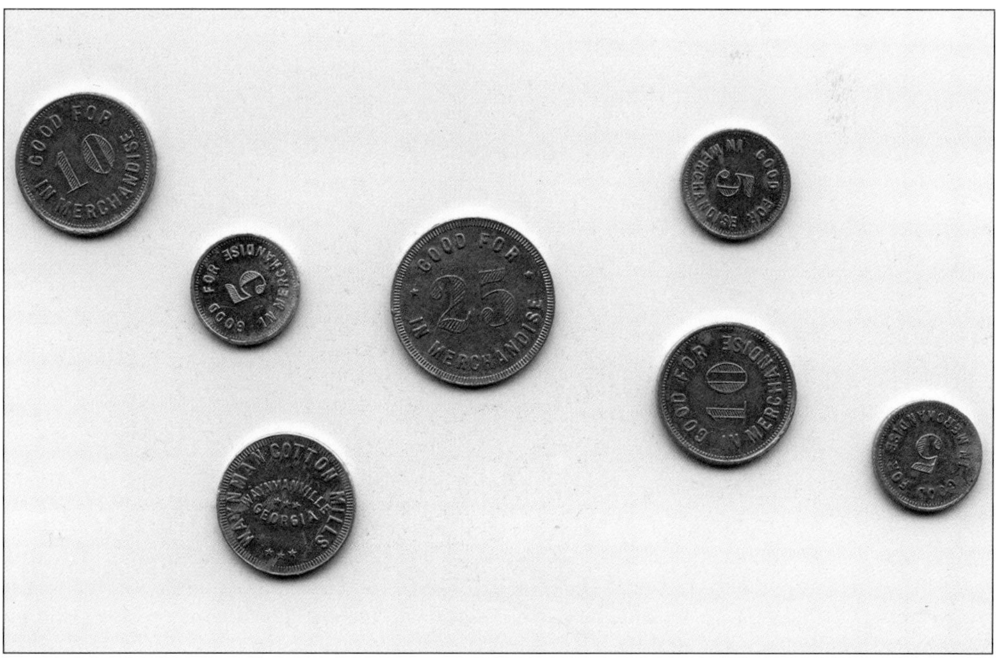

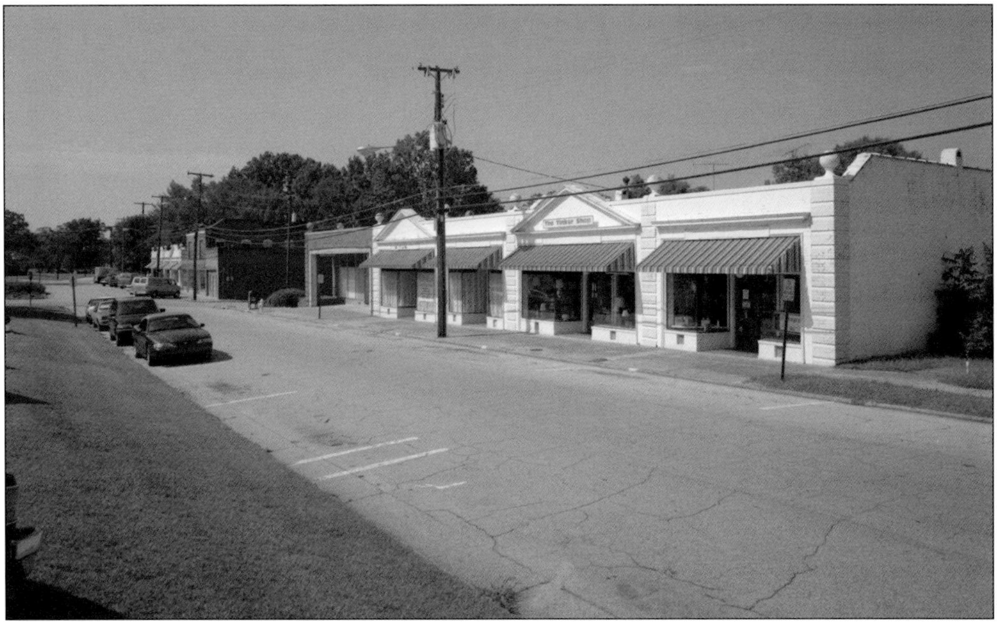

Callaway Mills hired Atlanta architects Ivey and Crook to design the Hillside commercial block in Southwest LaGrange in the early 1930s. Southwest LaGrange existed as an incorporated community from 1917 to 1920, encompassing four textile mills: Unity Cotton Mill, Unity Spinning Mill, Elm City Mill, and the Hillside Mill. The community became part of the city of LaGrange in 1920. (Courtesy LOC, HAER GA, 143-LAGR, 34–1.)

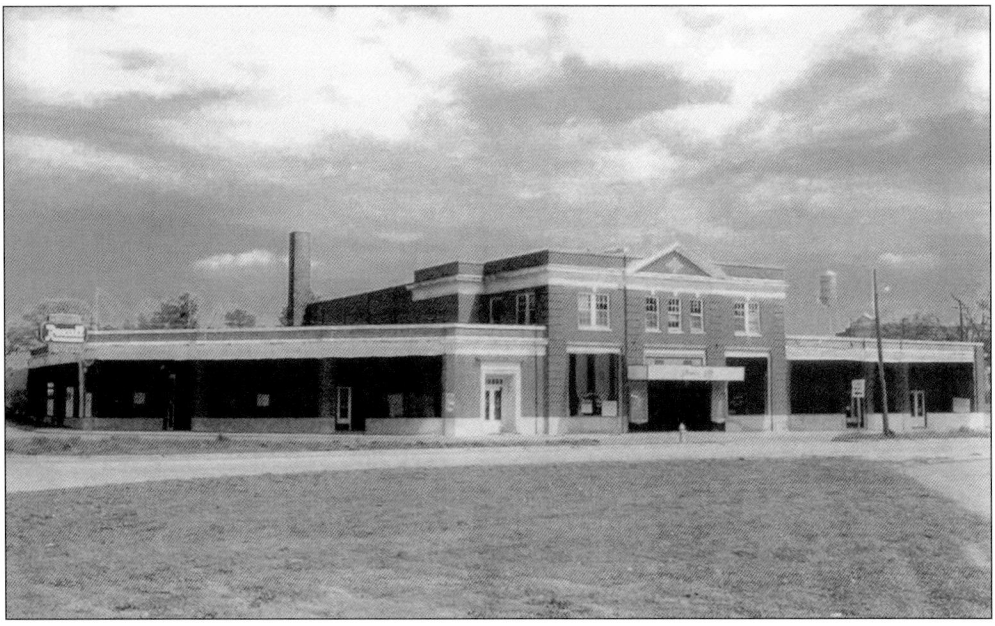

B.F. Goodrich began building the Silvertown mill village for operatives of Martha Mills near Thomaston in 1929. The village included a large brick community center with retail space for rent, operated by individuals rather than the textile company. The commercial block included a grocery store, drugstore, café, theater, beauty shop, and barbershop. The company doctor's office occupied the second floor. (Courtesy Thomaston-Upson Archives.)

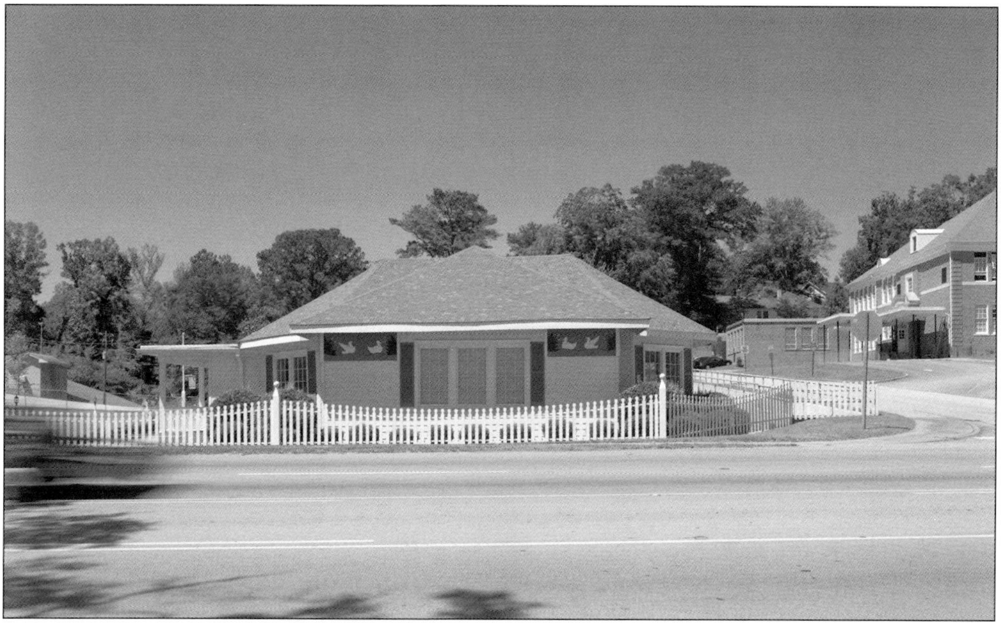

The West Point Manufacturing Company built the Langdale Kindergarten around 1915 in the spirit of welfare capitalism embraced by many textile mill companies in the South. More recently, it has served as a community center known as The Cotton Duck, a playful pun on the industrial cotton duck cloth produced by the community mills for so many years. (Courtesy LOC, HAER AL-167-C–2.)

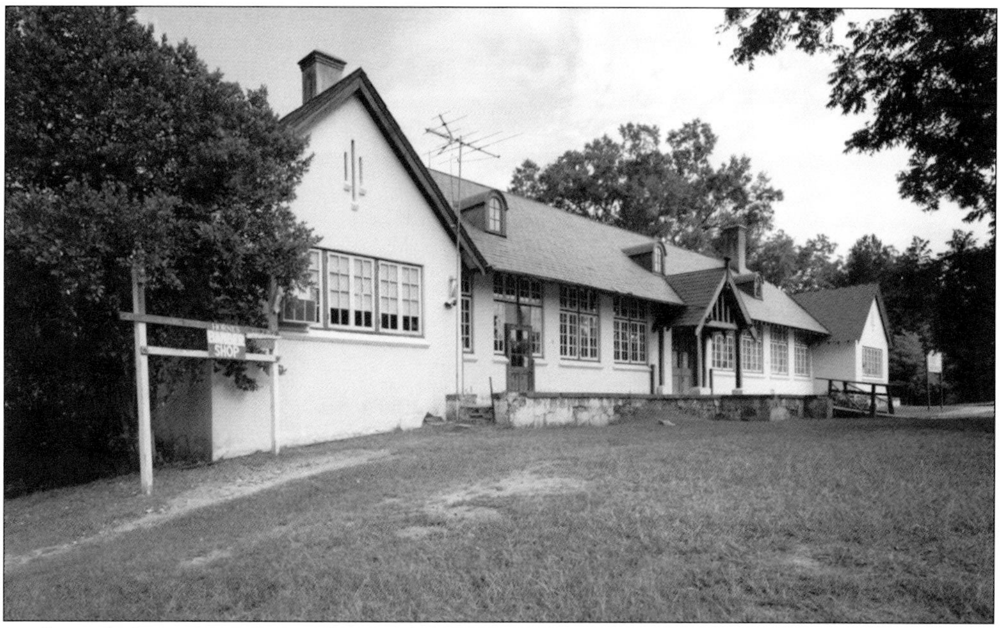

Lockwood Greene Engineers designed the Hogansville Mill Community Building in 1917. It included a swimming pool and bowling alley as well as meeting rooms and a gymnasium that doubled as an auditorium. The International Cotton Mills owned by Lockwood, Greene and Company bought the Hogansville Mill in 1913 and built Stark Mill in 1923. (Courtesy LOC, HAER GA, 143-HOVI, 5–1.)

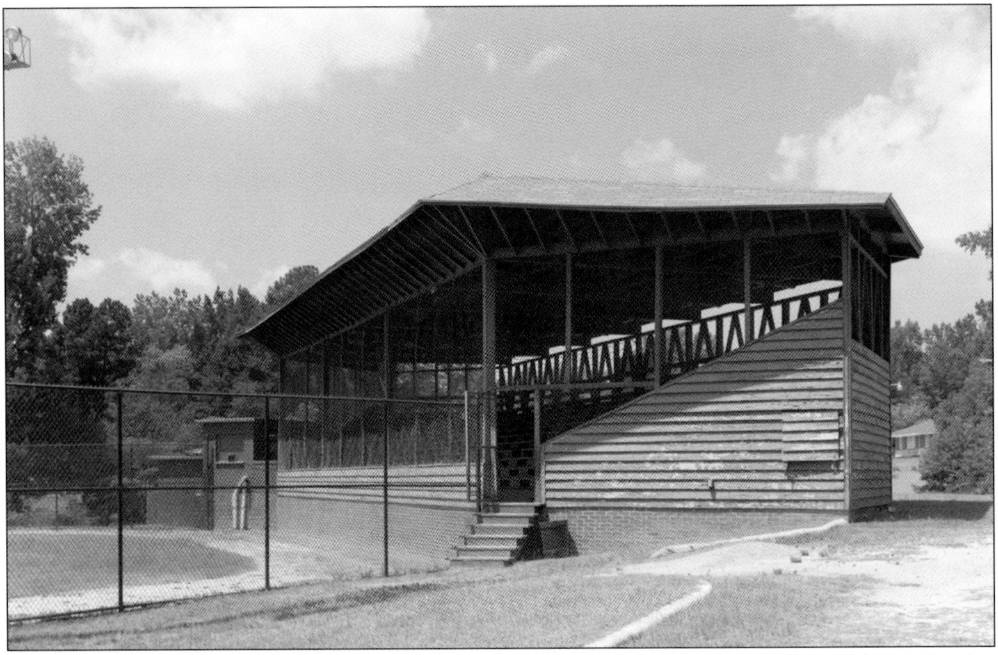

The West Point Manufacturing Company built this baseball field with grandstand for its Fairfax mill village employees around 1925. Although many southern textile mill villages once had ballparks, few remain intact with grandstand. The Towel Makers team name points to the mill's production of terry and crash toweling associated with the Martex brand after 1928. West Point Manufacturing built Fairfax as a toweling mill in 1915–1916 but temporarily shifted to cotton duck in response to military needs during World War I. The company hired Harvard-trained landscape architect William B. Marquis to lay out the village around the mill. (Both, courtesy LOC; above, HAER AL-168–2; below, HAER AL-182–1.)

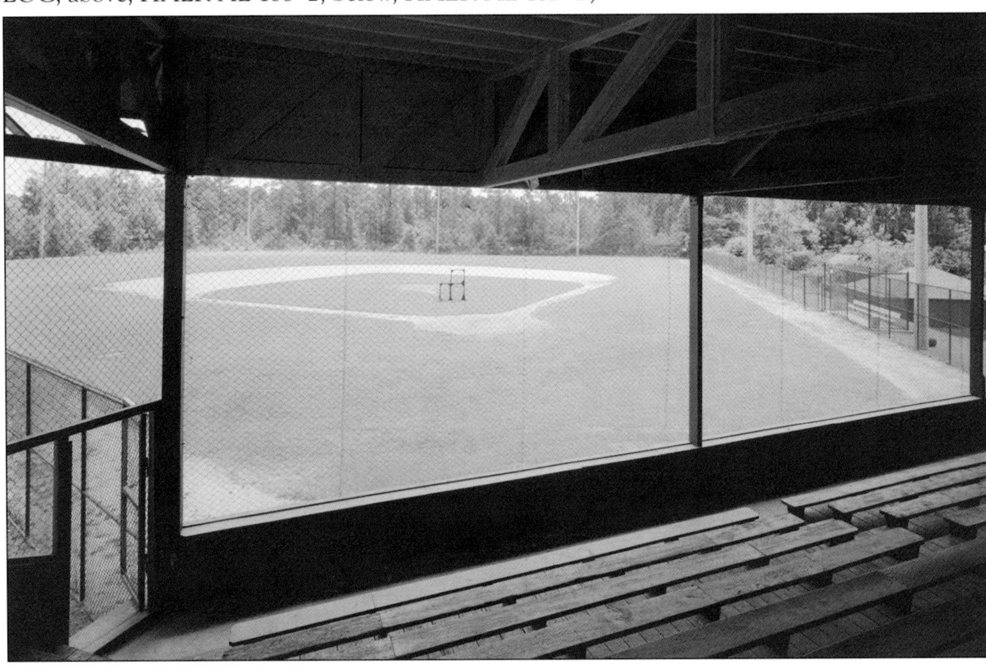

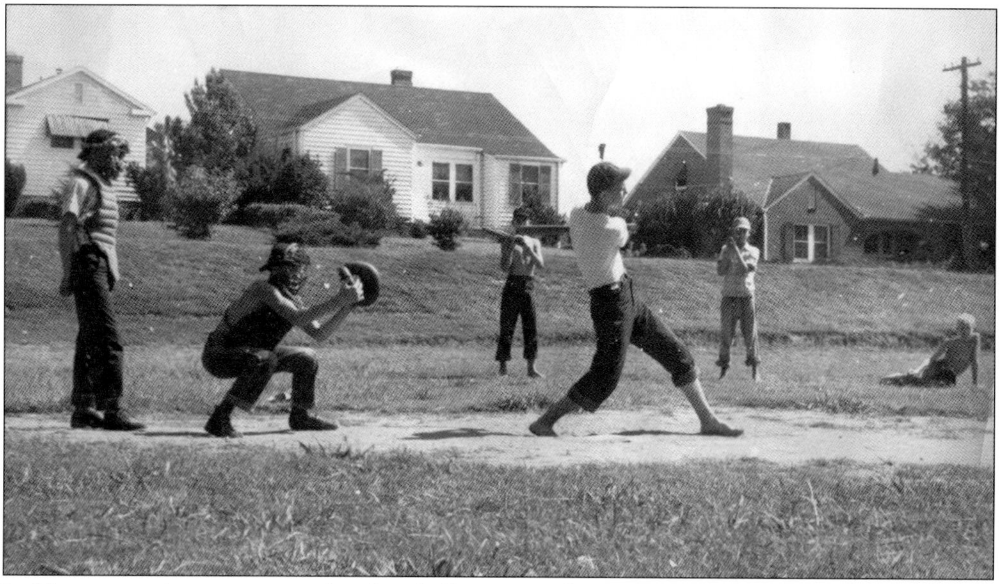

In Thomaston, boys enjoy a pickup baseball game on the open green space at the village center. Both the East Thomaston and Silvertown mill villages fielded semiprofessional baseball teams with ballparks. When the crosstown rivals faced off, particularly large crowds gathered at the village ballpark. (Courtesy Thomaston-Upson Archives.)

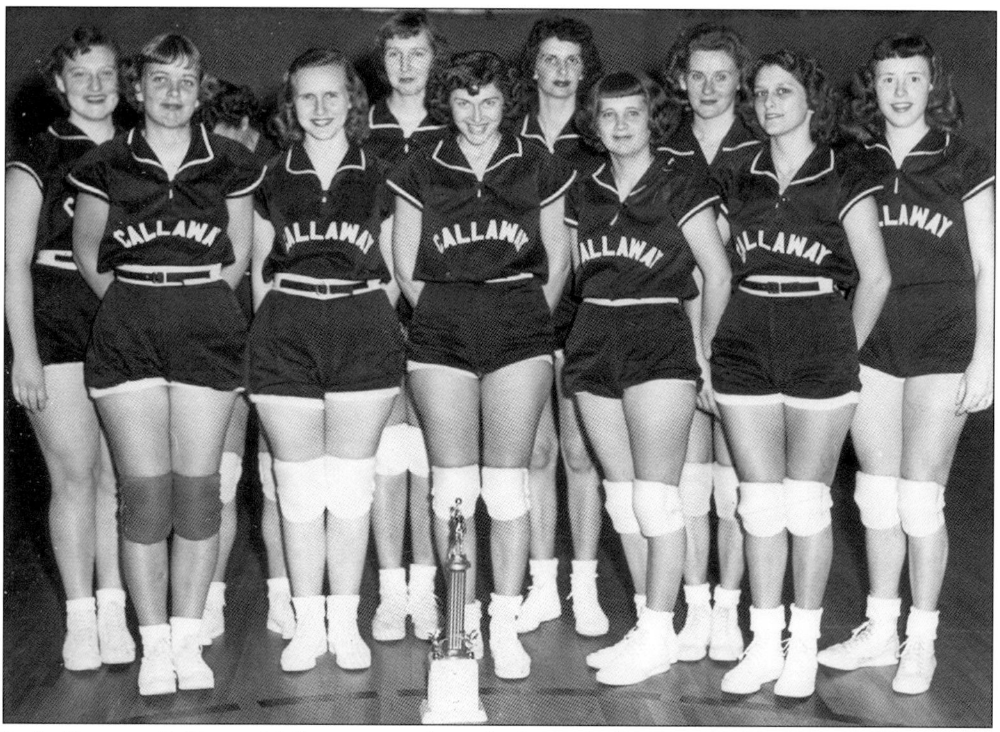

In LaGrange, Callaway Mills sponsored a girls' basketball team, as well as one for the boys. Community sports played a strong role in corporate culture and exemplified mill villages as social institutions and manufacturing centers. Mills provided these non-wage benefits to attract and keep a stable workforce. (Courtesy Troup County Archives.)

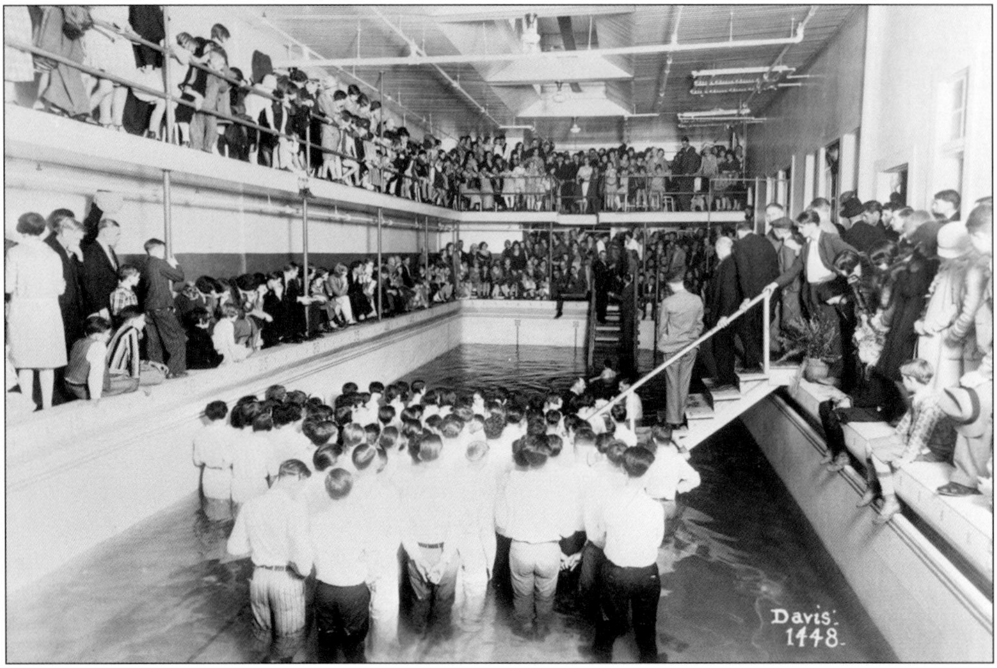

Around 1930, many gathered at the Callaway Mills pool to watch as a minister baptized a large group of young people. The mill village swimming pool was more often the focal point of summer fun and relaxation. (Courtesy Georgia Archives, Vanishing Georgia Collection, trp247.)

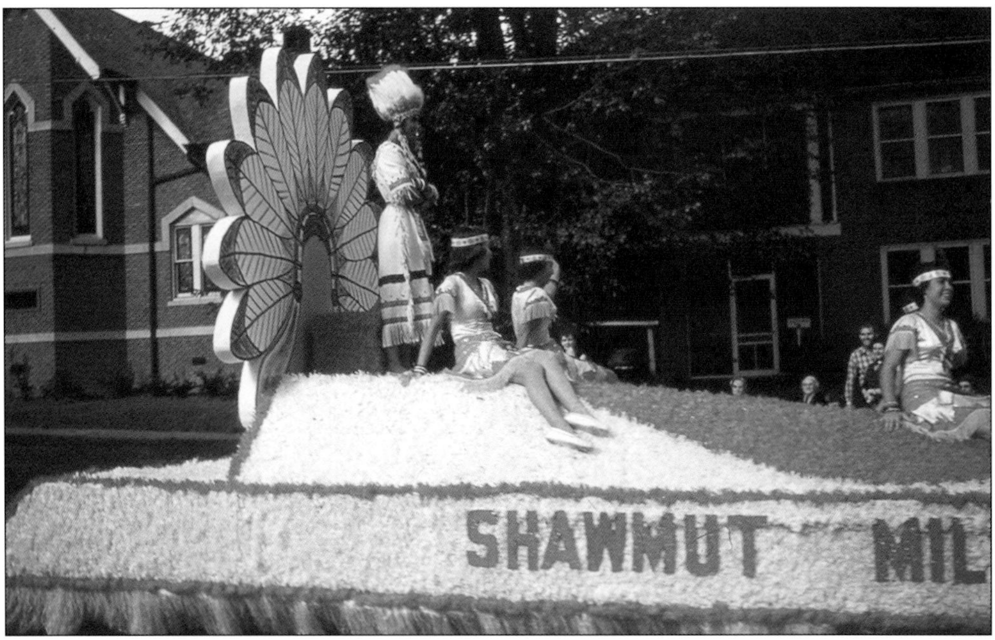

The West Point Manufacturing Company concluded a week-long celebration of its 75th anniversary with a parade on October 15, 1955. The Shawmut Mill contributed a float reflecting its connections to Boston investors and the Algonquin origin of its name. West Point merchants, school bands, civic groups, and even the US Navy and American Red Cross participated in the parade. (Courtesy Troup County Archives.)

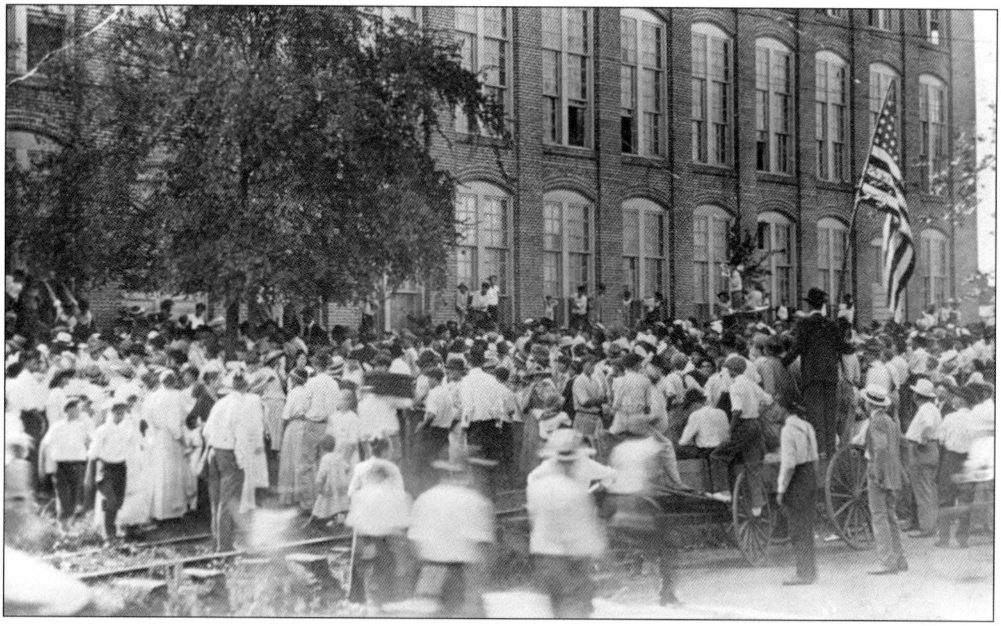

Workers at Swift Mills in Columbus rally during the national textile strike of 1934. Violence broke out in Columbus before the United Textile Workers (UTW) officially called for the strike. W.R. Sanders, a striker at the Georgia Webbing and Tape Company and a member of the UTW, was killed in a fight between picketers and other workers when management tried to resume operations on August 10. (Courtesy Columbus State University.)

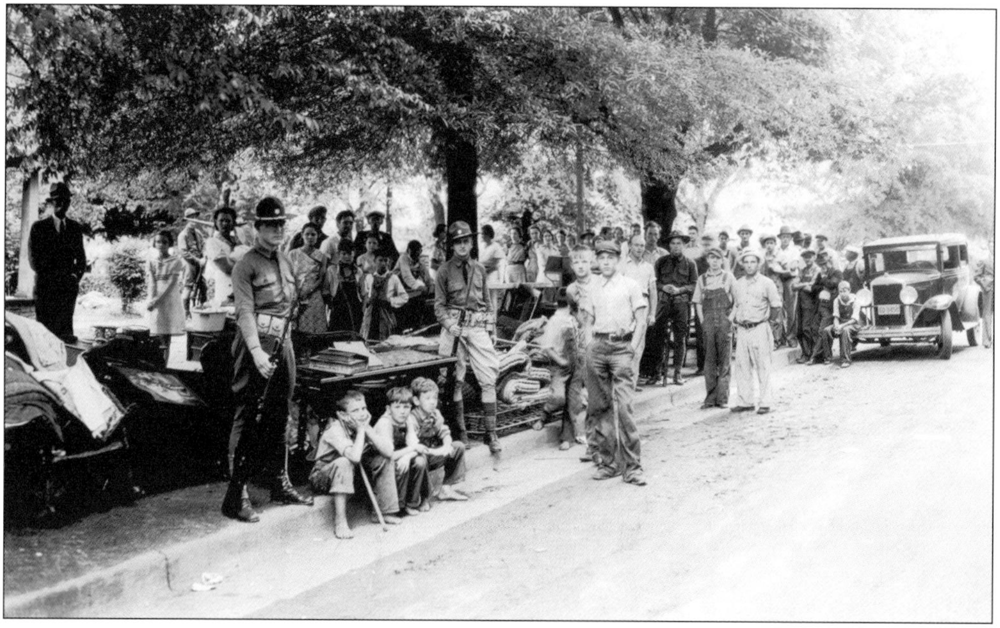

In LaGrange, the National Guard evicted striking workers from houses owned by Callaway Mills during the strike of 1934. Protests resulted from the National Industrial Recovery Act, a New Deal measure passed in response to the Great Depression. Campaign promises by Eugene Talmadge encouraged textile workers, but as the newly elected governor, he immediately activated the National Guard and effectively ended the strike in Georgia. (Courtesy Troup County Archives.)

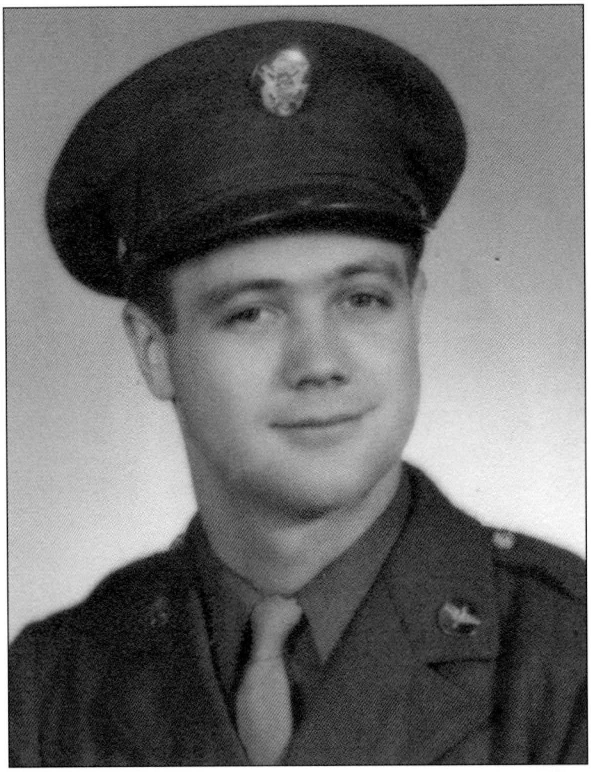

S.Sgt. Render T. Parham Sr. of the US Army Air Corps was a freshman at Georgia Tech when he dropped out and began working for Uniroyal in Hogansville. During World War II, Parham served in the Pacific Theater with the 871st Bomber Squadron. He returned to Stark Mill as an industrial engineer after completing his Georgia Tech degree under the GI Bill. (Courtesy R. Terrell Parham Jr.)

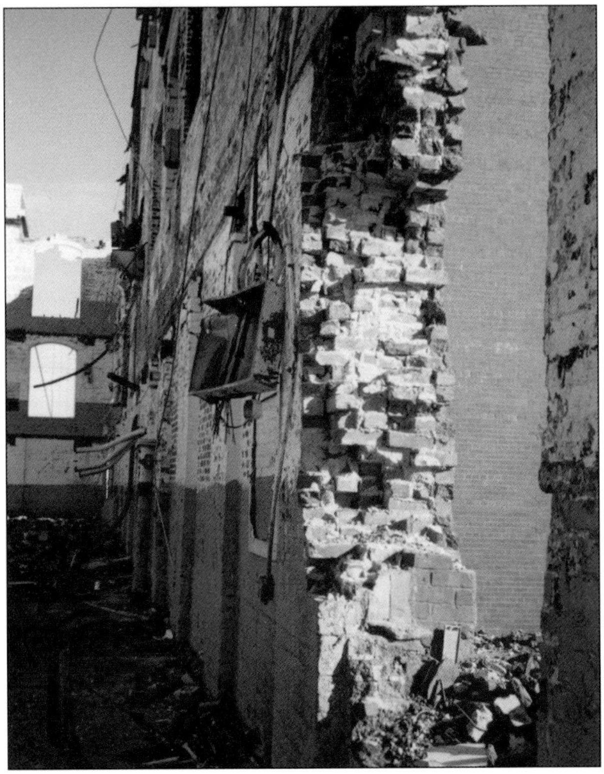

Like many southern textile mills, Thomaston Mills could not overcome the economic changes produced by NAFTA. In 2001, Thomaston Mills filed for bankruptcy. The textile mill, which had long been the center of the local economy and social scene, was demolished in 2005. It had already deteriorated, as seen here. (Courtesy Ellen Tew.)

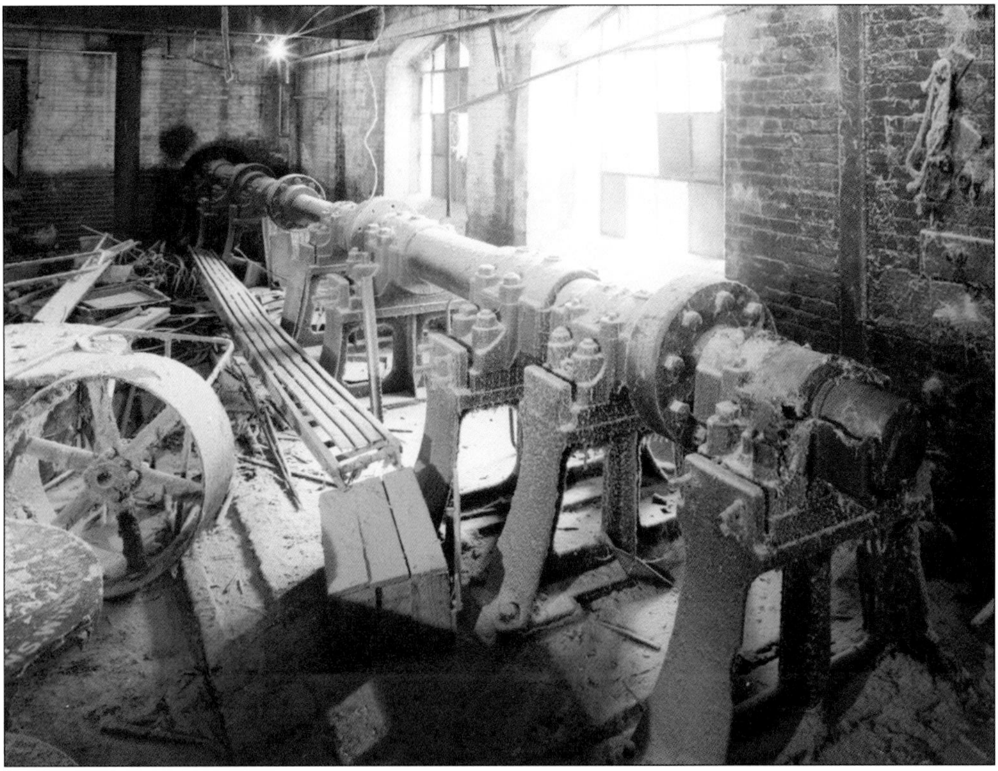

These two images show abandoned machinery at Bibb Manufacturing Company in Columbus after the plant closed in March 1998. As cotton manufacturing declined, company president William S. Manning began to sell Bibb Manufacturing's plants in Georgia in the 1970s. By 1996, the company declared bankruptcy. Bibb City was so affected by closures, it was forced to merge with Columbus. The mill burned in 2008. (Both, courtesy LOC; above, HAER GA, 108-COLM, 27–19; right, HAER GA, 108-COLM, 27–27.)

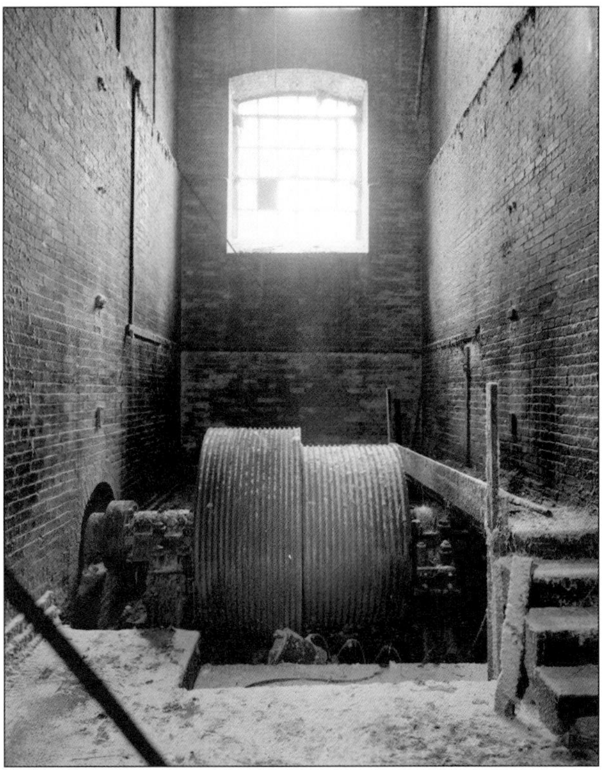

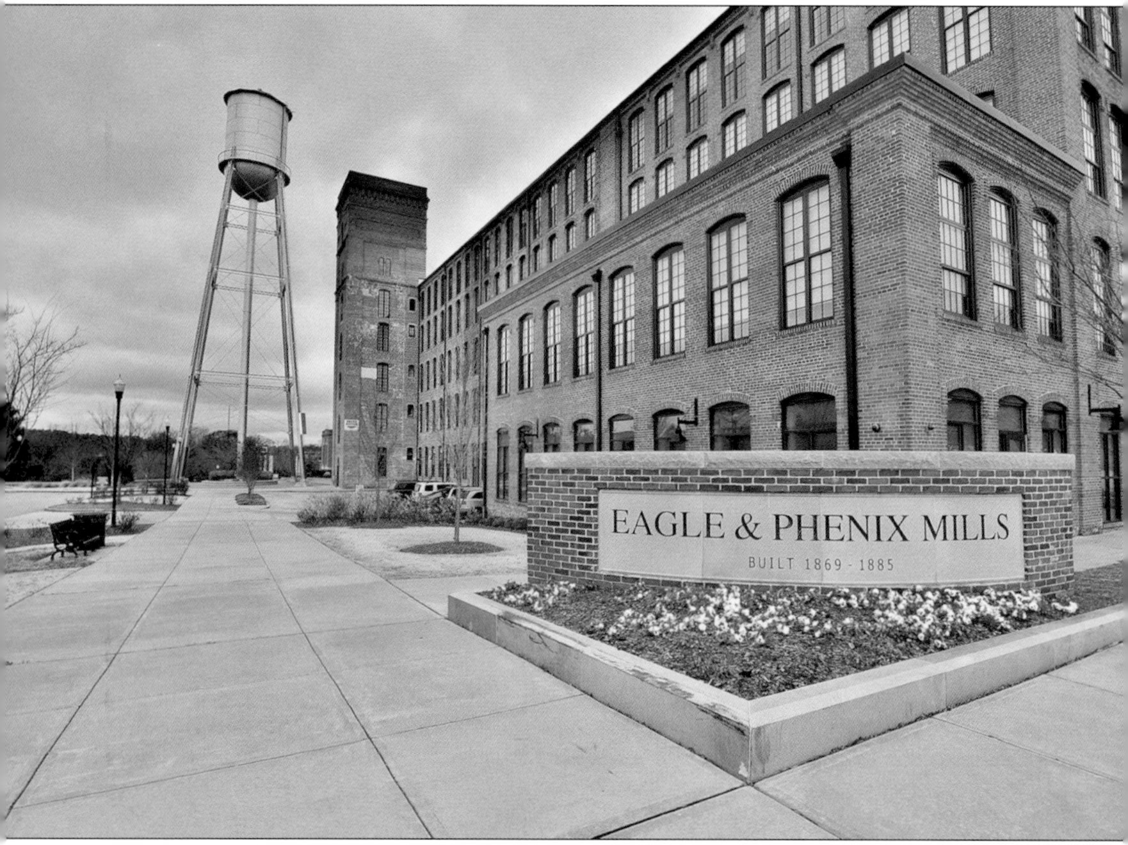

Columbus and its residents have worked to preserve some of the mill buildings as the textile industry declined. Eagle & Phenix Mill, shown here, was owned by several different companies, including Fieldcrest, which produced towels, and Pillowtex, which produced mattress pads. In 2003, W.C. Bradley bought the mill building and converted it into condominiums. (Courtesy Doug Roth Photography.)

Two

THE CENTRAL TRAIL

The Central Trail extends along US Highway 27 and the roads paralleling the railroad lines, such as US Highways 78 and 29. This section includes Carroll and Haralson Counties along the Alabama border and Coweta, Douglas, and Paulding Counties to the east.

Two small-scale cotton spinning mills emerged along rivers in this region during the antebellum period: Bowensville Manufacturing Company near Whitesburg in 1847 and Sweetwater Manchester Company near Lithia Springs in 1849.

After the Civil War, New South ideology and modern technology encouraged southern and northern investors to establish cotton mills in the growing towns along the new railroad lines. The largest growth in this region occurred at the turn of the 20th century with the construction of multistory brick mills, beginning with the Newnan Cotton Mill in 1888, followed by others in the railroad towns of Carrollton, Tallapoosa, Douglasville, Senoia, Villa Rica, and Dallas. Operated by steam and electric power, these mills produced cotton yarn and cloth. Company owners established mill villages filled with homes, churches, schools, stores, and other amenities.

Hosiery mills moved into the railroad towns in this region in the early 20th century, often alongside the cotton mills. By 1910, Grantville, Banning, Douglasville, and Dallas had hosiery or knitting mills. The greatest concentration opened in the 1920s. Carroll County boasted the largest number of hosiery mills in Georgia in 1935, located primarily in Carrollton and Villa Rica.

At the same time, the men's apparel industry emerged in Bremen. Brothers Robert, Roy, and Warren Sewell moved their clothing manufacturing company from Atlanta to Bremen in 1928, constructing manufacturing plants throughout Carroll and Haralson Counties and into Alabama over the next five decades. The apparel industry boomed, reaching its height of production in the 1970s and 1980s, when this region became known as the "Clothing Center of the South."

All of these textile operations declined in the late 20th century, first cotton and then hosiery. Some apparel manufacturing still takes place here, particularly for the military, although much has moved offshore.

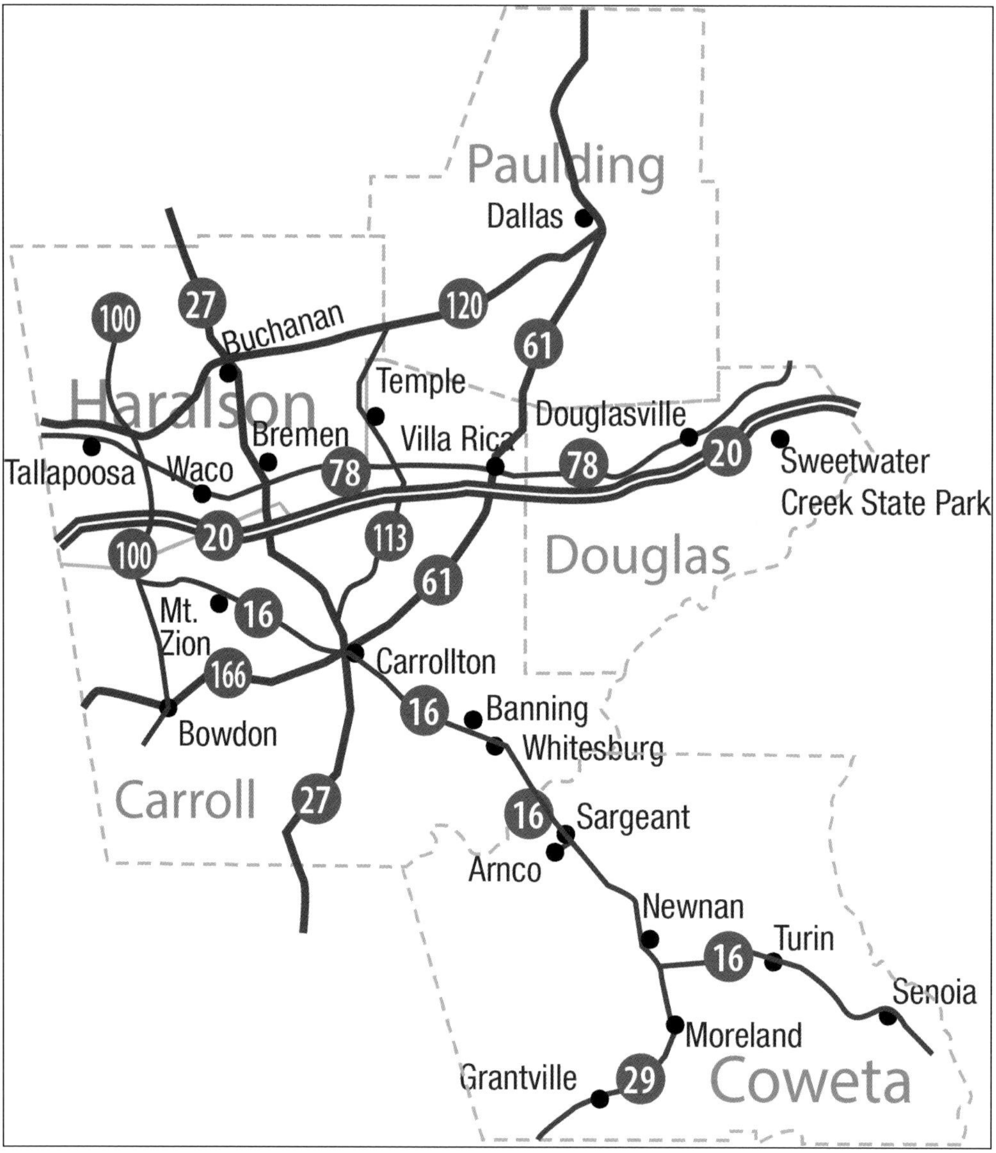

Cotton and hosiery mills in the central region follow the railroad lines established through the region in the mid- to late 1800s. The apparel companies began to establish plants in Carroll and Haralson Counties beginning in the 1920s, starting first with Bremen and Bowdon and then spreading into other railroad towns and rural communities.

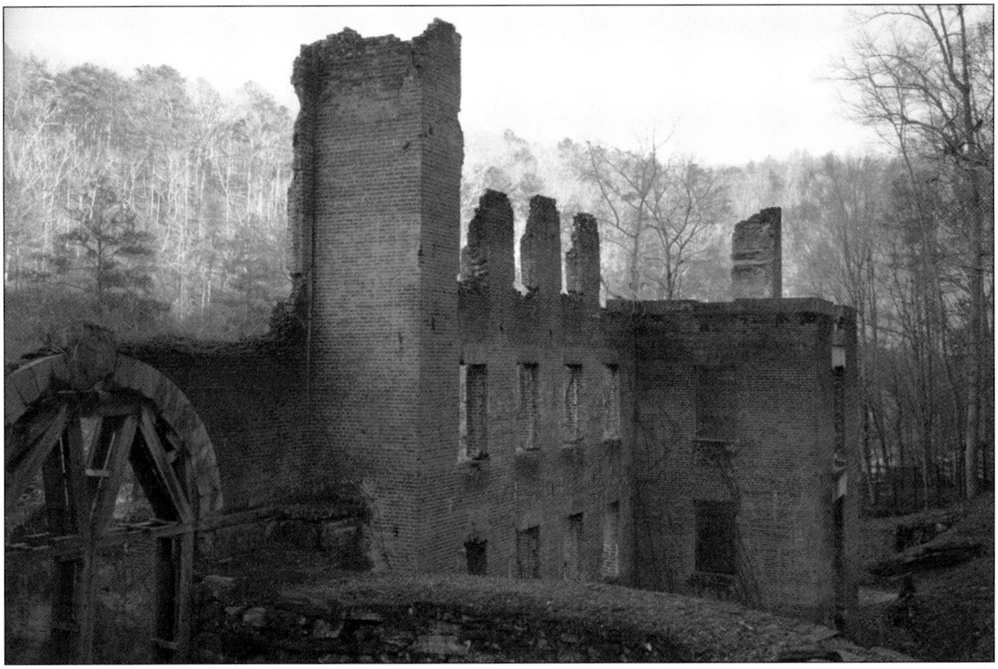

James Rogers and Charles McDonald funded this five-story brick mill along Sweetwater Creek in 1849. Sweetwater Manufacturing Company, later renamed New Manchester Manufacturing Company, produced yarn and cotton duck with labor from nearby farm families. On July 9, 1864, Union forces burned the mill and sent the women workers north into Kentucky and Indiana. Today, the mill is part of Sweetwater Creek State Park. (Photograph by Kymberli Darling)

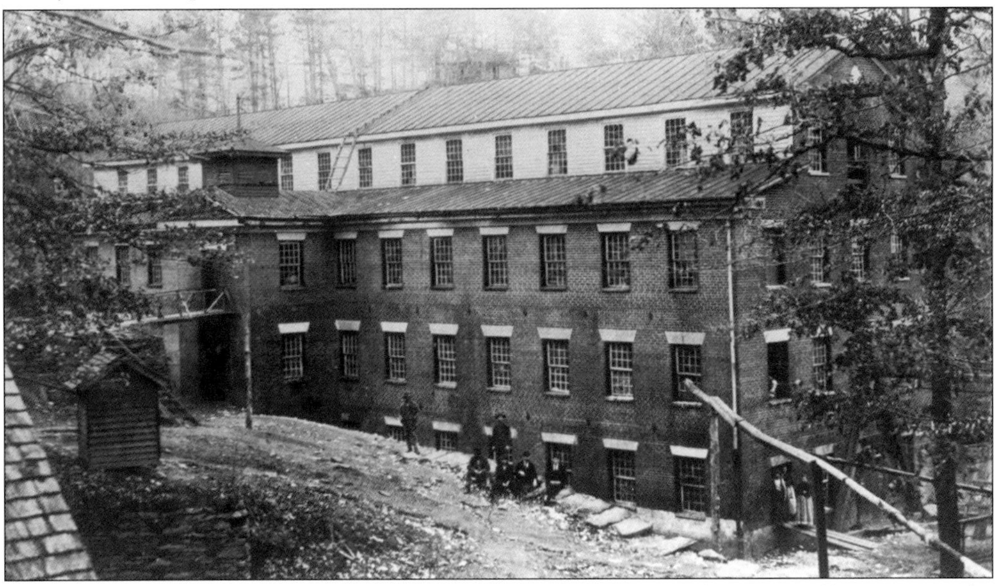

Four brothers established Bowen's Mill along Snake Creek in southern Carroll County in the 1840s. The small textile operation spun coarse yarn for osnaburgs. The mill burned in 1851. Some operations resumed in 1866 as Carroll Manufacturing, but it was not until 1878 that Arthur Hutcheson purchased and modernized the mill by adding new equipment. It first operated by waterpower, but by 1885, it ran by steam.

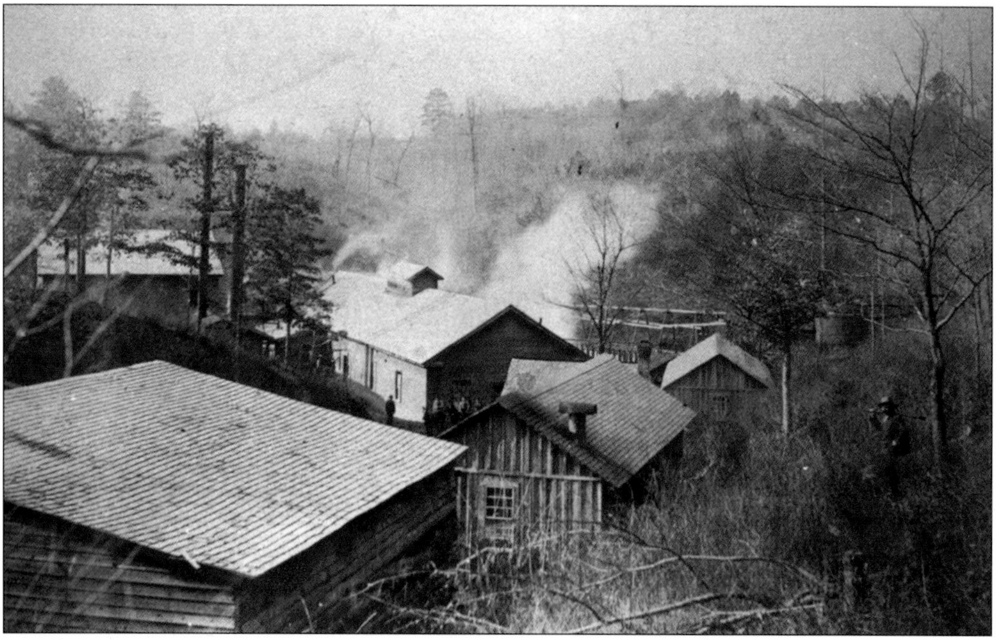

The location of Hutcheson Mill, tucked in the Snake Creek valley, was typical of the early water-powered textile operations in this region. In 1878, Arthur Hutcheson began to establish a village around the mill. By the early 1900s, when this photograph was taken, the community had houses for the workers; a company store, church, and school; and a sock mill, cotton gin, warehouse, and sawmill.

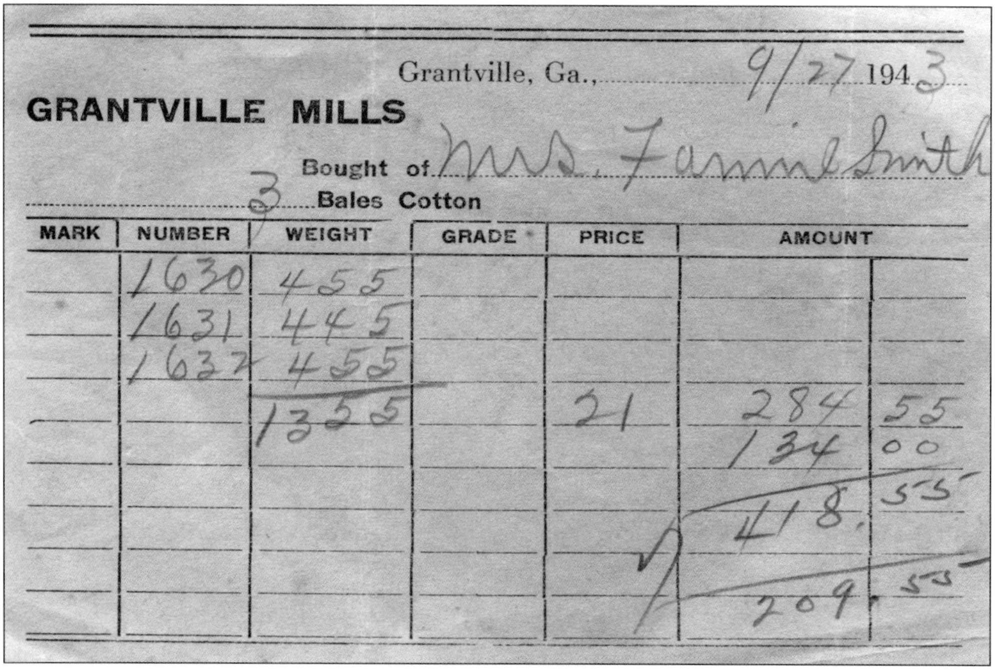

Grantville, Ga., 9/27 1943

GRANTVILLE MILLS

Bought of Mrs. Fannie Smith

3 Bales Cotton

MARK	NUMBER	WEIGHT	GRADE	PRICE	AMOUNT	
	1630	455				
	1631	445				
	1632	455				
		1355		21	284	55
					134	00
					418.	55
					209.	55

Many farm families sold their cotton to the mill companies, which often owned multiple cotton gins and warehouses. In this receipt from September 1943, Fannie Smith sold three bales of cotton to the Grantville Mills. (Courtesy Coweta County Genealogical Society.)

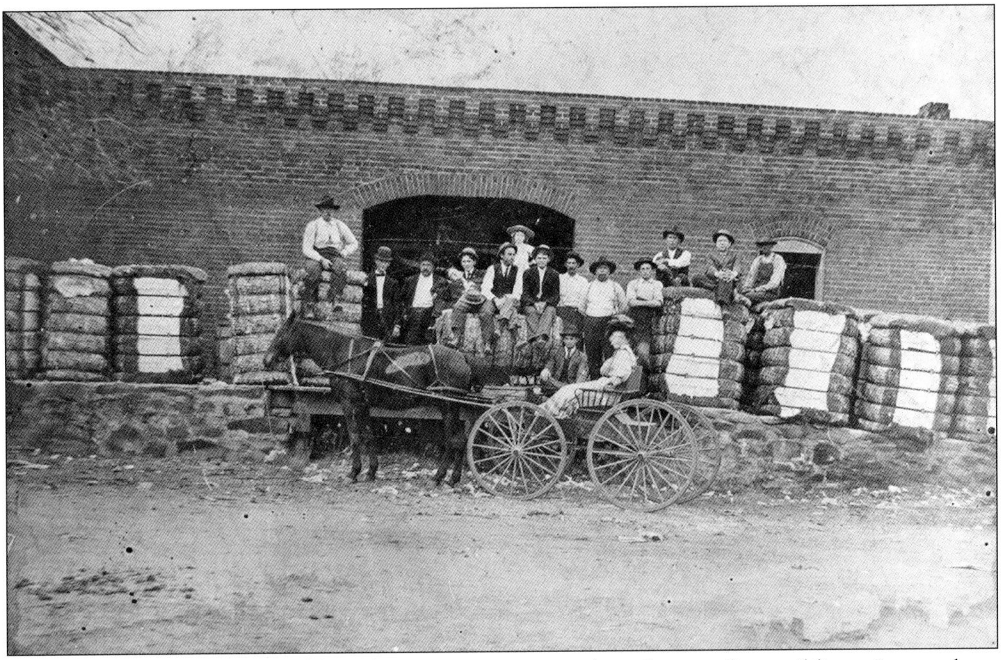

Rural communities benefited from being near major roads and expanding rail lines. It was along these railroads that local merchants and agents established cotton warehouses and platforms to store incoming and outgoing shipments of cotton bales, like those seen here in Turin in the 1890s. (Courtesy Georgia Archives, Vanishing Georgia Collection, cow185.)

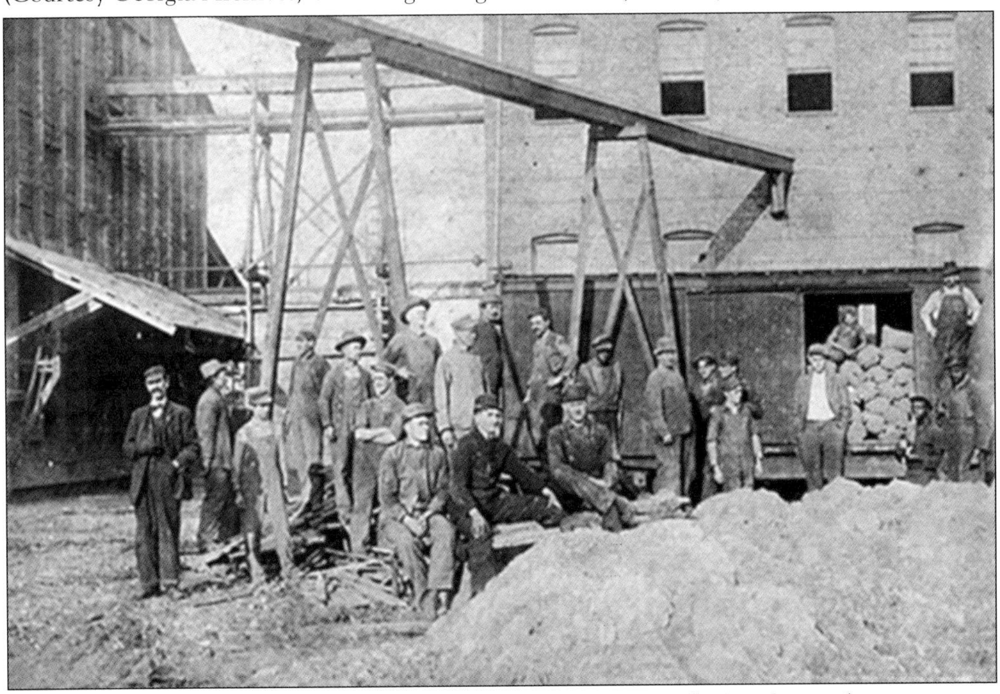

Local businessmen and mills operated cotton gins in towns, as well as in the rural communities. This 1890s gin in Grantville served area farmers by processing their raw cotton. (Courtesy Georgia Archives, Vanishing Georgia Collection, cow180-95.)

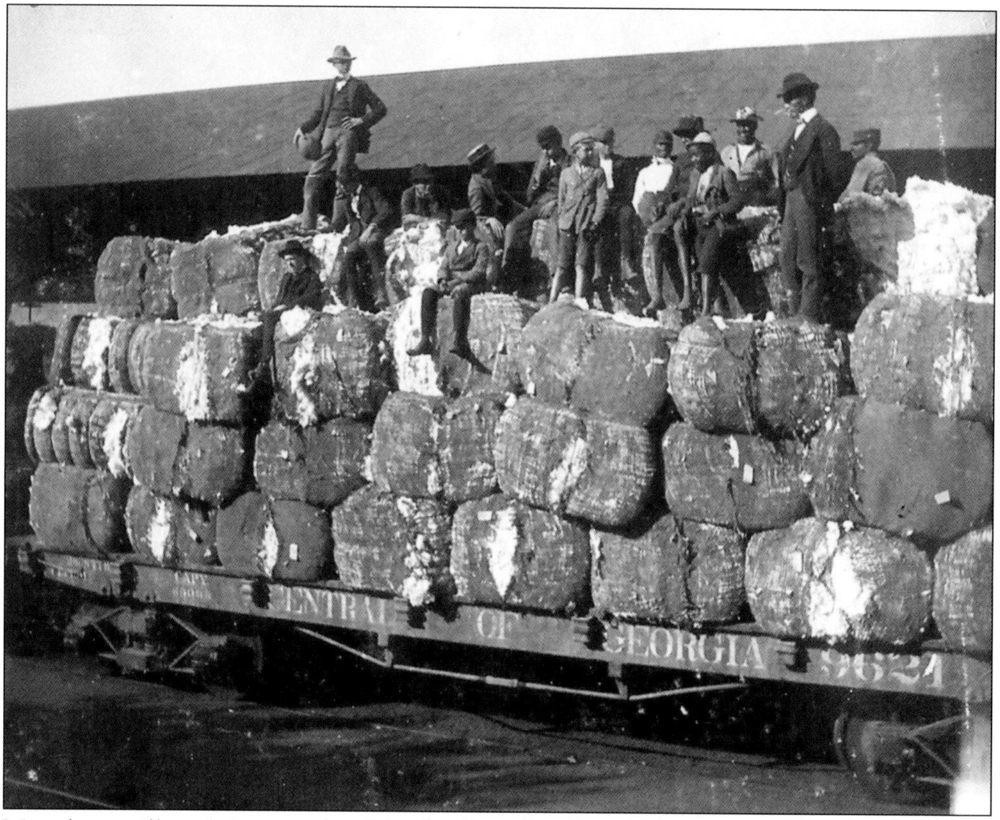

Many large mills and plants, such as Mandeville Mills of Carrollton, had their own spur lines from the railroad adjacent to the mill. The train platforms of Mandeville Mills and the town depot received raw product for processing and manufacturing and shipped finished products off to large regional or national markets on the railroad. (Courtesy Susan Patton Hamersky.)

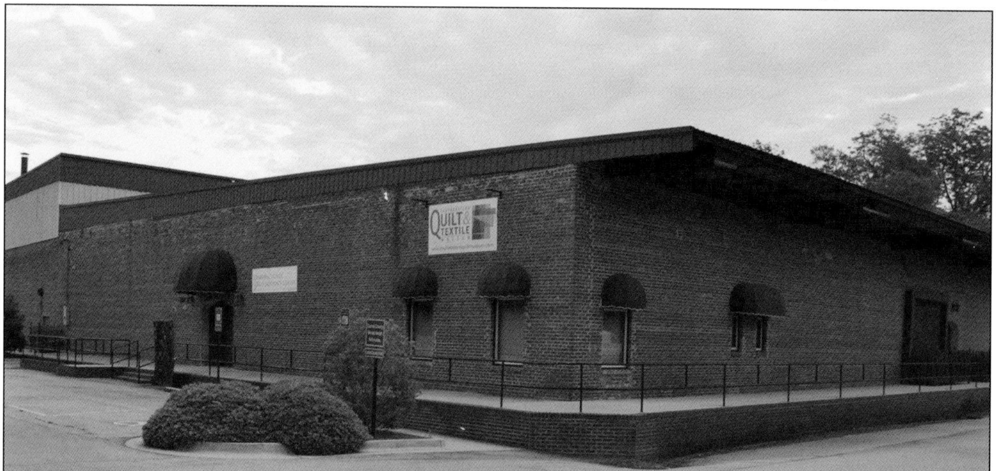

This building, now Southern Quilt and Textile Museum of Carrollton, was once a large cotton warehouse used by area farmers during the early to mid-1900s. Part of the building burned in 1937, but it was soon repaired and continued to be used as a cotton warehouse. Farmers often stored their bales here when cotton prices were low. (Photograph by Keri P. Adams.)

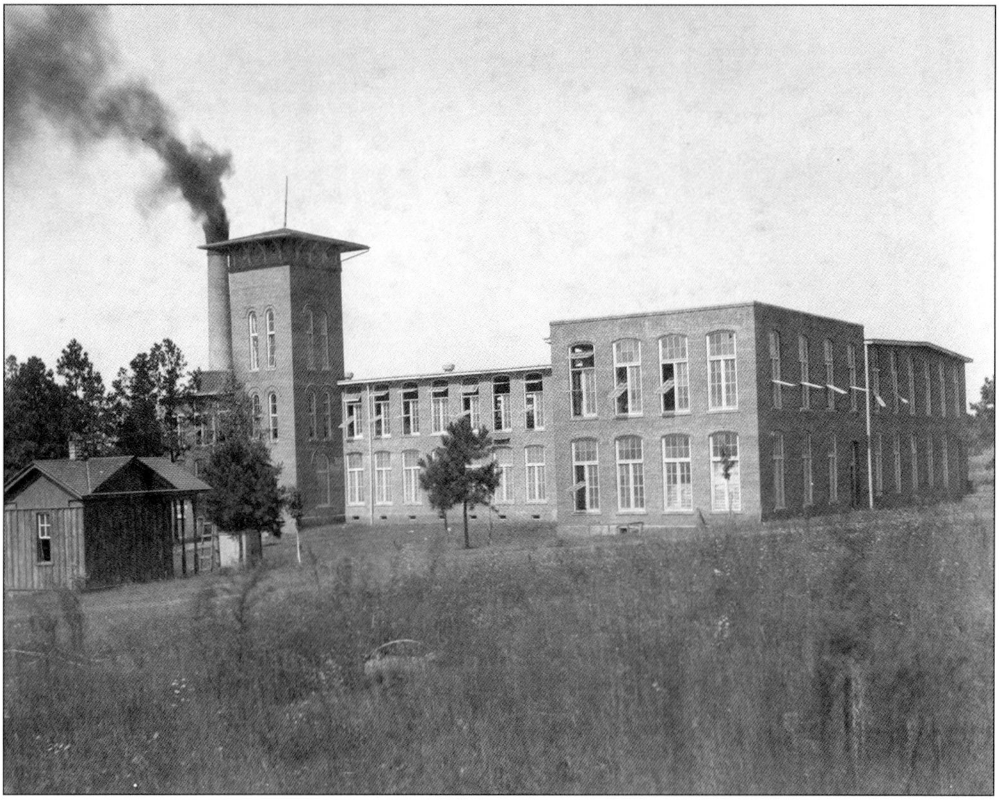

In 1899, Mandeville Mills became the first textile operation in the growing railroad town of Carrollton. The coal-burning steam engine that powered the mill produced the smoke seen in this c. 1900 photograph. In the early 1900s, the company employed over 200 workers to produce cotton yarn and fertilizer and to operate several gins on the property. By 1910, the mill had added 120 looms.

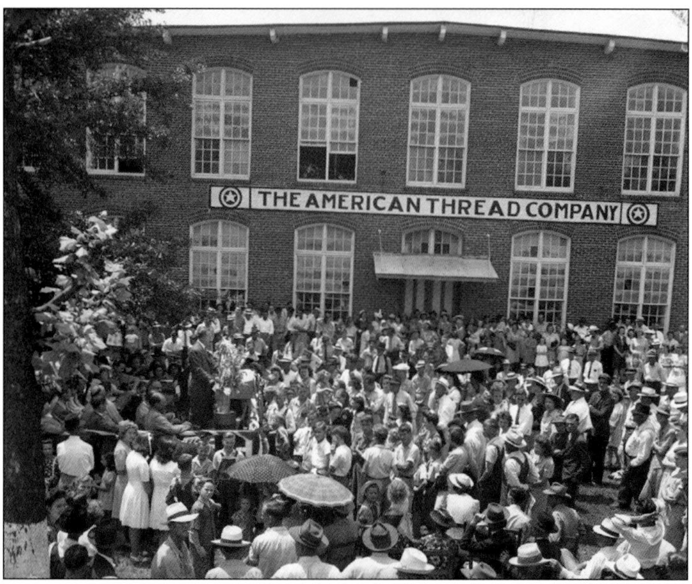

Tallapoosa Mills opened in the booming railroad town of Tallapoosa in 1908, employing 200 workers by the 1920s. After operating part time during the Depression, the mill closed in 1939. American Thread Company (ATCO) purchased the mill in 1943 to make combed yarn. The reopening on January 28, 1944, featured speeches and a flag-raising. (Courtesy Special Collections and Archives, Georgia State University Library.)

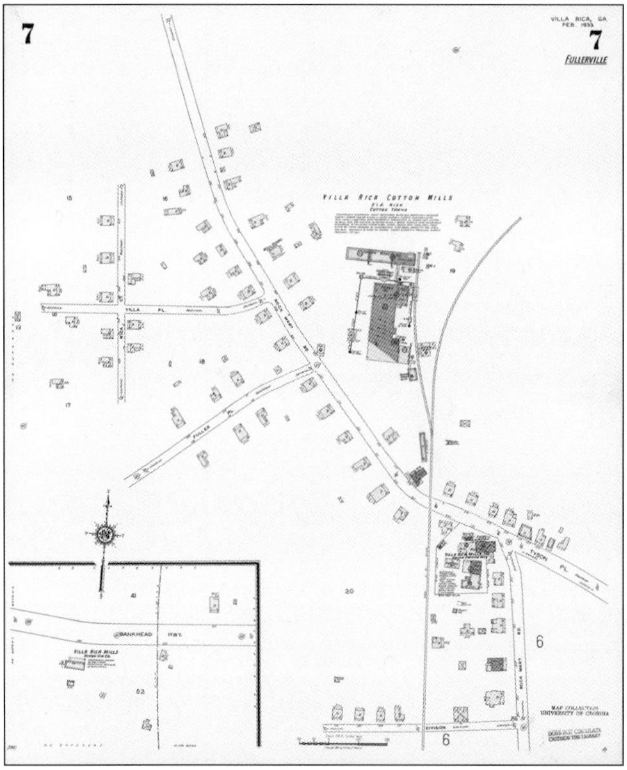

This 1933 map depicts the mill community of Fullerville adjacent to the city of Villa Rica. Note the close relationship between the Villa Rica Hosiery Mill, the Villa Rica Cotton Mill, and the mill village. The company built houses with several plans, including a square duplex and a double shotgun design. The Fuller family started the cotton mill in 1906 and added the hosiery mill in 1911. (Courtesy the Sanborn Library LLC.)

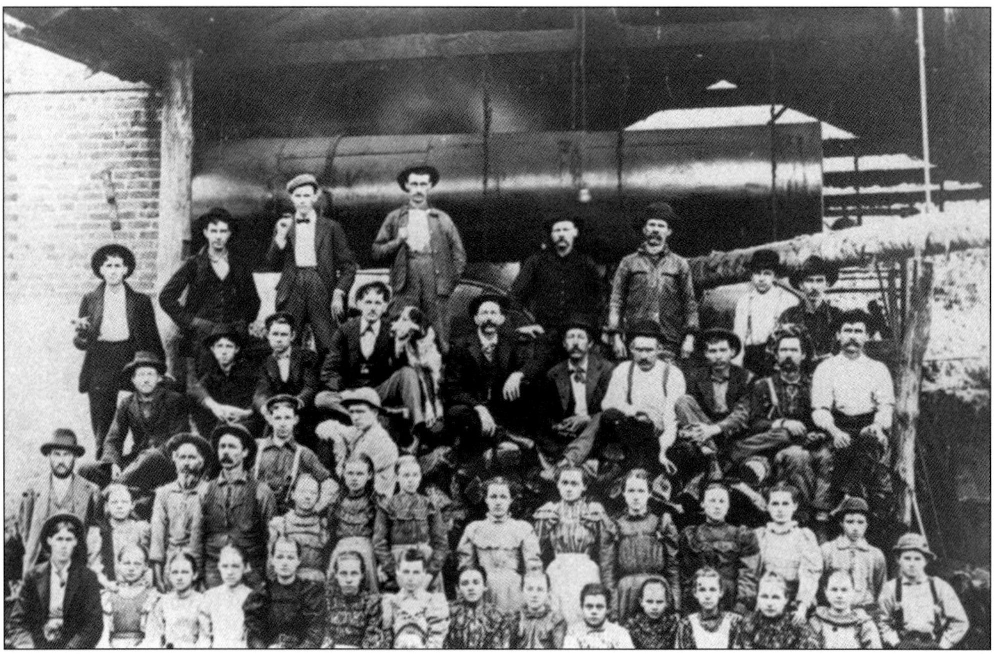

Hutcheson Manufacturing Company at Banning employed a varied workforce that included children and young women in low-paying, unskilled jobs. Many came from the country to get "public work." As one former worker recalled, "They were farmers and later they moved to the mill. I had two older sisters that got old enough to work in the mill and we moved to Banning."

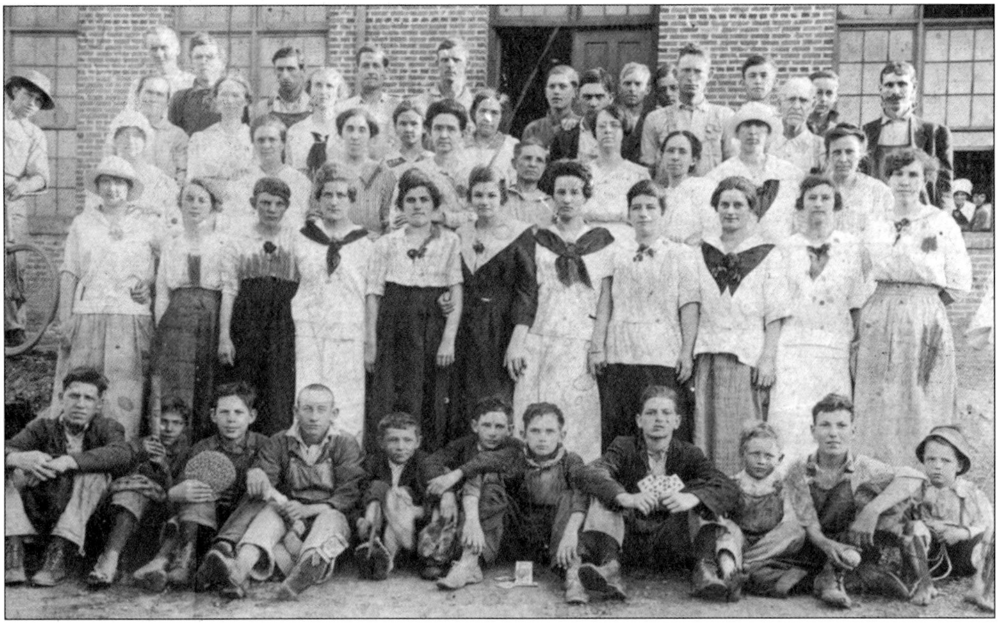

This c. 1910 photograph shows some of the workers employed at the Tallapoosa Cotton Mill. Incorporated in 1907, the mill employed 125 workers by 1910. The Cotton Mill produced yarn, and women and children made up the majority of the workforce. Tallapoosa was a booming railroad town at this time and offered work opportunities for those from the countryside. (Courtesy West Georgia Museum of Tallapoosa.)

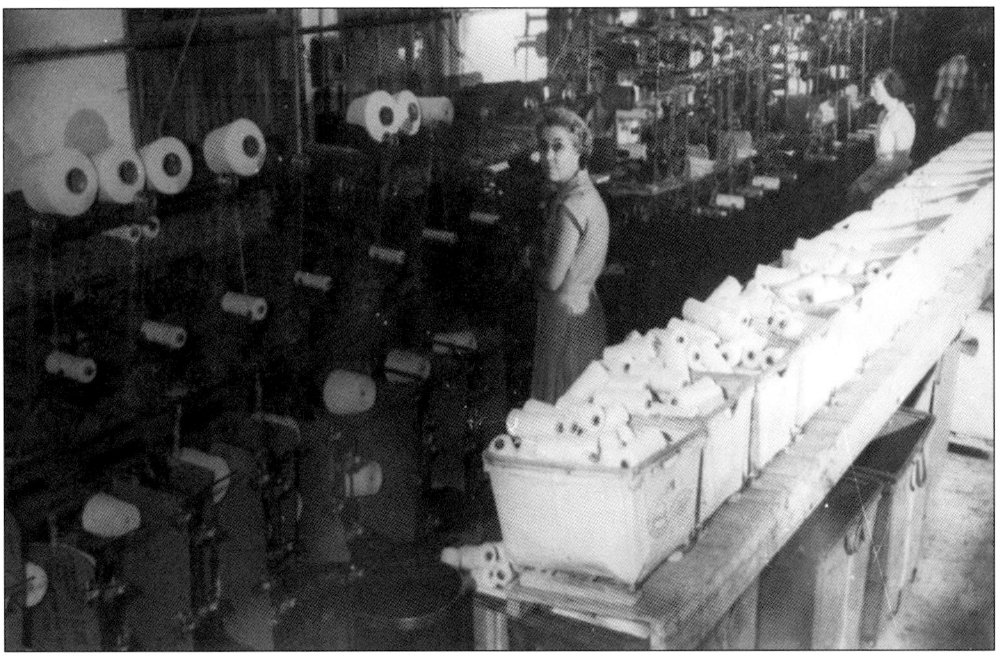

One of the most common jobs for women working in cotton mills was operating the spinning frame. Recalled one former spinner, "My dad didn't want me to spin, because he said it was too hard. And spinning was hard, but I loved it." Here, two women work at the spinning frame at Wellington Mill near Whitesburg in the early 20th century.

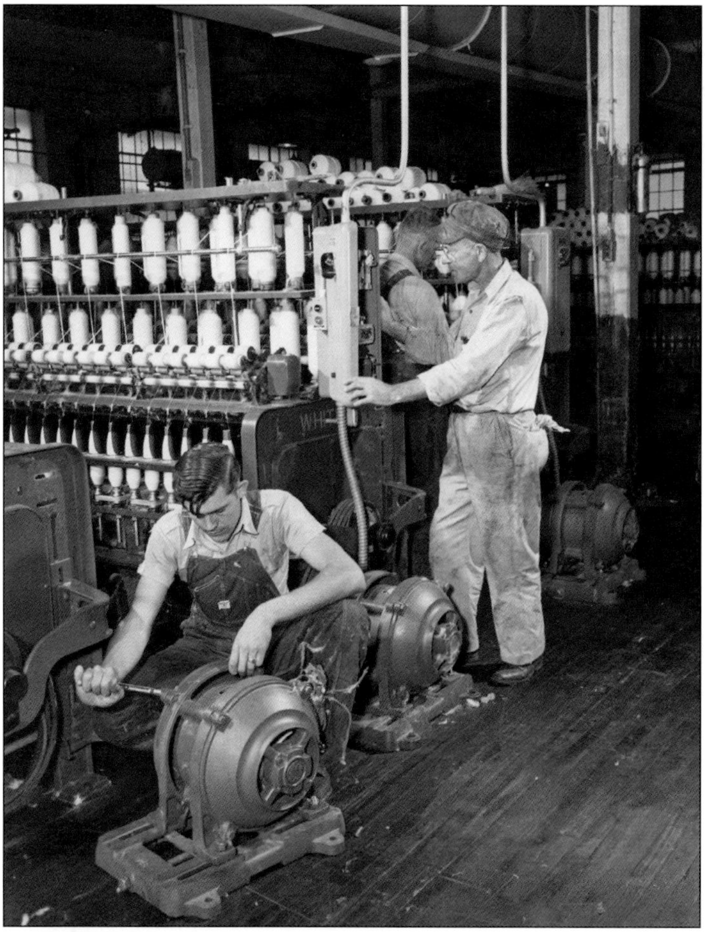

Master mechanic Marvin L. Holloway (standing) and James Jones work on a spinning frame at Arnall Mills in Sargent around 1960. Holloway became the head mechanic with only a second-grade education. He worked at the Sargent mill for 50 years until Bibb Manufacturing Company purchased both the Arnall and nearby Arnco Mills in 1963. (Courtesy Karen Payton and Patricia Eidson.)

Two women operate the looms at the Hutcheson Manufacturing Company in Banning in the early 1900s. For much of its history, the mill produced yarn, but the owners added a weave shop that operated for several years in the early 20th century. Women typically operated the looms in the textile mills.

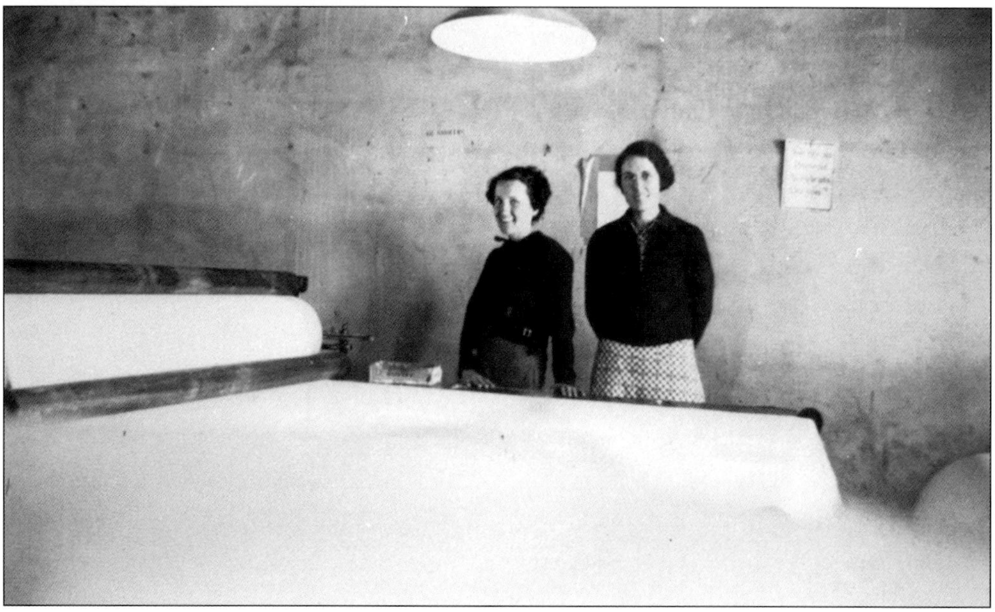

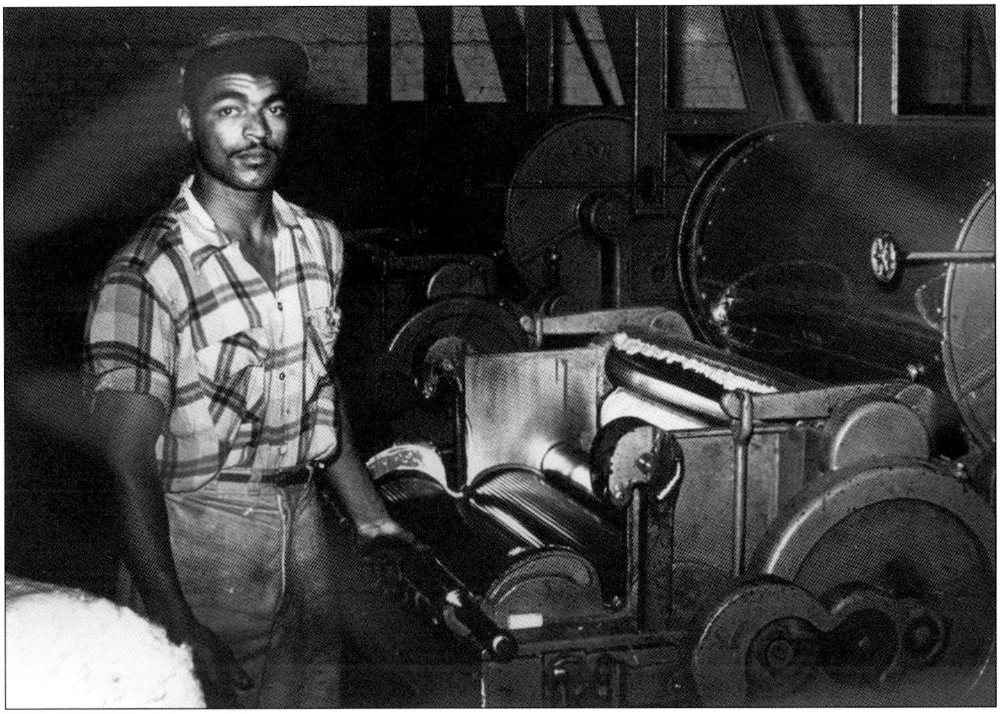

Some textile mills in the central region, such as Arnall Mills in unincorporated Sargent, operated cotton gins on the same property as the mill. In this c. 1960 photograph, an African American employee is shown working in the cotton gin, where raw cotton was processed in preparation for threading and weaving in the mill. (University of West Georgia, Ingram Library, Special Collections.)

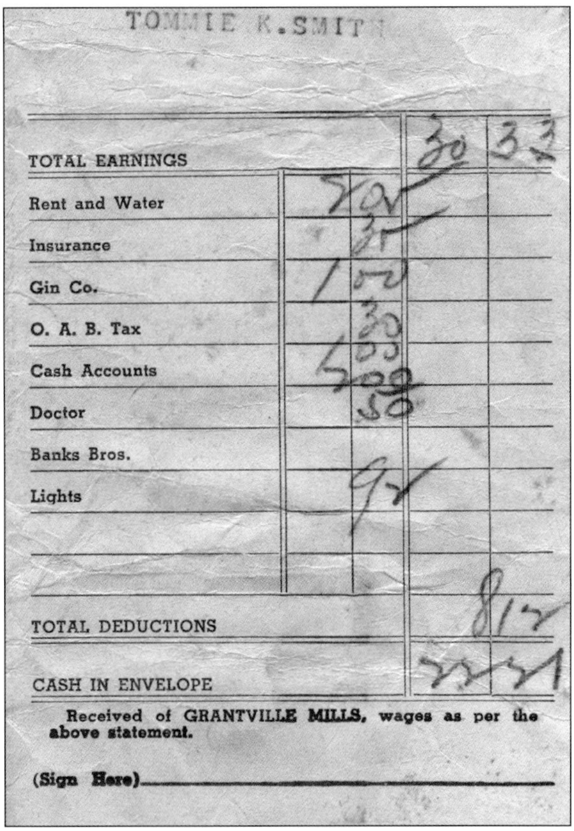

TOMMIE K. SMITH

TOTAL EARNINGS	
Rent and Water	
Insurance	
Gin Co.	
O. A. B. Tax	
Cash Accounts	
Doctor	
Banks Bros.	
Lights	
TOTAL DEDUCTIONS	
CASH IN ENVELOPE	

Received of GRANTVILLE MILLS, wages as per the above statement.

(Sign Here)__________

This 1942 paycheck from Grantville Hosiery Mills shows the weekly pay the employee received and the deductions taken by the company. Note the rent the worker paid for a company house, as well as lights, water, and insurance. The house an employee could rent often depended on the number of family members working for the company and the types of jobs they held. (Courtesy Coweta County Genealogical Society.)

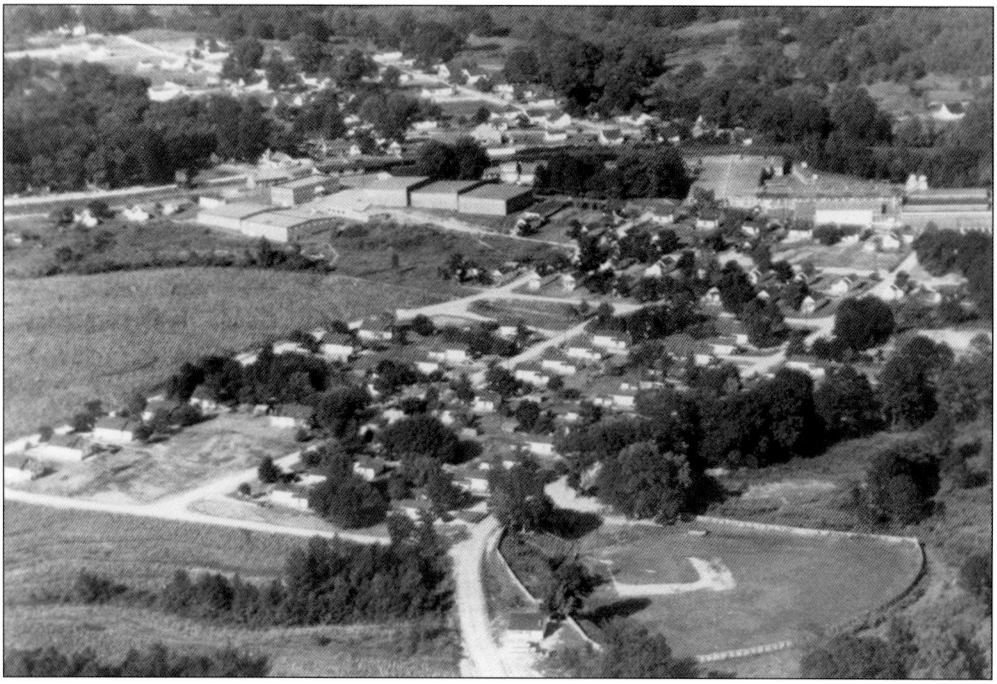

This c. 1960 aerial view shows the Arnall Mill and village in Sargent, a small industrial community in northeastern Coweta County. The Wilcoxon Manufacturing Company opened a mill to produce yarn at this site in 1866. The company was reorganized as Wahoo Manufacturing in 1888 and then purchased and renamed Arnall Mills in 1919. Note the rows of matching company houses. (University of West Georgia, Ingram Library, Special Collections.)

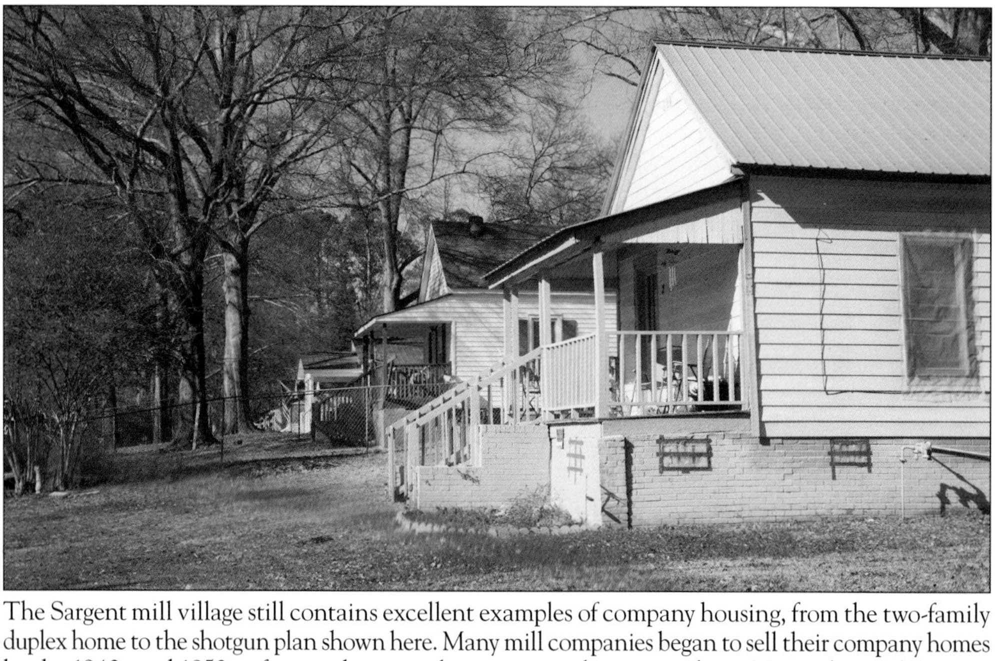

The Sargent mill village still contains excellent examples of company housing, from the two-family duplex home to the shotgun plan shown here. Many mill companies began to sell their company homes by the 1940s and 1950s, often to those employees currently renting them. Notice how subsequent owners have remodeled and personalized their homes. (Photograph by Kymberli Darling.)

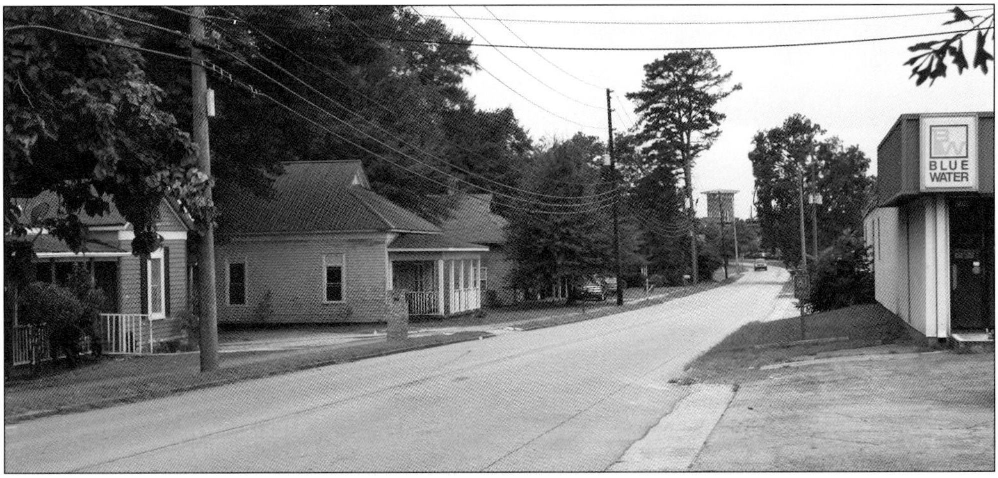

The Mandeville Mills village features roads spreading out in all directions from the mill. Several types of mill houses sit amidst the platted landscape, with gardens and outhouses behind the homes. Each street typically had matching houses. More skilled employees usually rented the larger homes. Mill villages included segregated housing for African American employees on the edge of town. (Photograph by Keri P. Adams.)

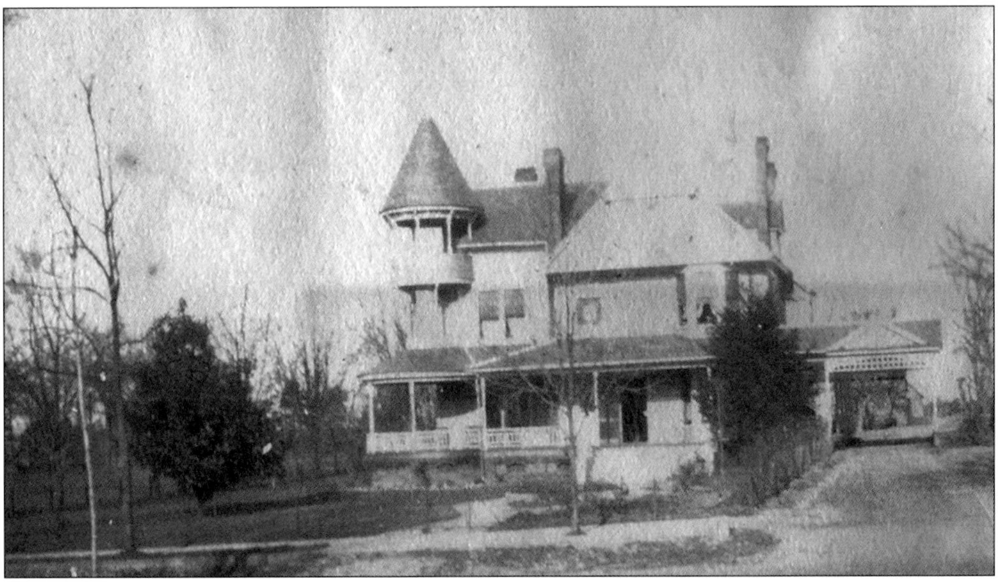

Mill owners lived in larger, stylish homes built at a distance from their workers. The Queen Anne–style home of Mandeville Mills president and founder Leroy C. Mandeville was built in the 1890s on the main road just east of the mill village. The house received many updates and additions in recent decades to serve as a restaurant, sports bar, and events facility. (Courtesy Susan Patton Hamersky.)

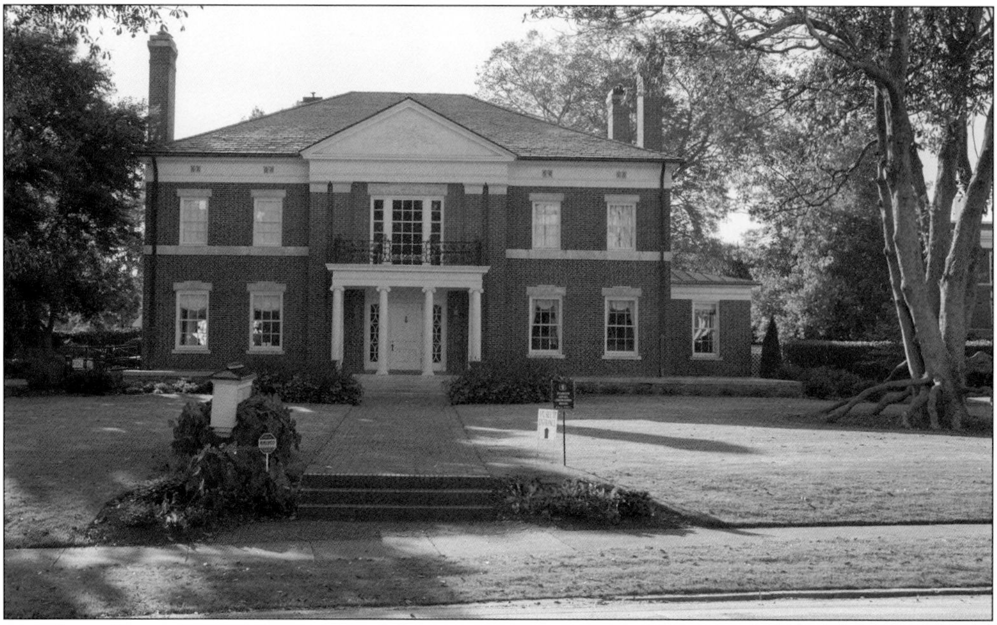

Arnall Mills president Ellis H. Peniston and his wife, Mildred Willcoxon Arnall Peniston, built this home in a wealthy Newnan neighborhood in 1937. The stylish exterior and modern conveniences illustrate the profits their families earned from the textile industry. Peniston introduced automated, high-speed machinery in his mills in the late 1950s to stay competitive. The Newnan-Coweta Historical Society recently renovated the home into the McRitchie-Hollis Museum. (Photograph by Patrick J. Elias.)

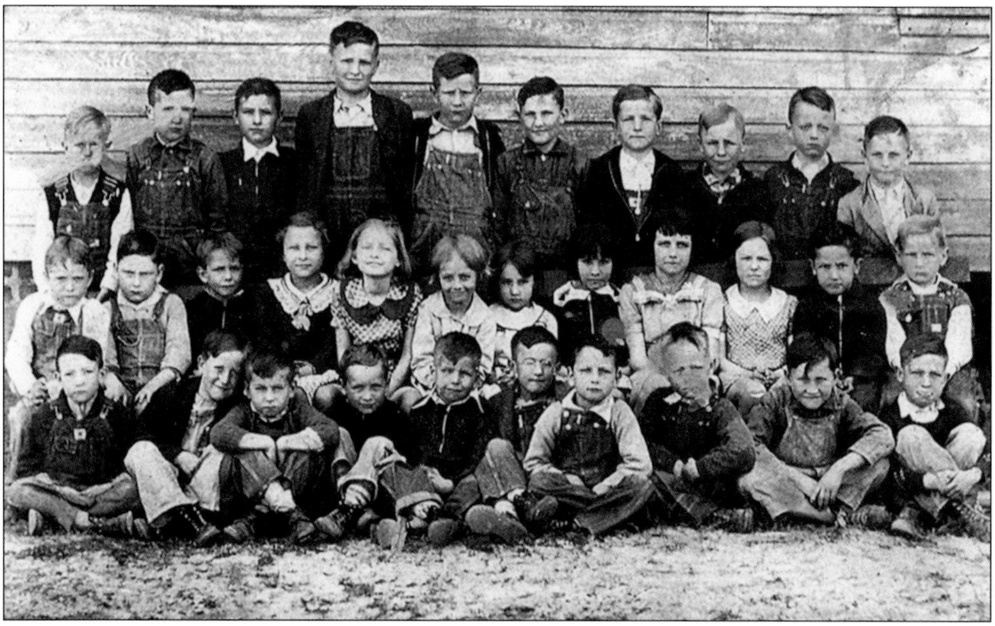

Textile mills established schools for mill village children to provide an education for their future workforce. This 1936 photograph shows the Fullerville School, which served children from the hosiery and cotton mills. Children often attended school until they were old enough to work in the mills to earn money to contribute to the family income. (Courtesy Teddy Williamson.)

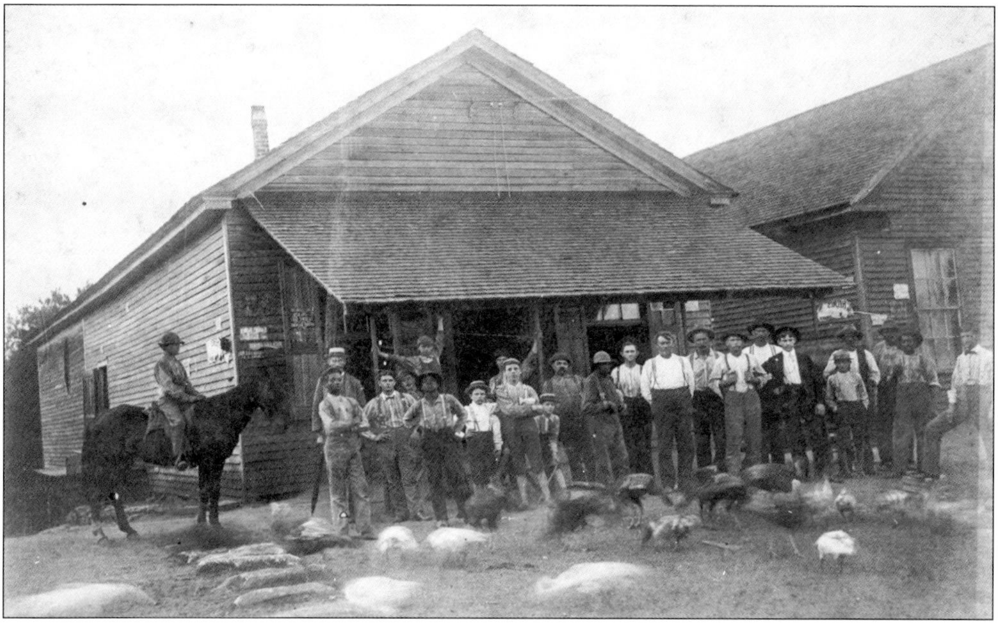

Hutcheson Manufacturing Company operated this store for its workers in the remote community of Banning. "When you got paid, you got so much beaucoup money and the only place you could spend it was the company store," recalled one worker. "Everyone in the village went shopping there. That was where you bought your groceries." Residents bought salt, soda, flour, meal, and canned goods as well as hog and cow feed.

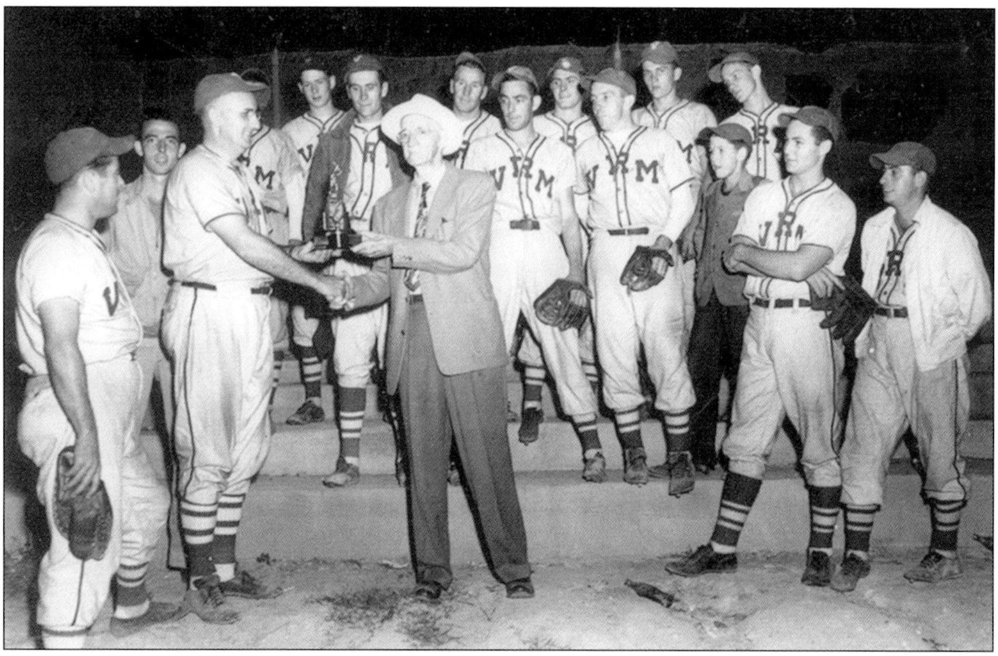

Mill baseball teams were a source of pride and entertainment. Fullerville workers celebrated their team's athletic achievements, especially when they defeated local rival Mandeville Mills in Carrollton. Mill companies often recruited talented athletes to play on the team and offered them good jobs in the mill. (Courtesy Teddy Williamson.)

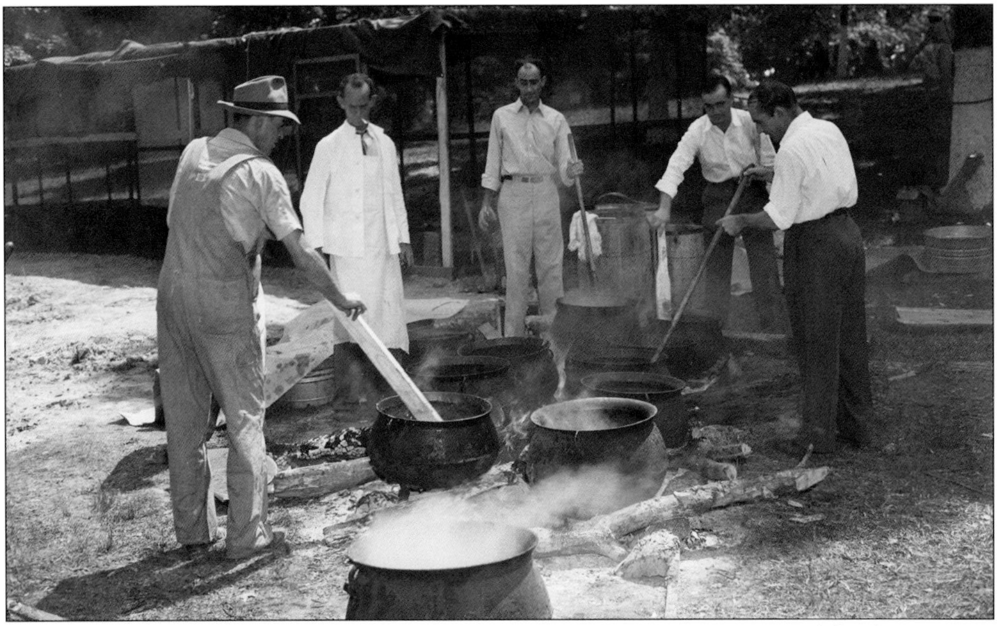

Textile companies often organized barbecues to celebrate important events and develop a strong sense of community among mill workers and their families. Here, the American Thread Company prepares a barbecue for the 3,000 to 4,000 people who attended the re-opening of this 1908 mill in Tallapoosa. African American men who worked at the mills usually prepared the barbecue. (Courtesy Special Collections and Archives, Georgia State University Library.)

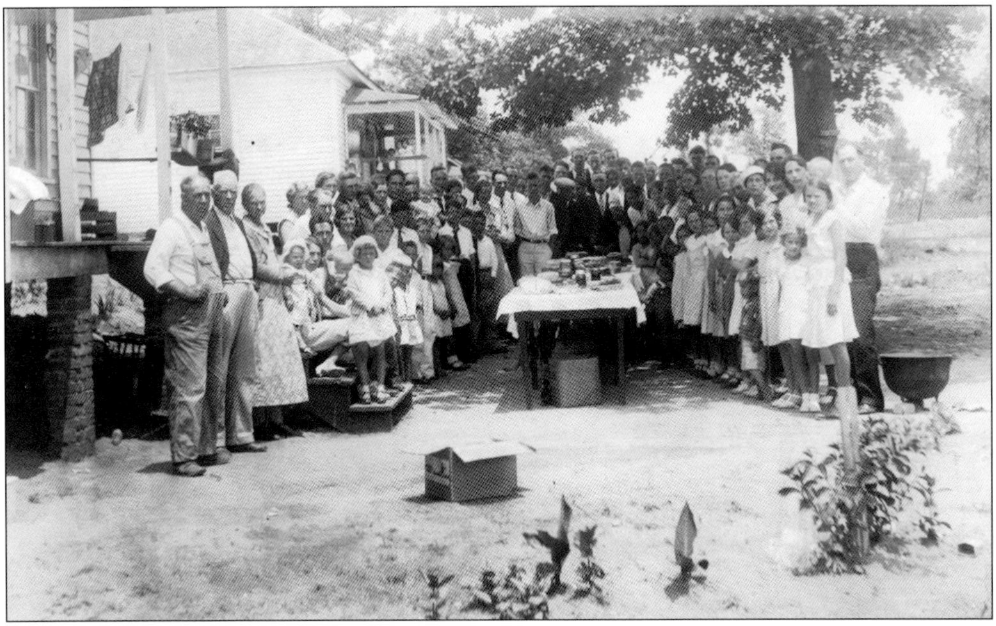

Millworkers often married other residents in the mill village, creating strong family networks. Here, the extended family of Nathan and Naomi Shedd gather for a family meal and get-together at their home on Cooper Street in the Lois Cotton Mill Village in Douglasville. Note the view of the mill village behind the dinner table and the matching company houses on the street. (Courtesy W. Jeff Bishop.)

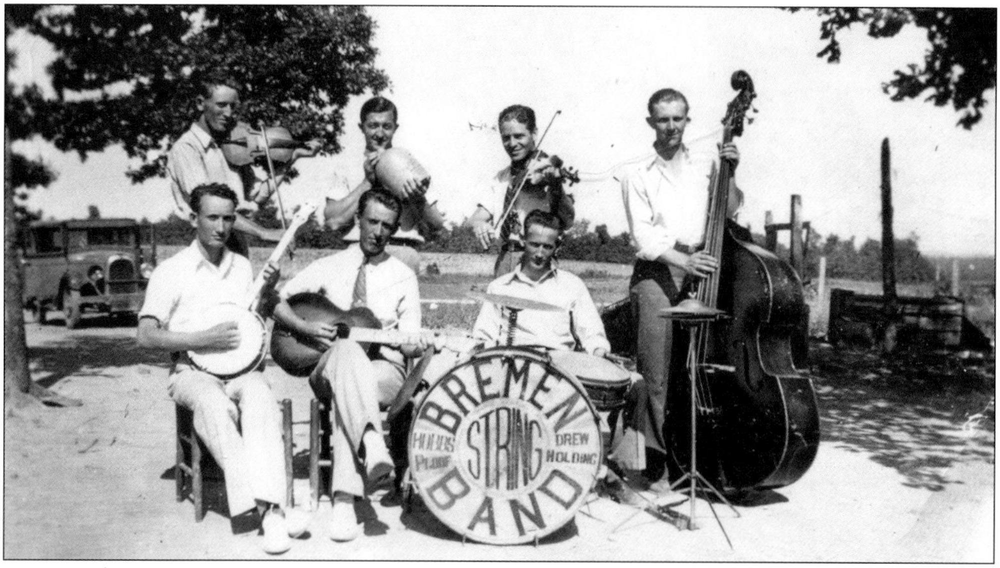

The roots of country music date back to the southern cotton mill villages in the early 20th century, where farm families brought and shared their music traditions on the front porches of mill homes. This photograph shows textile workers who formed a band in Bremen. The group includes Harold Shedd, who would become a major music producer in Nashville. (Courtesy W. Jeff Bishop)

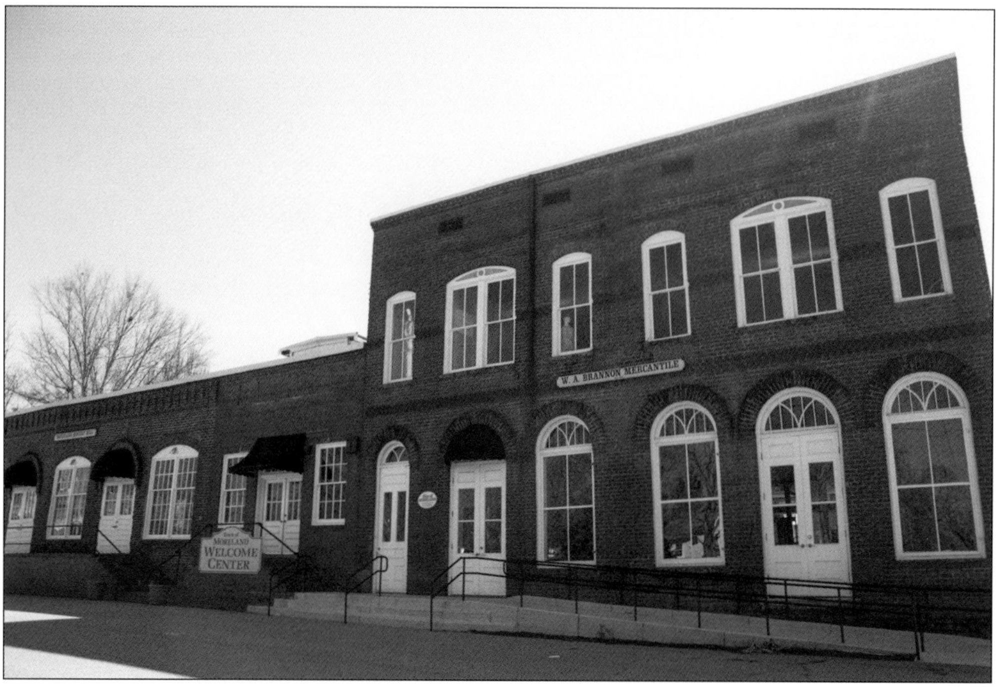

In 1920, an old cotton warehouse and fertilizer plant in Moreland, built around 1904, was converted to use as a hosiery mill. The Moreland Hosiery Company, which produced seamless socks, continued operations here until 1978. The Moreland Museum, which now occupies the space, features some of the original knitting machines. (Photograph by Kymberli Darling.)

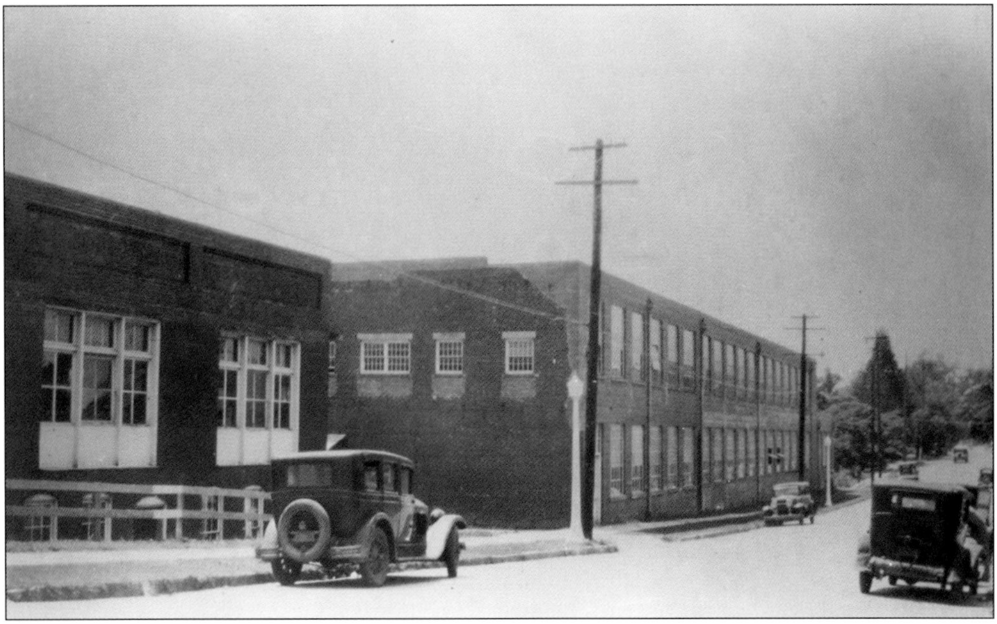

In 1924, local entrepreneurs and investors in the Mandeville Mills established Carroll Mills, a hosiery company, on Depot Street in an old Coca-Cola bottling plant. By the 1920s, hosiery mills and cotton warehouses replaced the livery stables and small dwellings once located here, creating a thriving industrial district near the railroad depot. Carroll Mills continued to operate into the early 2000s, making yarn braids and knitted tubing for the meat industry.

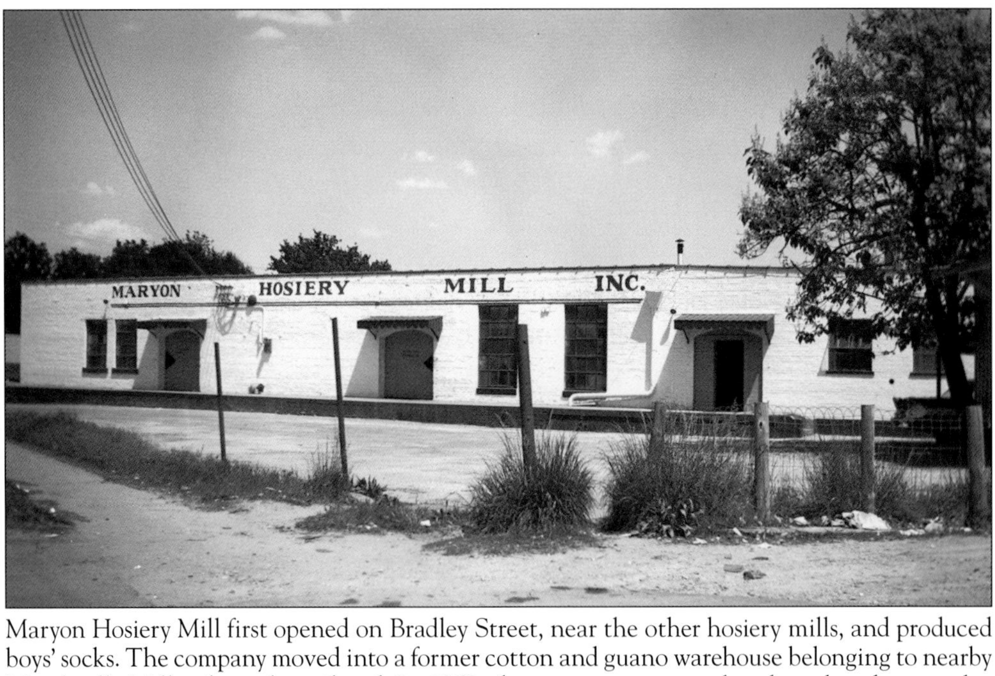

Maryon Hosiery Mill first opened on Bradley Street, near the other hosiery mills, and produced boys' socks. The company moved into a former cotton and guano warehouse belonging to nearby Mandeville Mills, along the railroad. In 1963, the company patented and produced a stretchy, knitted headband. This photograph dates to about 1950. (University of West Georgia, Ingram Library, Special Collections.)

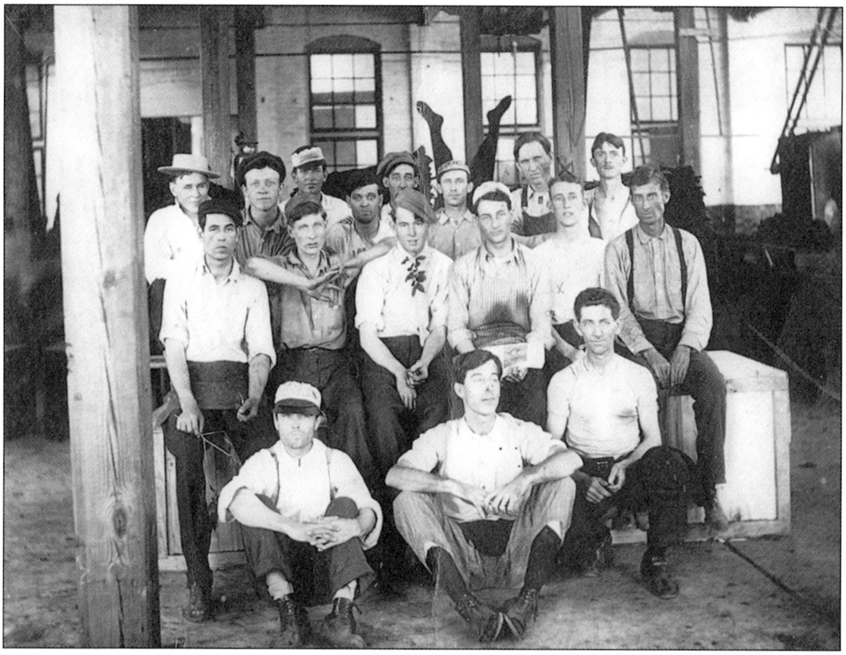

These two photographs show workers at the Villa Rica Hosiery Mill in Fullerville. Founded in 1911, this company employed 50, both men and women, by the 1920s. Above, a group of men pose in the Boarding Room. Notice the "legs" behind the men. Hosiery companies used boards such as these to shape the socks. As in the cotton mills, the hosiery mills typically hired more women than men, as shown below. Observe the working conditions, with socks piled on the table to the left, bins to the right, and pieces of socks and cotton on the floor. To learn more about Fullerville's history, pick up a walking trail brochure at the Villa Rica Visitors Center and explore the mill community. (Both, courtesy Teddy Williamson.)

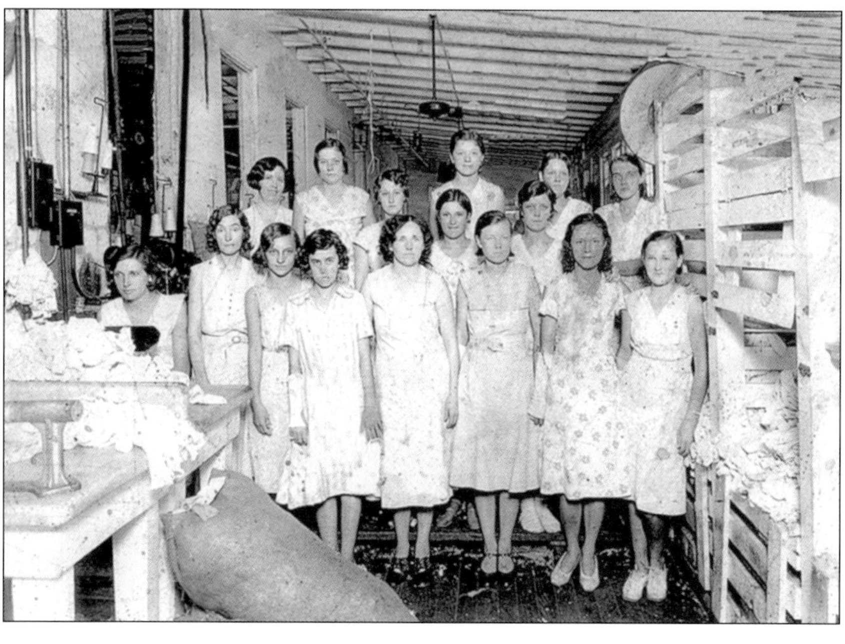

OUR PEOPLE Are the GREATEST Asset In Our Industry

WE SALUTE THEM ON LABOR DAY, 1952

This group of employees has been with Lawler Hosiery Mill since the plant was moved into the present building in 1932. They are typical of the loyalty and cooperation that exists among our people who are among the most skilled in the industry. There a e others who have joined the organization over a period of years who are compiling the same kind of record that makes us proud of them.

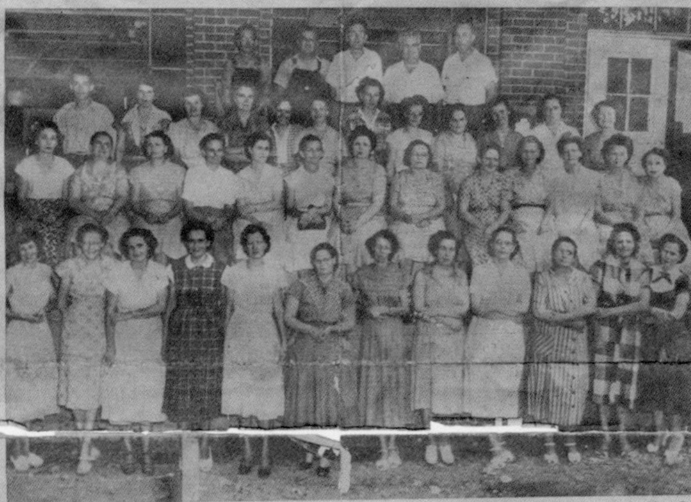

FIRST ROW, left to right, Opal Dean, Agnes Wilson, Ophelia Pearce, Nellie Miles, Imogene Payne, Nina Phillips, Mary Folds, Iva Muse, Ovie Long, Mary Askew, Clara Duffey, Nettie Barnes. SECOND ROW, Elizabeth Shoemake, Pauline Akers, Annie Mae Duffey, Clara McCravey, Leila Stitcher, Minnie Gray, Edna Crawford, Connie Gillespie, Velma Davis, Cora Webb, Johnnie Lou Webb, Nera Story, Betty Fisher. THIRD ROW, Alton Stitcher, Lois Simpkins, Moville Griffin, Ruth Long, Ethel League, Mary Jiles, Irene Nix, Verdie Dean, Leola Caldwell, Edna Nicholson, Leville Rooks, Estelle Reid. FOURTH ROW, Jasper Gray, W. L. Warren, Dovard Gray, Rhody Ayers, J. D. Davis.

Not present when the picture was made: Glenn Parks, Bannie Causley, Ruby Kilgore, Josie Parks, L. D. Palmer, Odelle Cottle, Avis Pollard, Maude Hutson, Evelyn Gable, Geneva Golden, Vassie Crutchfield, Nora Shoemake, Katie Smith, Pearl Warren, Letha Chambers, Sally Mullenix, Wilsie Hannah and Gladys Fuller.

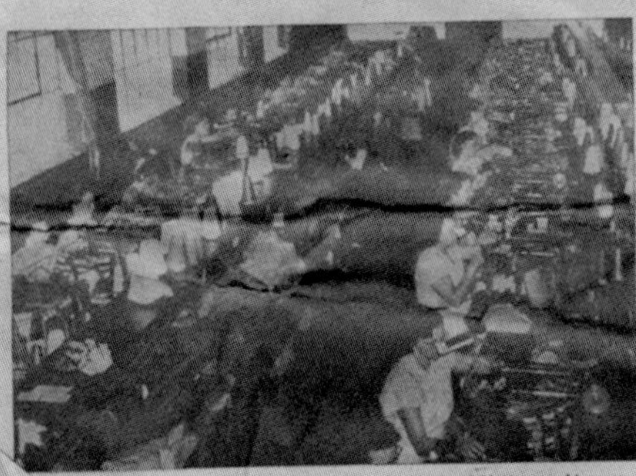

This picture shows a section of the plan t where hundreds of looping machines are operated by skilled hands in the manufactu re of a wide variety of socks for all ages.

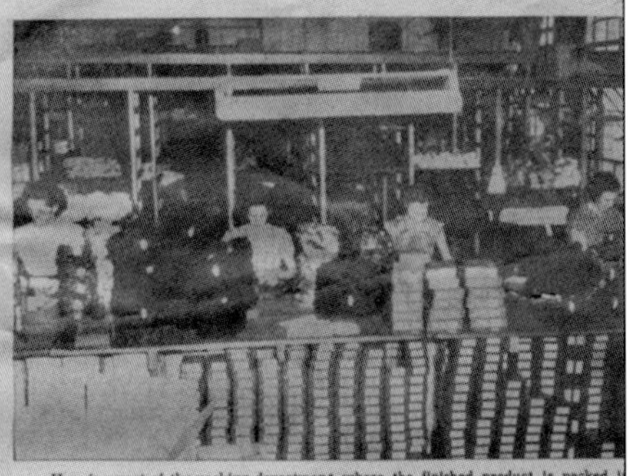

Here is a part of the packing department where the finished product is packed in boxes ready for shipment to wholesale houses all over the nation.

Lawler Hosiery Mill

Carrollton, Georgia

Established in 1926, the Lawler Hosiery Mill built a two-story brick facility on Depot Street in 1934. Note the primarily female workforce. Recalled a child of one of the workers here, "My mother started working in the hosiery mill while we lived back in the country. I had an aunt that was working there too. They rode back and forth in a T-model." Founder Thomas J. Lawler owned three hosiery companies in Carrollton.

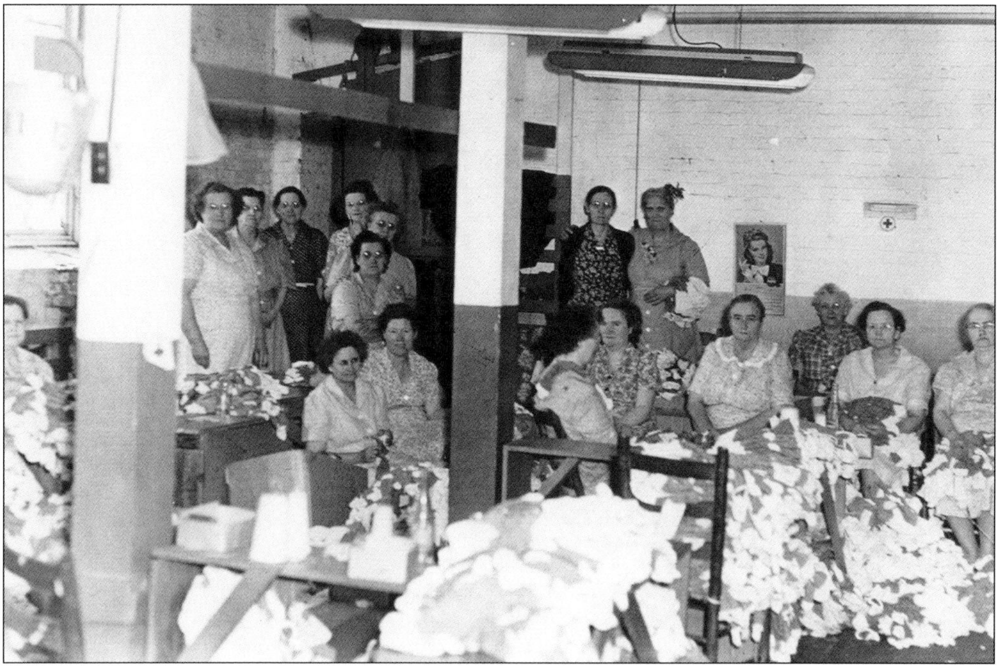

The Grantville Hosiery Mill shown here began operations in 1896, adding a yarn mill in 1906. By 1922, the company employed 210 people, most of whom were women, to produce seamless cotton hose and half hose and yarn. This photograph shows the inside of the Quality Control Room. West Point Pepperell purchased the mill and operated it until it closed in 1980. (Courtesy Darwin B. Palmer.)

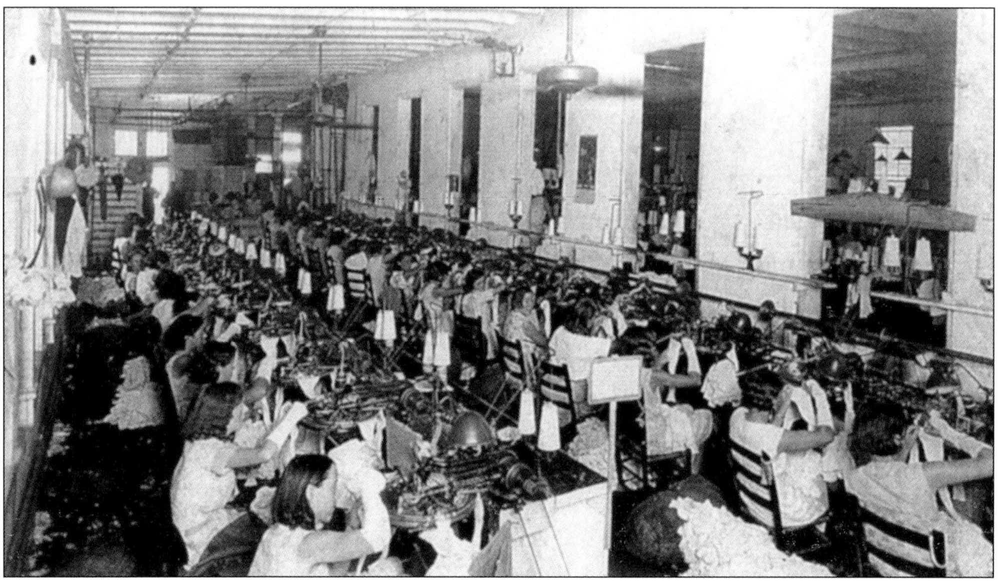

The hosiery machines in this photograph of the Villa Rica Hosiery Mill produced socks for men, women, and children. Note the rows of knitting machines operated by the primarily female workers. The machines knit the socks and stockings in a circular fashion, thus creating the popular "seamless" design. One worker recalled that "they were more unisex back then. There was just one cotton sock with the ribbed top." (Courtesy Teddy Williamson.)

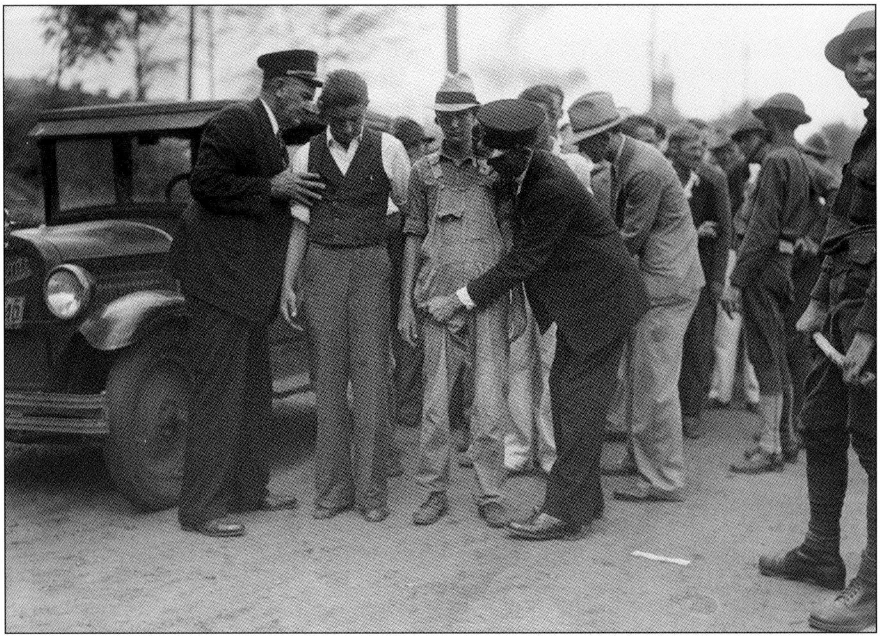

By the early 1930s, nearly 44,000 Georgia workers participated in the General Textile Strike of 1934, including many from this region. The first strikers to be arrested were at the East Newnan Cotton Mills and nearby Arnall Mills in Sargent. In these photographs by *Atlanta Constitution* photographer Kenneth Rogers, the Georgia National Guard and local civil authorities are inspecting workers of Newnan Cotton Mills for weapons and arresting the picketers. With bayonets in hand, the National Guard loaded the workers into military trucks to move them to Fort McPherson in East Point, outside of Atlanta. There, workers were kept in outdoor detention facilities used by German prisoners during World War II. (Both, courtesy Kenan Research, Atlanta History Center; above, VIS 82.148.02; below, VIS 82.518.01.)

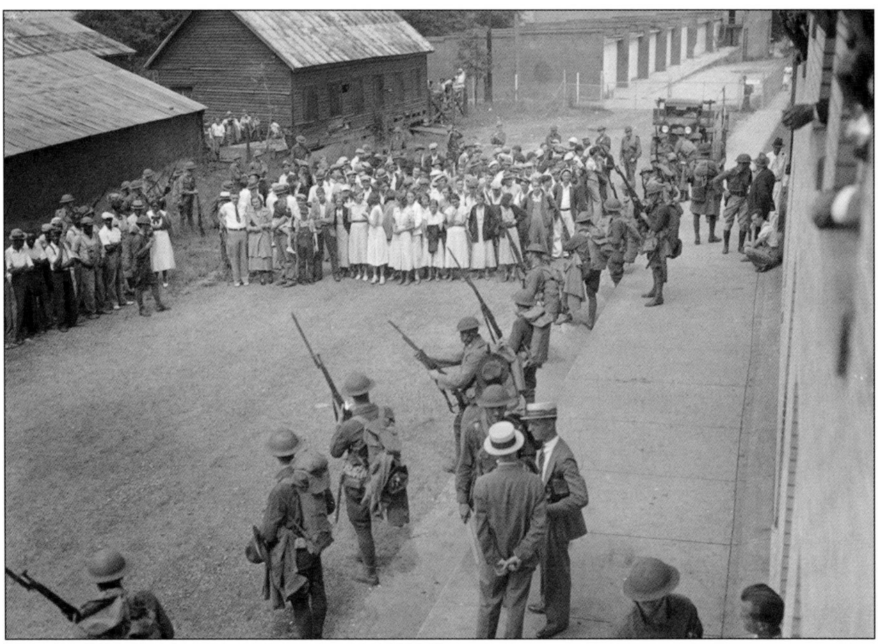

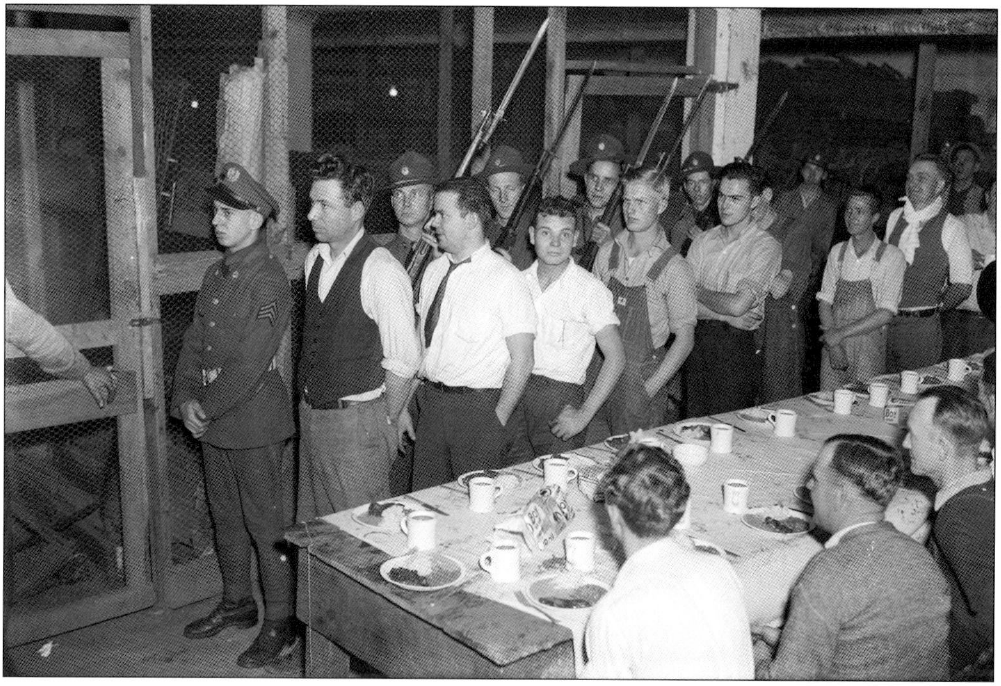

The Georgia National Guard held the Newnan and Sargent strikers at Fort McPherson for three weeks, until the strike ended. In this photograph, armed guardsmen escort textile workers who are eating in their presence. After the strike, employees returned to the same working conditions. Some strikers were blacklisted and forced out of company homes. Many turned away from unions after this event. (Courtesy Kenan Research Center, Atlanta History Center, VIS 82.148.19.)

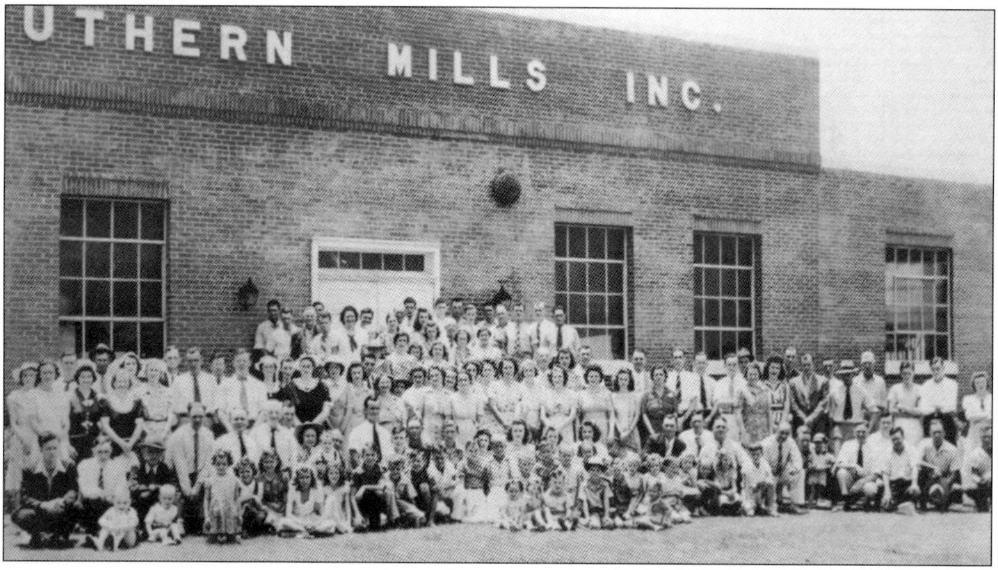

Like many textile operations throughout the region, Southern Mills in Senoia contributed to military production during World War II. Here, workers and their families proudly gather for a group photograph in front of the mill. Although the plants typically employed more women than men, notice the large number of women in this photograph because so many of the men were serving in the military. (Courtesy Newnan-Coweta Historical Society.)

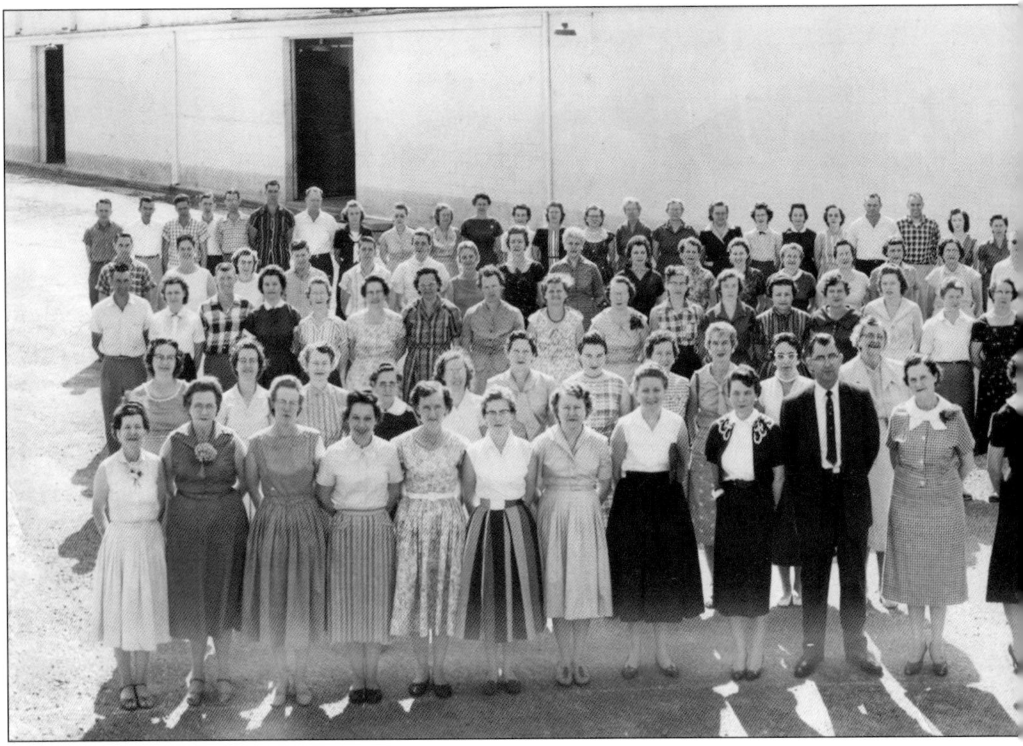

Another prominent textile industry of the trail's central region was men's apparel. In the late 1920s, both New York–based Cluett, Peabody & Co. Inc. and Sewell Manufacturing Company, begun in Atlanta, established the area's first apparel plants in Bremen. Both companies expanded operations several times in the coming decades, building plants in nearby Buchanan, Bowdon, Temple, Douglasville, and Rome, Georgia, as well as Heflin, Alabama. Group portraits like the

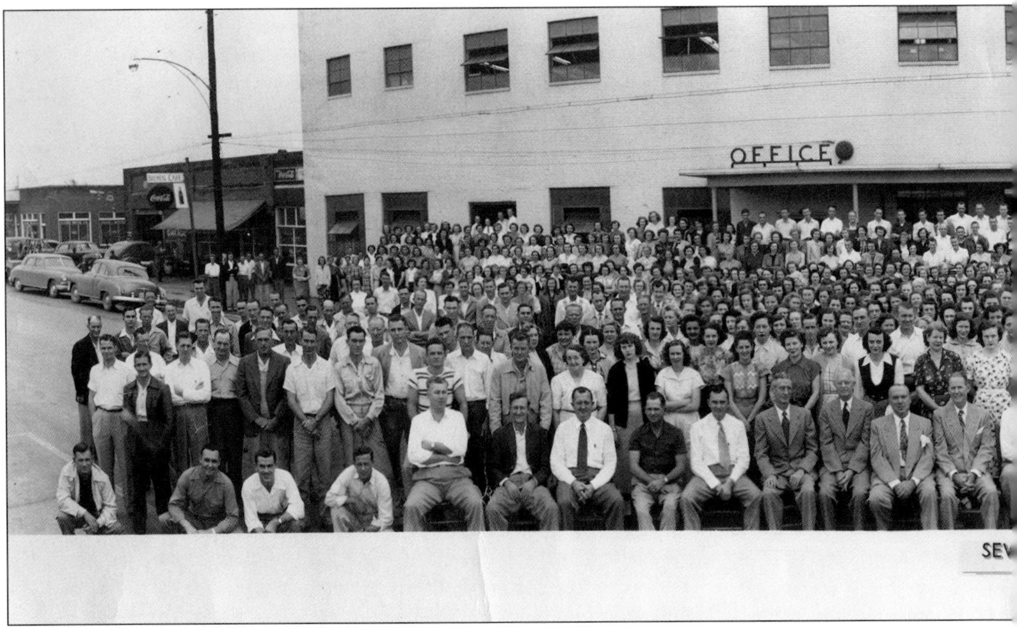

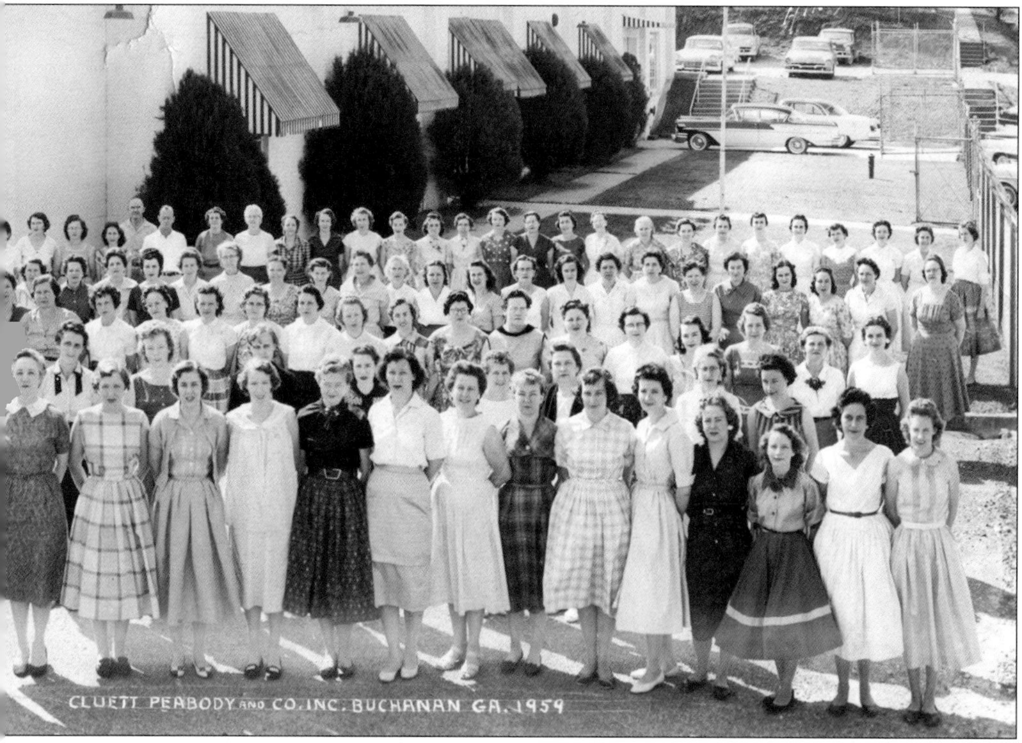

1959 photograph of the Cluett plant in Buchanan (above) and the 1950 photograph of Sewell's plant number one in Bremen (below) were a common practice among the local apparel industries and not only document the workforce, but the buildings as well. Area apparel plants employed hundreds of local residents, most of whom were women who had left farmwork. (Above, courtesy Haralson County Historical Society; below, courtesy Mary Jackson.)

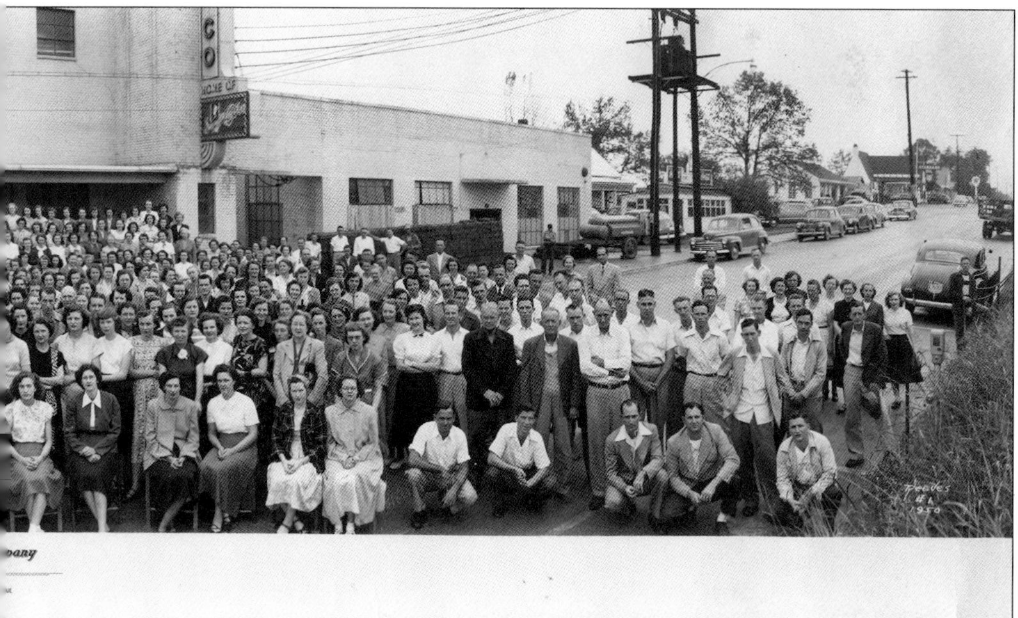

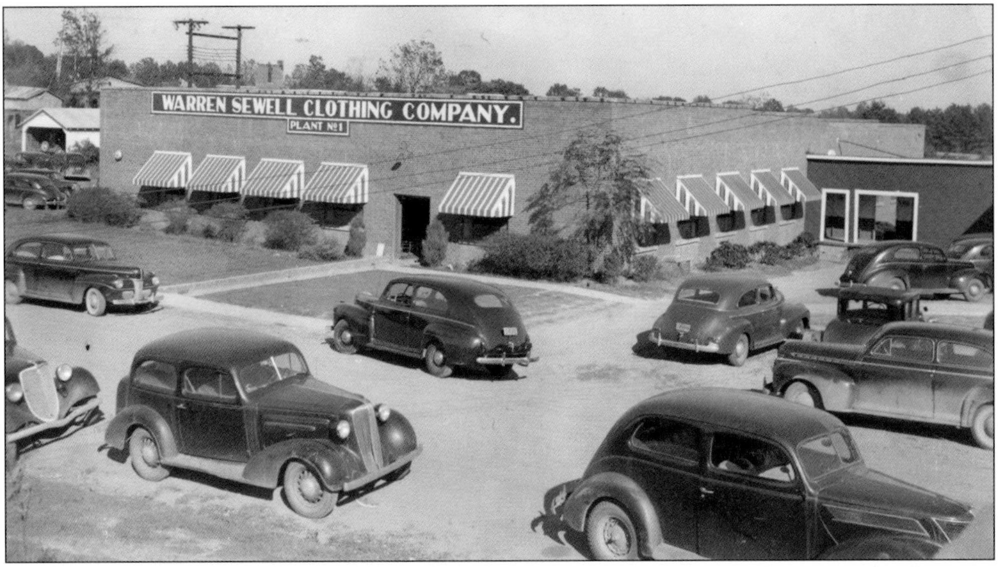

The Warren Sewell Clothing Company plant, shown here in 1945, was the first apparel industry in Bowdon. This facility opened in 1934 as a plant of Sewell Manufacturing Company headquartered in Bremen. Shortly after its transfer from Sewell Manufacturing to Warren Sewell Clothing Company, the Bowdon operation was renamed Bremen-Bowdon Investment Company (BBIC). Until around 2005, when the two companies split, BBIC served as the manufacturing arm of the Warren Sewell Clothing Company. (Courtesy Bremen Museum Project.)

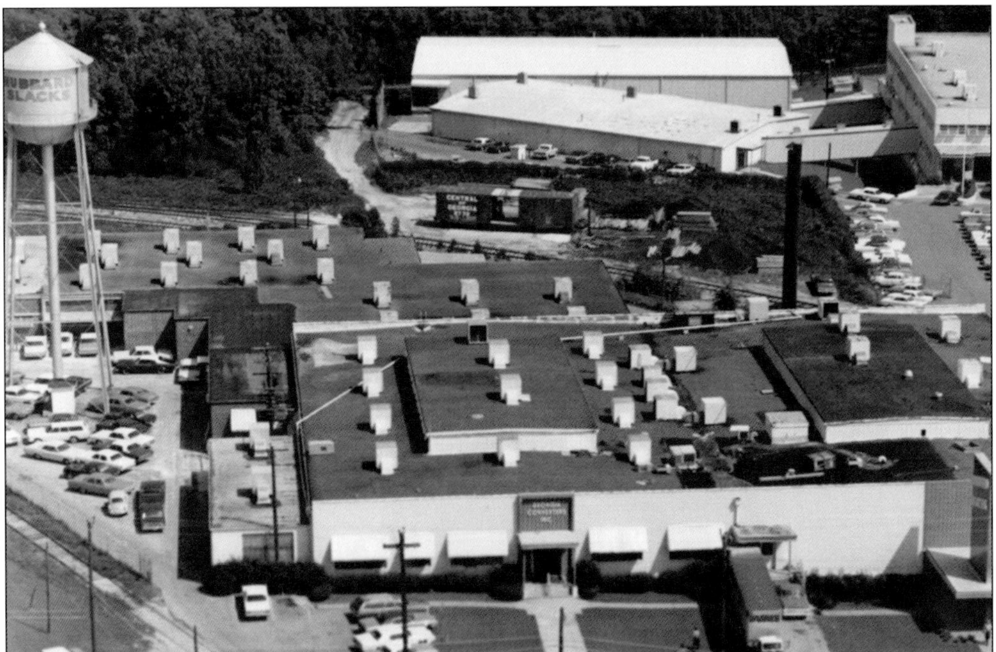

Samuel W. Hubbard founded the Hubbard Pants Company in 1935. By the 1960s, Hubbard was manufacturing a full line of menswear and had a separate manufacturing company called Georgia Converters Inc. that was incorporated into the original plant building, as seen in this c. 1979 aerial photograph. (Courtesy Bremen Museum Project.)

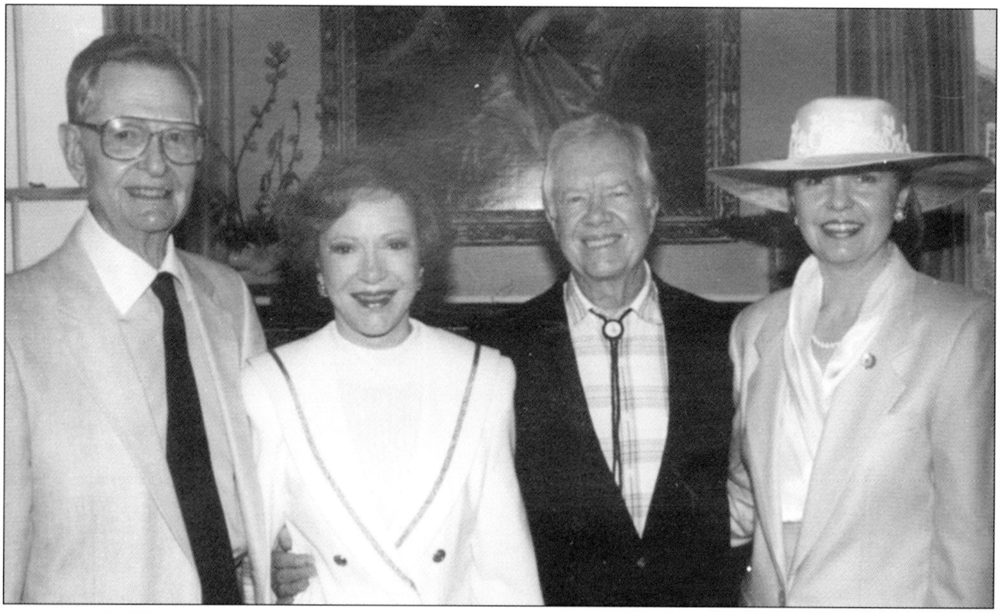

From the 1930s through the 1980s, the Sewell family dominated the region's apparel industry with several business expansions, partnerships, and new companies. Warren Sewell's son-in-law Lamar Plunkett founded LaMar Manufacturing Company in Bowdon around 1955. His company made suits for Pres. Jimmy Carter. Here, Plunkett and his wife, Shirley Johnson Barrett Plunkett, pose with President Carter (who is wearing a suit made by LaMar) and his wife, Rosalynn. (Courtesy Bowdon Area Historical Society.)

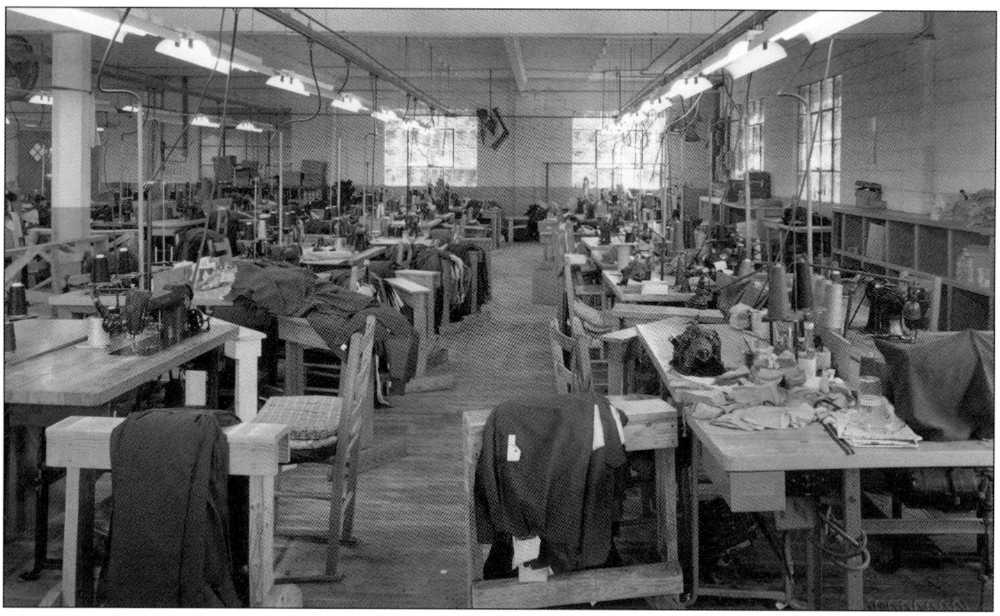

The Ray Sewell Company began in 1955 in the home of its 28-year-old founder, Ray Sewell Sr., when he filled a contract order for men's pants with a Louisiana company. The Ray Sewell Company soon expanded operations into Mount Zion; Buchanan, Georgia; and Wedowee, Alabama. This 1950s photograph shows the interior of the company's pants "shop," or plant, in Mount Zion. (Courtesy Sharon Sewell.)

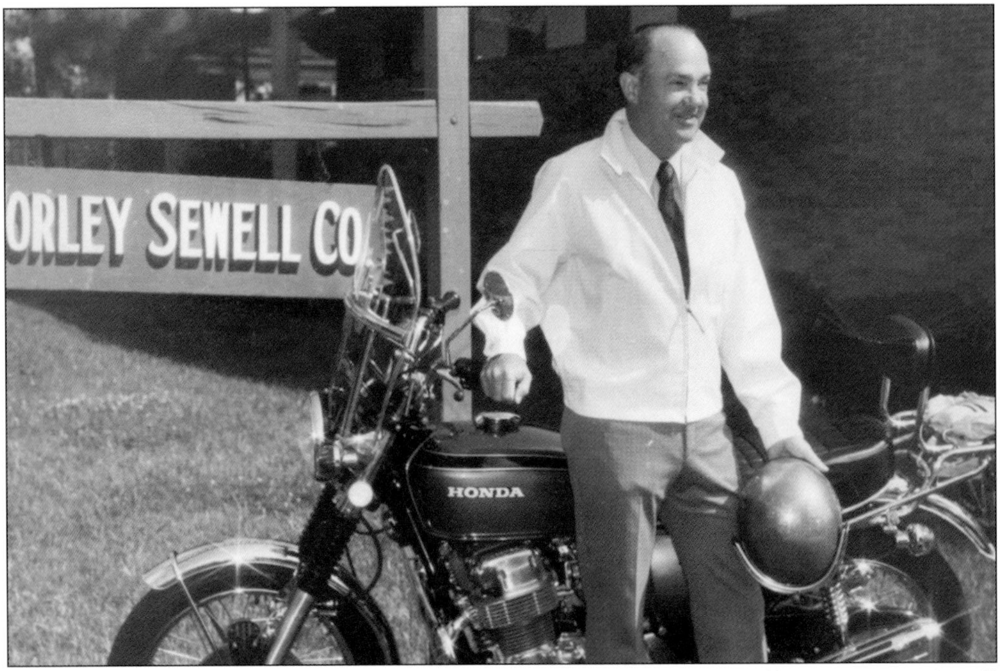

Jack Worley began working as a salesman for his father-in-law, Warren Sewell Sr., at Warren Sewell Clothing Company after serving in World War II. Worley opened his own business, Worley-Sewell Company to produce all-weather jackets and tuxedos. The headquarters were in Bremen, seen here in 1969, with a manufacturing facility in nearby Waco. Many of the smaller apparel companies found a niche in the industry. (Courtesy Robin Sewell Worley.)

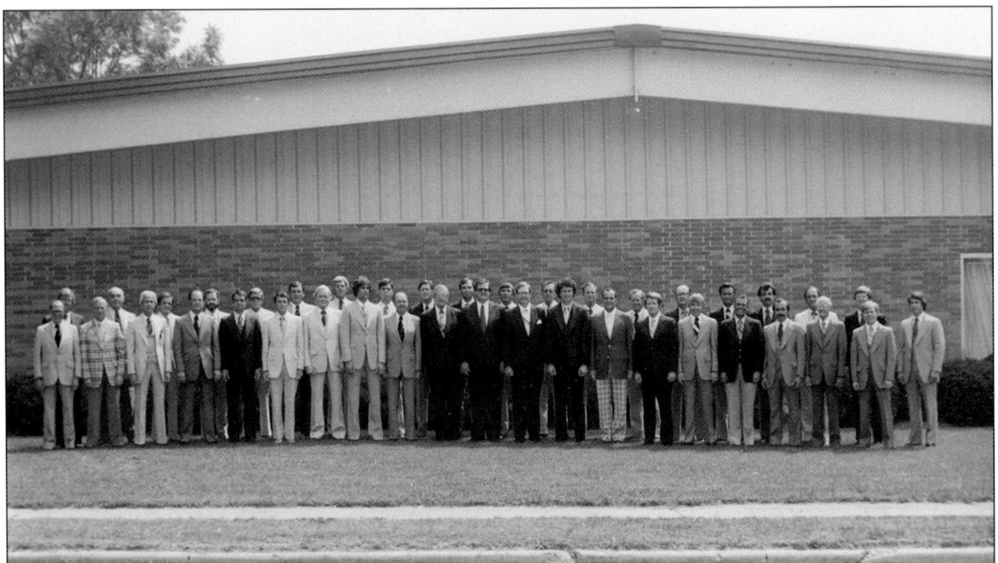

The area's apparel companies hired a large contingent of traveling salesmen to market their products throughout the country. These salesmen traveled to hometown men's apparel stores to market their new styles every season. This c. 1979 photograph shows Warren Sewell Clothing Company salesmen in front of one of the company's sales buildings in Bremen. (Courtesy Bremen Museum Project.)

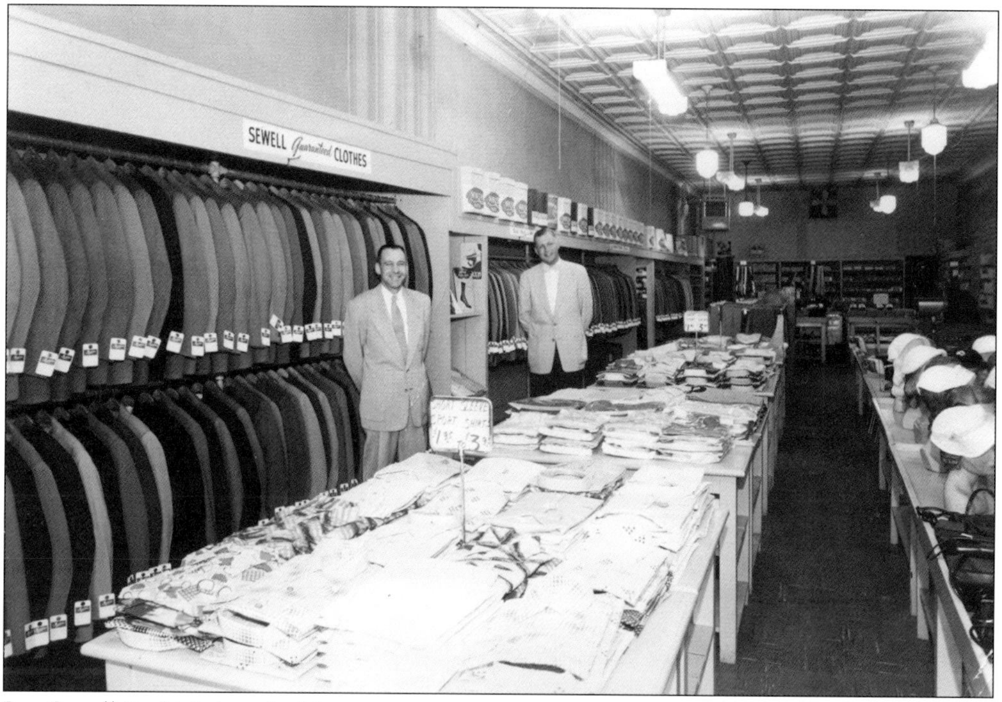

Ray Sewell Sr. (right) worked for his uncle at Sewell Manufacturing Company. He began in the cutting department and later became a traveling salesman before launching his own company in 1955. In this c. 1960 photograph, Sewell poses with his sport coats on display in a menswear store. (Courtesy Sharon Sewell.)

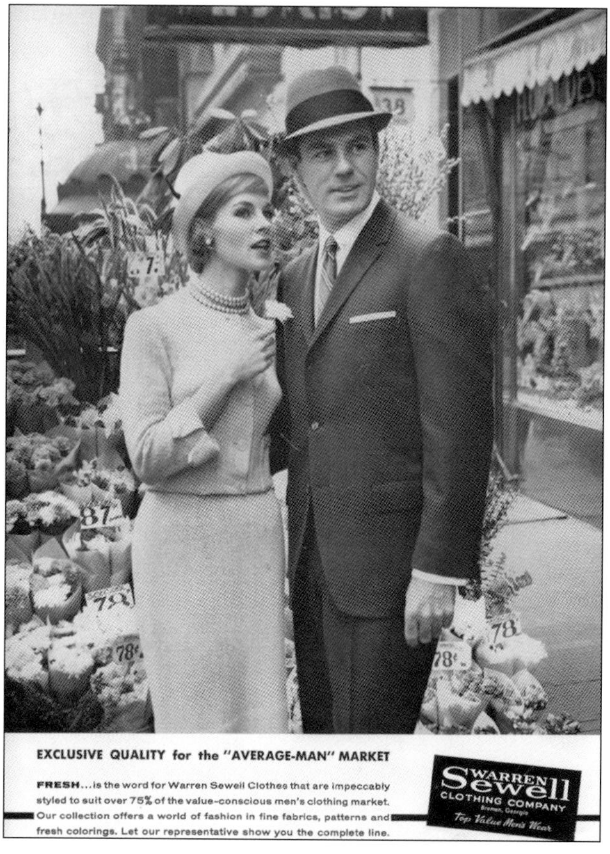

The apparel companies in Bremen and nearby cities and towns manufactured stylish men's suits, pants, and sport coats. This Warren Sewell Clothing Company advertisement from the early 1960s is indicative of the more formal and professional apparel look, which predates the "dress-down" culture that began in the 1970s. (Courtesy Robin Sewell Worley.)

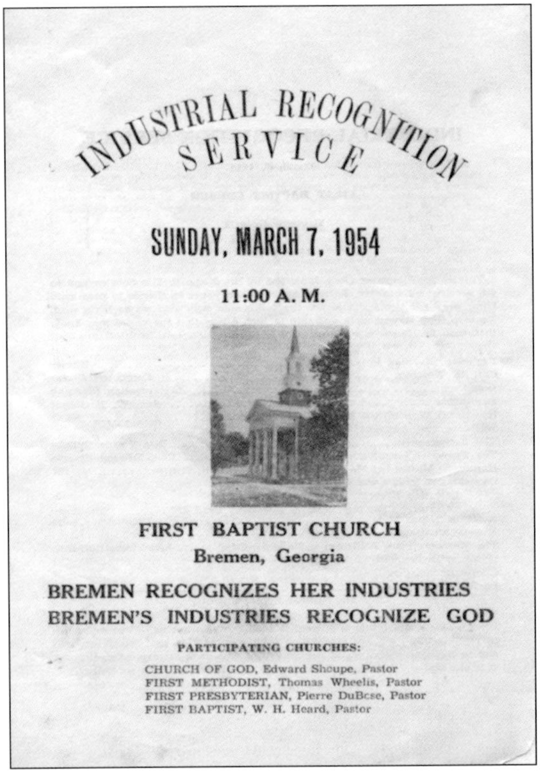

INDUSTRIAL RECOGNITION SERVICE

SUNDAY, MARCH 7, 1954

11:00 A. M.

FIRST BAPTIST CHURCH
Bremen, Georgia

BREMEN RECOGNIZES HER INDUSTRIES
BREMEN'S INDUSTRIES RECOGNIZE GOD

PARTICIPATING CHURCHES:

CHURCH OF GOD, Edward Shoupe, Pastor
FIRST METHODIST, Thomas Wheelis, Pastor
FIRST PRESBYTERIAN, Pierre DuBose, Pastor
FIRST BAPTIST, W. H. Heard, Pastor

The apparel industries of Haralson and Carroll Counties created strong communal bonds similar to that of other textile workers who lived in more traditional mill villages. In 1954, apparel plant owners and employees came together for a special church service that recognized the significance of the industries operating alongside one another in Bremen. (Courtesy Bremen Museum Project.)

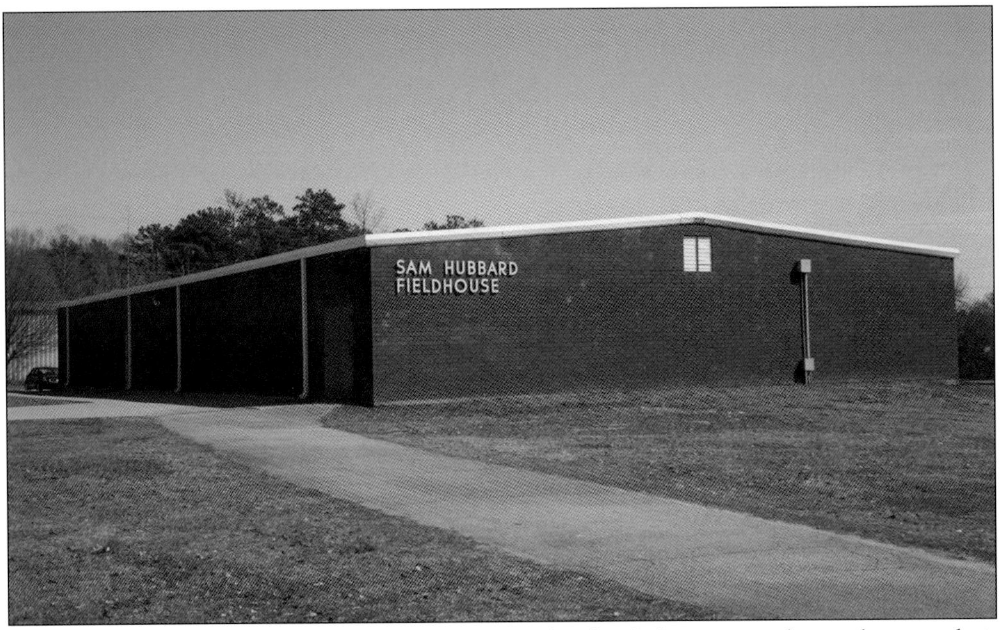

Local apparel company owners did not need to provide schools, housing, and stores because their industries relied on the infrastructure of cities like Bremen and Bowdon. Yet, many company founders supported local churches and schools in these communities. Samuel W. Hubbard provided funds to build this field house at Bremen High School, and Warren and Ava Sewell established a charitable foundation to serve the region. (Photograph by Kymberli Darling.)

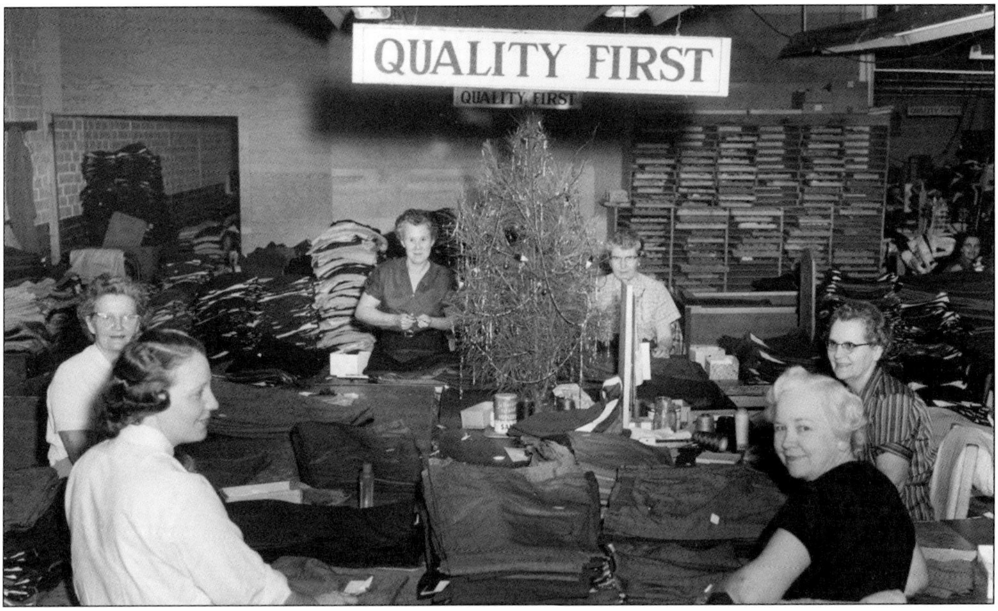

Apparel employees created community and fellowship in their workplace. In this 1950s photograph, women in Sewell Manufacturing's plant in Temple decorate a small Christmas tree on their work table. Holiday celebrations and potlucks were a common practice among many employees and were often featured in the company's newsletter, *Sewell Confidential*. (Courtesy Harold Brock family.)

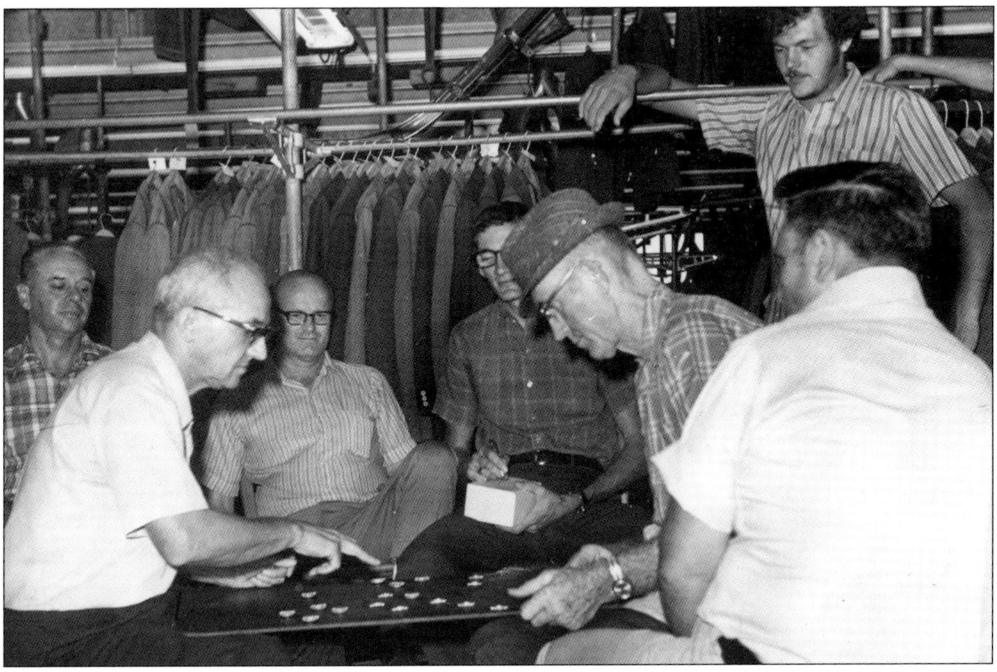

In this 1960s photograph, LaMar Manufacturing Company employees play checkers during their break at the company plant in Bowdon. The apparel workers of Bremen and Bowdon had several scheduled breaks during their workday. Workers used their breaks to relax, eat, and shop at the stores in town. During their lunch break, apparel workers were given preference at local cafés. (Courtesy Bowdon Area Historical Society.)

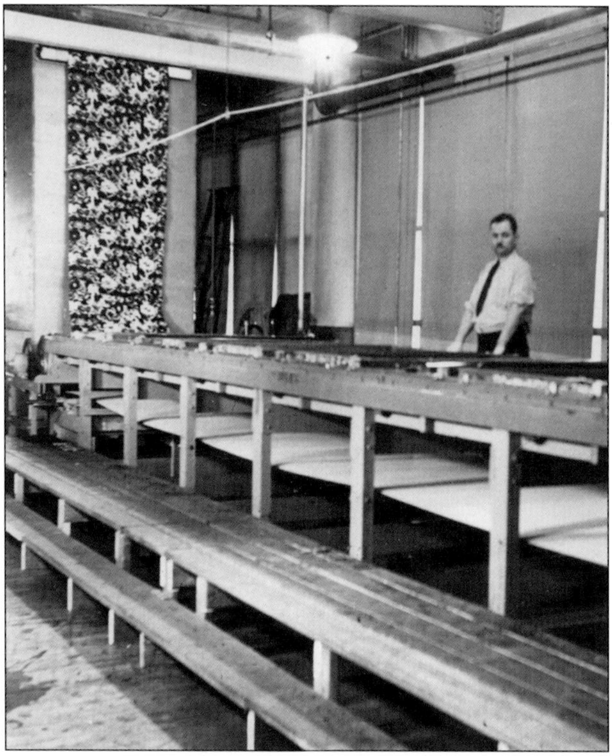

Textile operations became increasingly diverse in this region in the second half of the 20th century, catering to more specialized markets. Printed Fabrics reflects the changes occurring in the textile industry at this time. This New York–based company moved south from Pennsylvania to Carrollton in search of cheaper labor. The company purchased the two Mandeville Mills buildings in 1954, the year after Mandeville closed. At left, workers screen prints onto fabric used for furniture upholstery and other purposes. The photograph below shows the diverse workforce that evolved after the Civil Rights Act of 1964. The men seen here worked in the same department. At its peak, Printed Fabrics employed over 300 workers. The company closed in 2002. (Left, courtesy Southeastern Quilt and Textile Museum.)

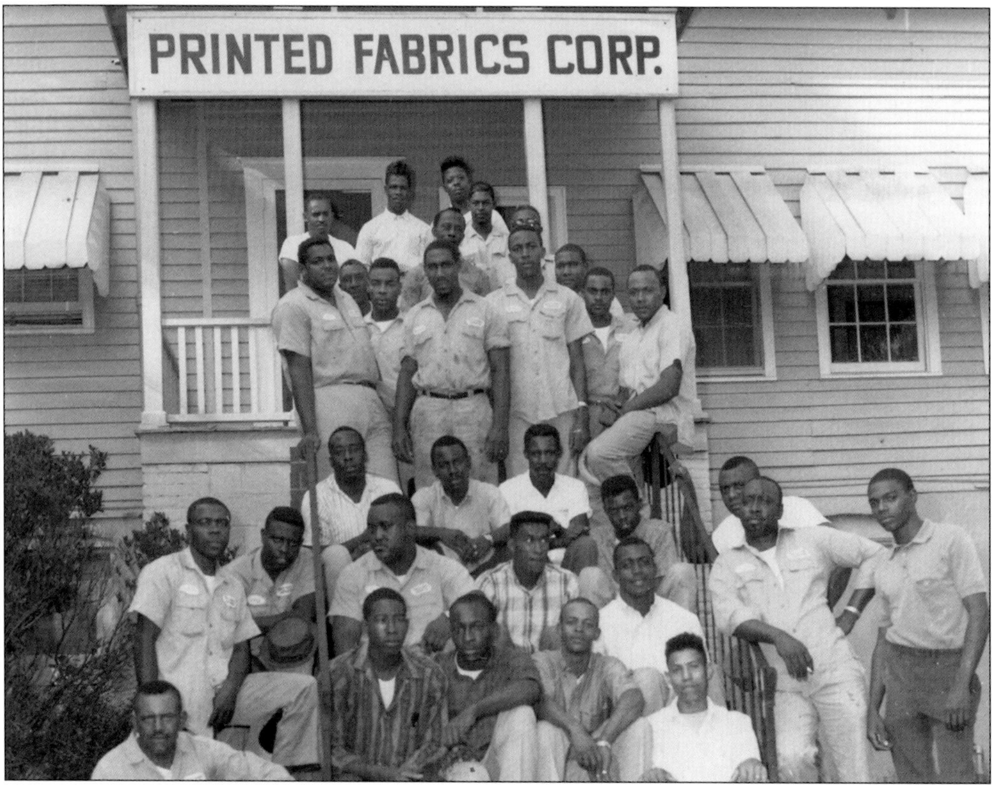

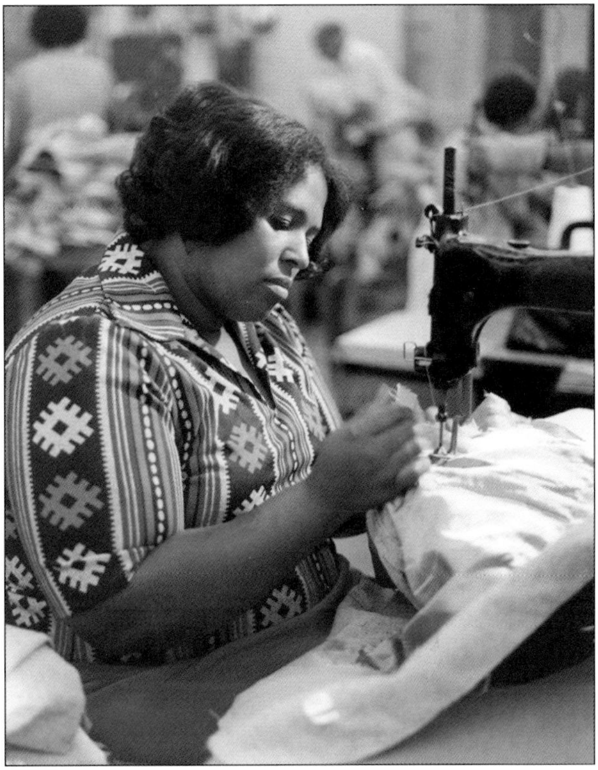

African American women had few opportunities to work in the textile and apparel industry before the Civil Rights Act of 1964. The new legislation required all companies to integrate their workforce. "That was big," recalled a former Bowdon supervisor. "Whites had never worked with Blacks before. We had to let it be known in very, very strong terms that we were going to enforce that law. It hit the people hard. They were stunned by it." These c. 1979 photographs of African American women working at BBIC highlight the diversity and change in the region's workforce in the decades after the law passed. In the image below, notice the computerized equipment that the company had acquired by this time. Apparel companies updated their operations to compete with overseas competition. (Both, courtesy Robin Sewell Worley.)

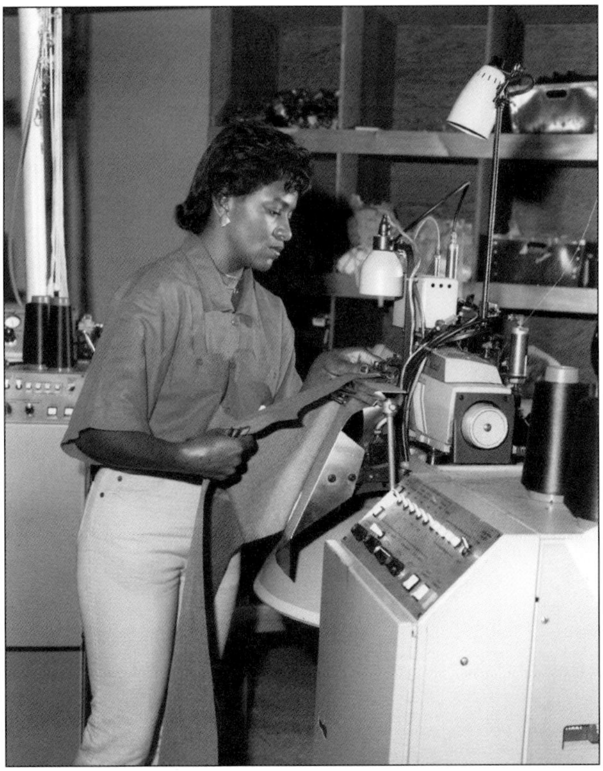

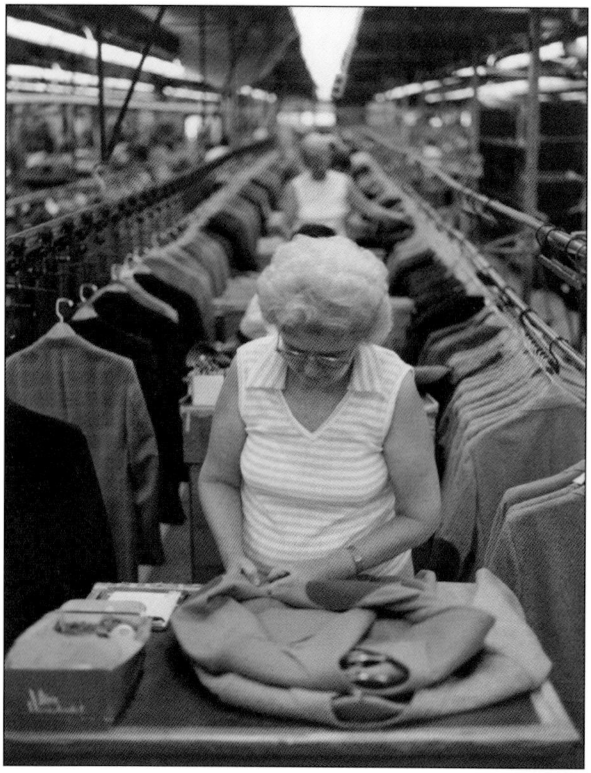

Although many of Bremen's apparel industries were affected by the casual dress-down culture that began in the 1970s, Warren Sewell Clothing Company remained successful by marketing new lines of menswear, including Zino, LaCrosse, and Cotton Brothers, and tapping into larger markets such as Belk and Nordstrom department stores. Here, a BBIC employee is seen during part of the final inspection process of sport coats around 1979. (Courtesy Robin Sewell Worley.)

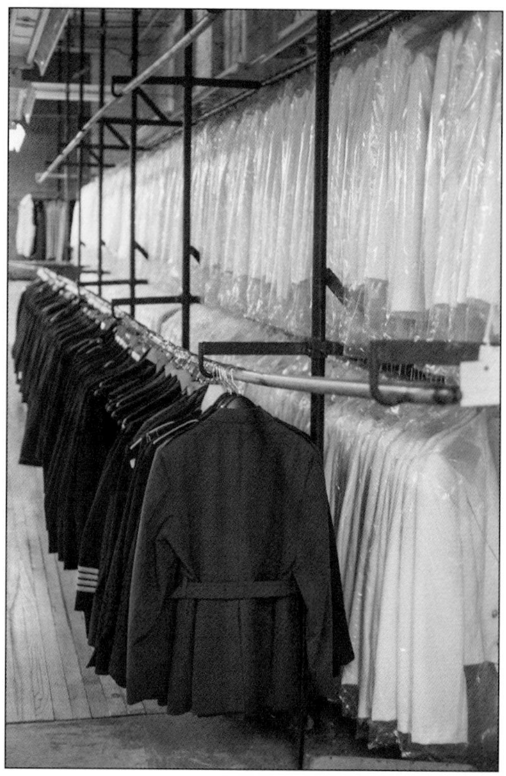

BBIC and The Sewell Companies, both still operated by grandchildren of Warren Sewell Sr., secured government contracts to produce military garments and maintain production in their local facilities after NAFTA. In this 2013 photograph, finished uniform pieces of the US armed forces hang in the stockroom of The Sewell Companies headquarters. (Photograph by Rachel Opolka.)

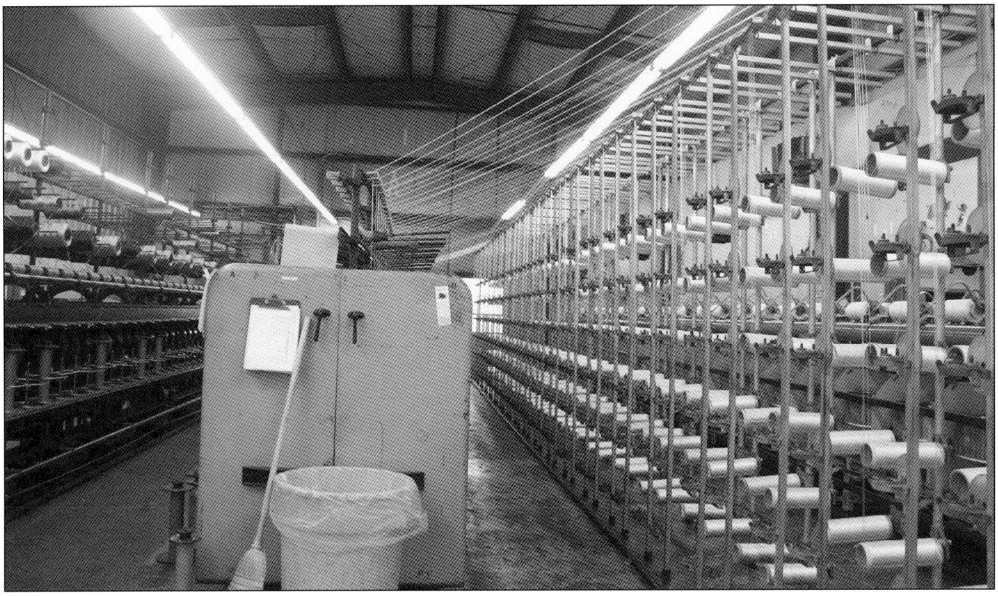

In 1954, a year after Mandeville Mills closed, the last president and Mandeville descendent, J.R. Newell Sr., began producing cotton rope and decorative twisted yarn next to the old mill. His son J.R. "Dick" Newell Jr. developed his father's rope factory into BlueWater Ropes, which produces an internationally known, state-of-the-art climbing rope. Newell and his wife were both spelunkers and wanted a better rope. Newell began by experimenting in his basement in the late 1960s, and in 1969, he manufactured the first American-made kernmantle caving rope. The family opened a modern operation, as seen in these 2015 photographs, to produce this dynamic climbing rope next to the rope factory. Today, his son Scott Newell carries on the family tradition of textile manufacturing. The old Mandeville Mills can be seen down the road, with homes from the mill village on the left. (Both photographs by Kymberli Darling.)

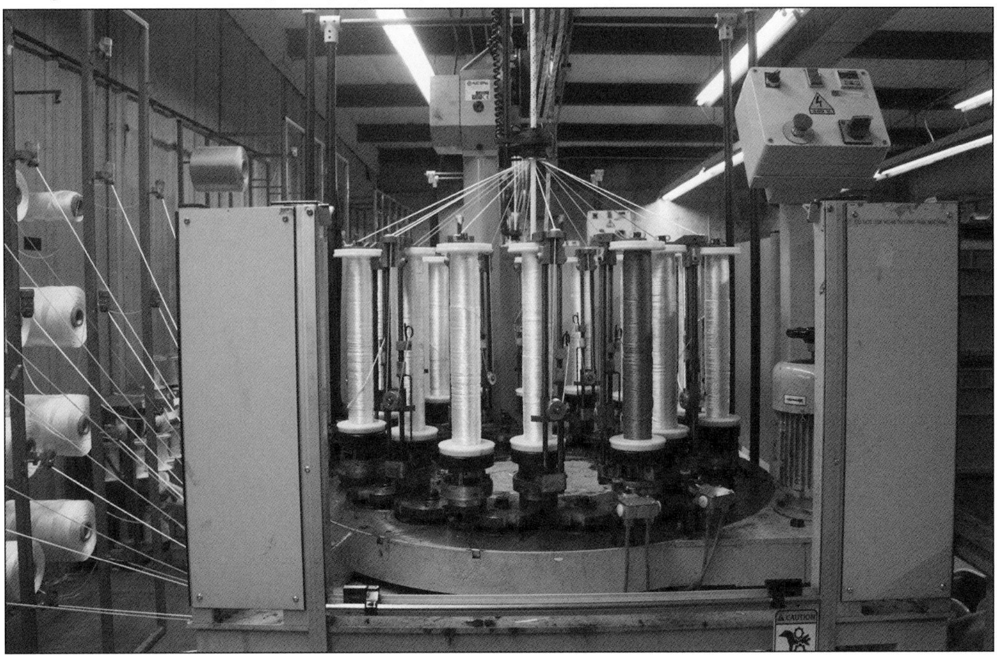

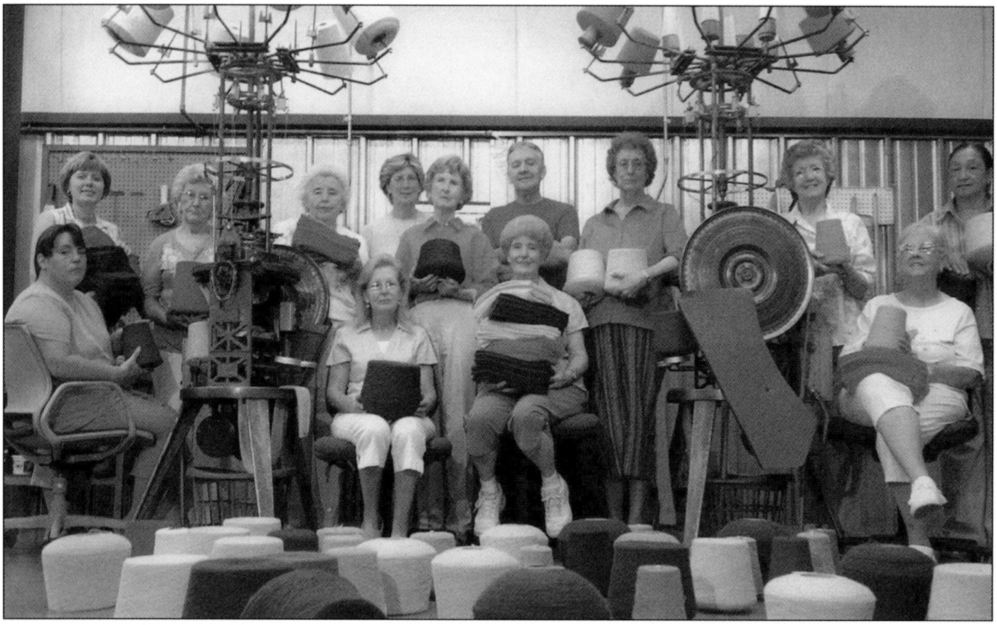

Pam Bruce, the granddaughter of E.T. Doyal, former president of Villa Rica Hosiery Company, opened Villa Rica Knitters in the old company building. This photograph shows the small workforce of predominantly retired hosiery workers who she employed to knit hats, scarves, "snugglers," and other knitted items. Her father, Emmet Doyal, operated the hosiery company through the 1980s before she took over the business. Her operation closed in the late 2000s.

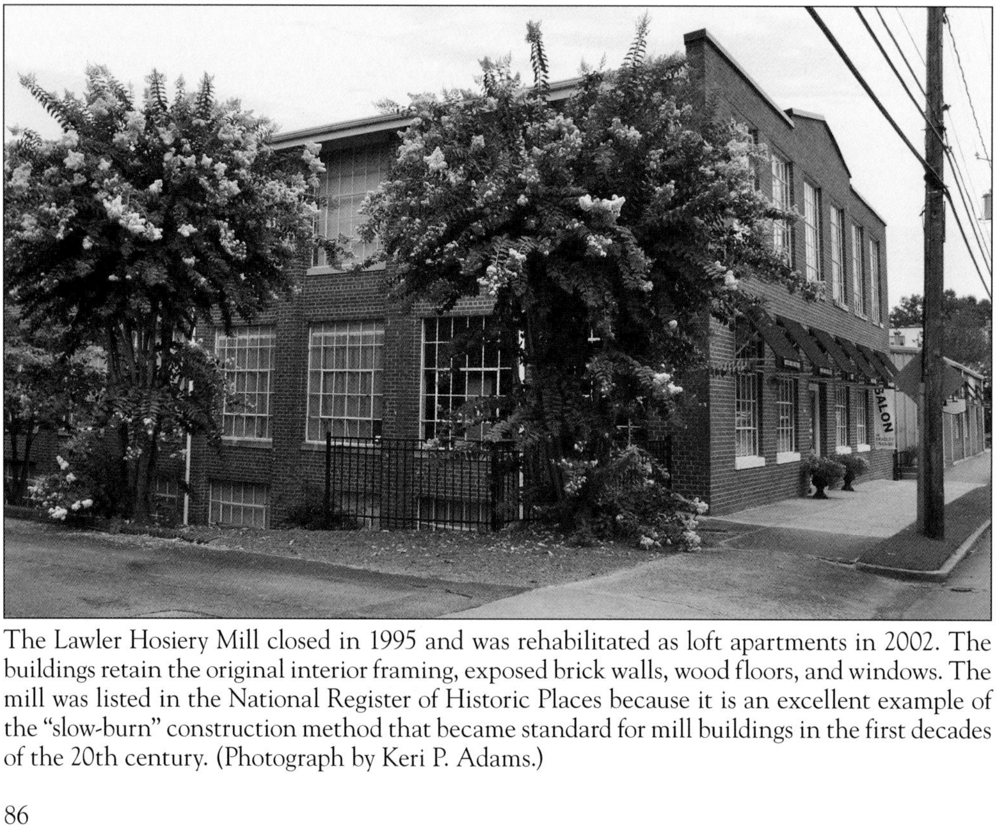

The Lawler Hosiery Mill closed in 1995 and was rehabilitated as loft apartments in 2002. The buildings retain the original interior framing, exposed brick walls, wood floors, and windows. The mill was listed in the National Register of Historic Places because it is an excellent example of the "slow-burn" construction method that became standard for mill buildings in the first decades of the 20th century. (Photograph by Keri P. Adams.)

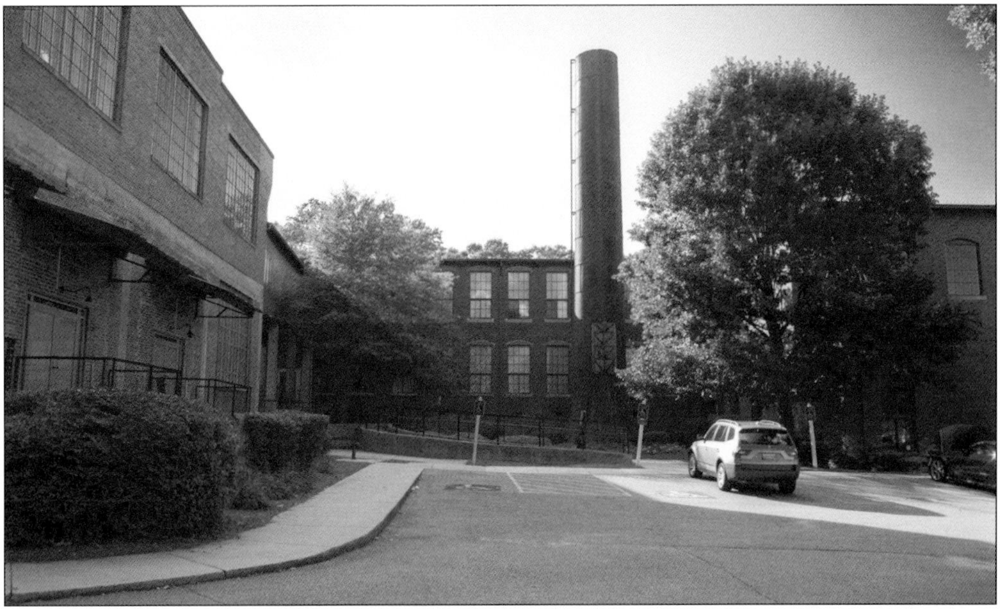

In 1950, the Newnan mills employed over 1,000 workers. Over the next two decades, the mills were purchased by national companies: Mount Vernon Mills, then West Point–Pepperell, and Bibb Manufacturing. Operations ceased in 1970. In 2001, the mill was rehabilitated as a mixed-use loft development known as Newnan Lofts. The property is listed in the National Register of Historic Places for its industrial history, community planning, and architecture. (Photograph by Patrick J. Elias.)

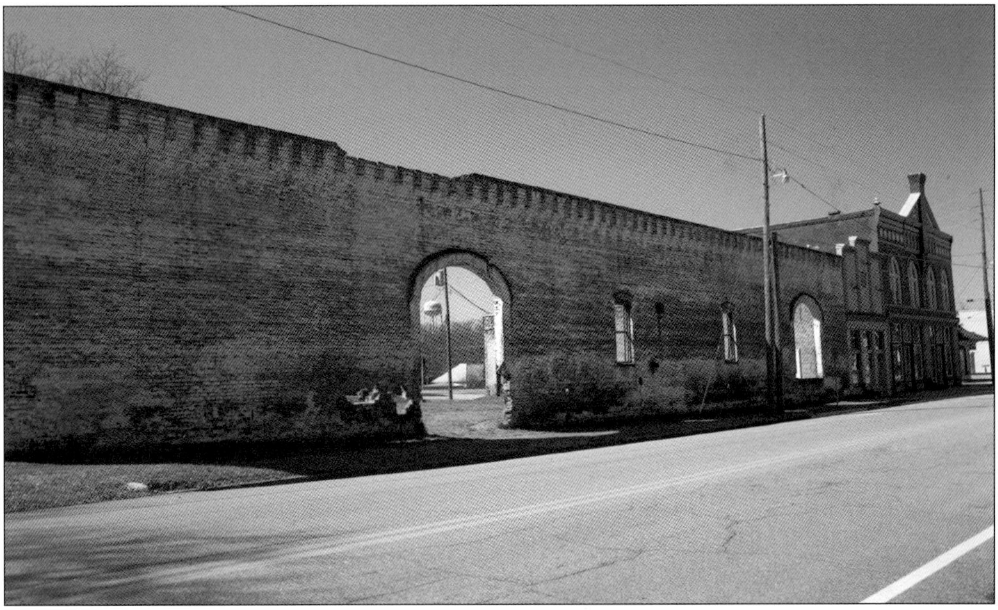

The Grantville Hosiery Mill closed in 1980, but its brick shell still survives. Located in the historic downtown, this structure has been used in recent years to film AMC's *The Walking Dead* television series. The show has featured the mill prominently, leading visitors to come to Grantville from around the world. Now, the old mill is once again a meeting ground for this small, southern Coweta County town. (Photograph by Kymberli Darling.)

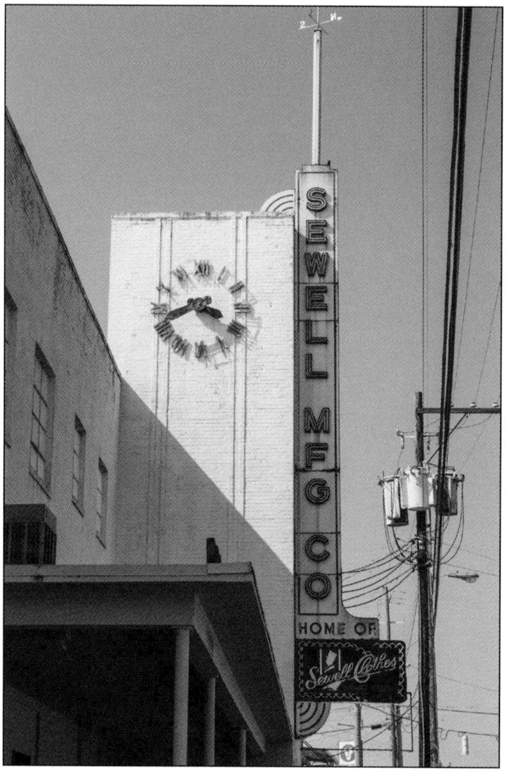

Known as plant number one of Sewell Manufacturing Company, this building has been used as the headquarters for The Sewell Companies since 2008. The building features the distinctive 1950s addition of the Sewell Manufacturing sign and clock tower. Today, visitors can shop in the company store, which sells men's and women's clothing. (Photograph by Rachel Opolka.)

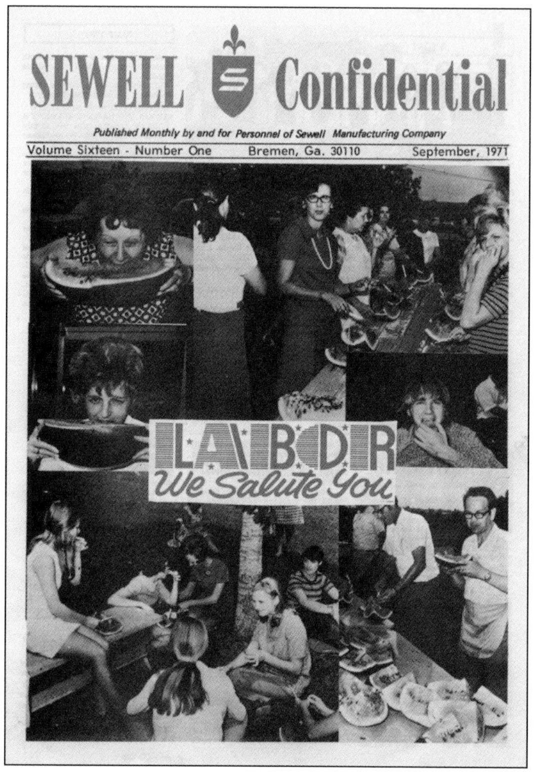

SEWELL Confidential

Published Monthly by and for Personnel of Sewell Manufacturing Company

Volume Sixteen - Number One Bremen, Ga. 30110 September, 1971

LABOR We Salute You

Sewell Manufacturing Company produced its own newsletter, as did many companies in the years after World War II. *Sewell Confidential* was edited and published by Sewell employees. Archival records such as these tell the stories of this company's rich history. Copies of this publication are available for research at the University of West Georgia Center for Public History. (Courtesy Bremen Museum Project.)

Three

The Northern Trail

The northern section of the West Georgia Textile Trail covers the region from the foothills of Polk County to the mountains of north Georgia. Dalton serves as the northern hub.

Local entrepreneurs established Trion Cotton Mill along the Chattooga River in October 1845. The textile boom at the turn of the 20th century brought large brick mills to many of the railroad towns by 1910. Several major northern companies established some of the largest cotton mills here, including the Massachusetts Mill of Georgia in Lindale and Aragon Mills. Hosiery mills appeared by 1900, with several in this region by the time Lewis Hine visited in 1913. The first knitting mills produced socks, but some of the 1920s companies produced underwear as well. Several cotton mills produced yarns for hosiery. Both cotton and many early hosiery mills constructed mill villages.

In the 1920s, national companies began to invest in this region. Goodyear purchased cotton mills in Cedartown and Cartersville and built a new plant in Rockmart to produce tire cord and fabric. American Chatillon Corporation, an Italian American business, established a new operation in Rome to produce rayon, a popular synthetic fiber. These late 1920s companies continued to build mill villages and embraced the spirit of corporate paternalism. The Northwest Georgia Textile League supported baseball teams for many of these larger mills.

The commercial chenille industry started here as part of the Appalachian crafts revival when Catherine Evans Whitener sold her first tufted spread in 1900. Chenille quickly grew from a small handicraft business to a regional enterprise. By the 1930s, clotheslines filled with hand-tufted products lined "Bedspread Boulevard" along US Highway 41. Tourists traveling to and from Florida along this stretch of the Dixie Highway stopped to purchase the popular chenille. By the 1930s, the process moved into factories and utilized machines, but chenille remained popular through the 1960s.

Carpet production evolved from tufted chenille and grew dramatically in this region from the 1950s onward. By the 1970s, the majority of the carpet companies in the United States were located around Dalton. Now, three of the four leading carpet companies in the country are based in Dalton: Shaw, Mohawk, and Beaulieu.

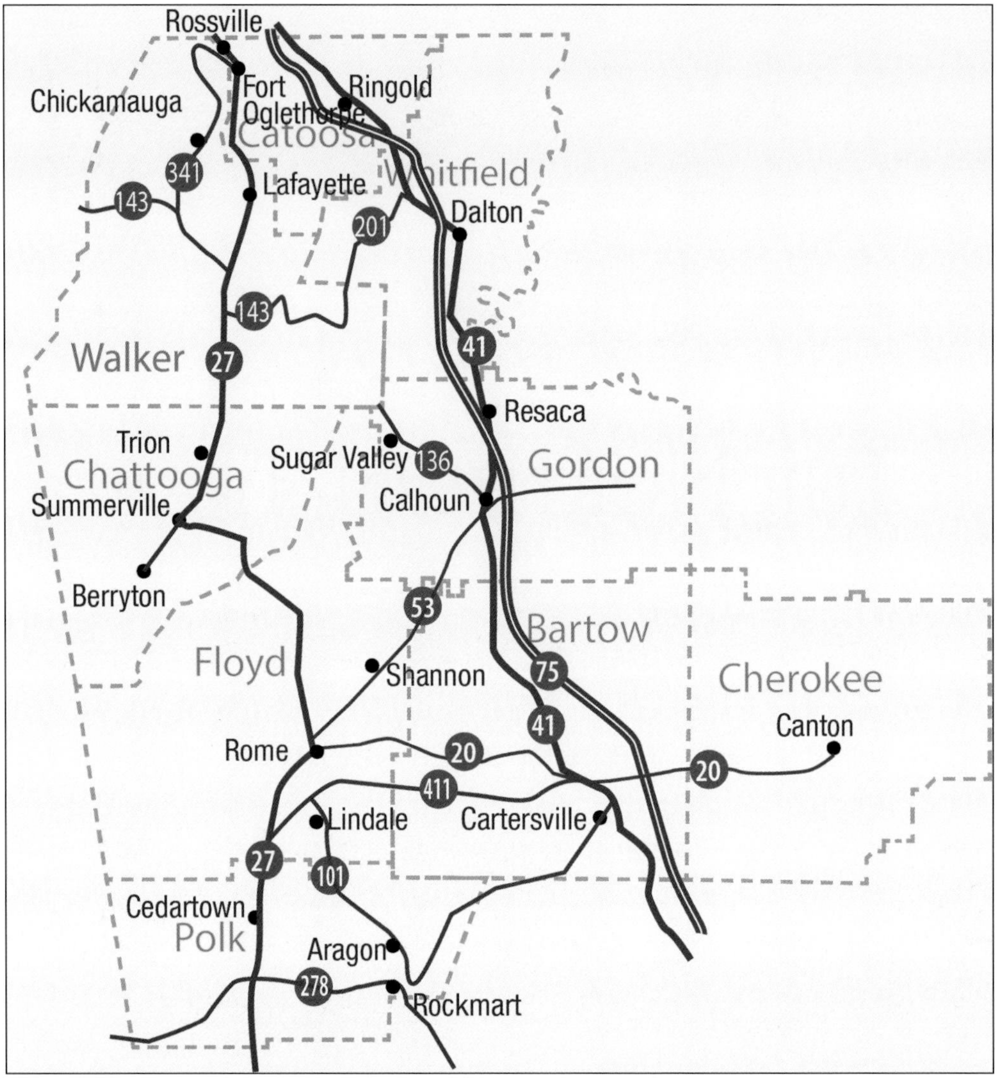

The cotton and hosiery industries developed along major transportation arteries, first rivers and then railroads and highways. Commercial chenille production began around Dalton but followed the Dixie Highway (US Highway 41) from the mountains south through Cartersville, the stretch also known as Bedspread Boulevard and, later, Peacock Alley. The carpet industry still dominates the economy.

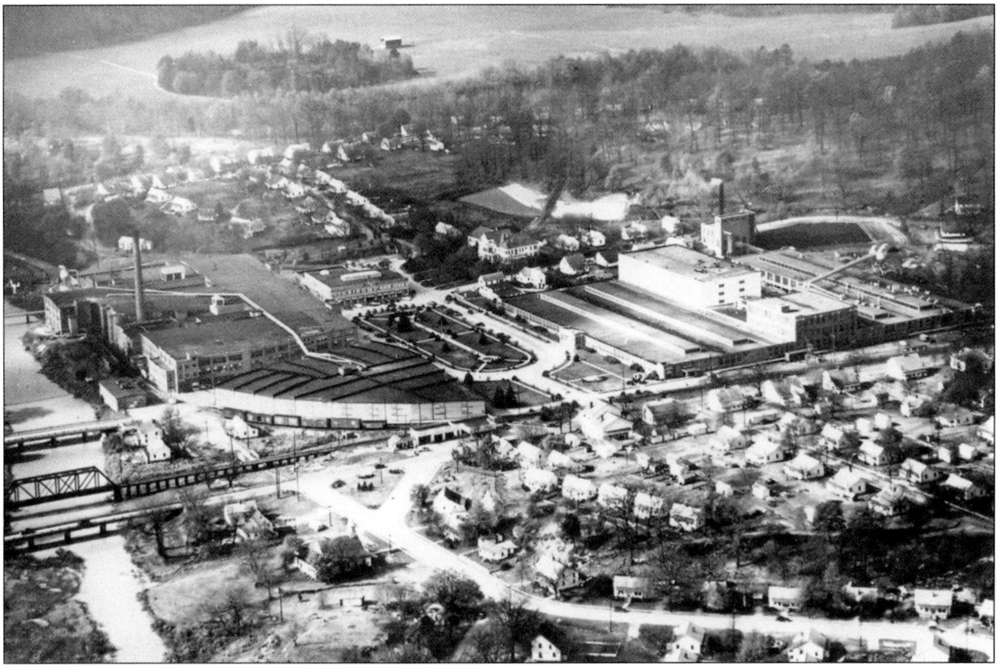

In 1847, businessmen Andrew Allgood, Spencer Marsh, and W.K. Brier organized the first and only antebellum cotton mill in northwest Georgia. Located along the Chattooga River, the water-powered Trion Cotton Mill employed 49 workers to produce yarn and osnaburg sacks. The mill grew dramatically until it burned in an 1875 fire. Six months later, the company built a new two-story brick mill, shown here, that has continued to grow. (Courtesy Trion Public Library)

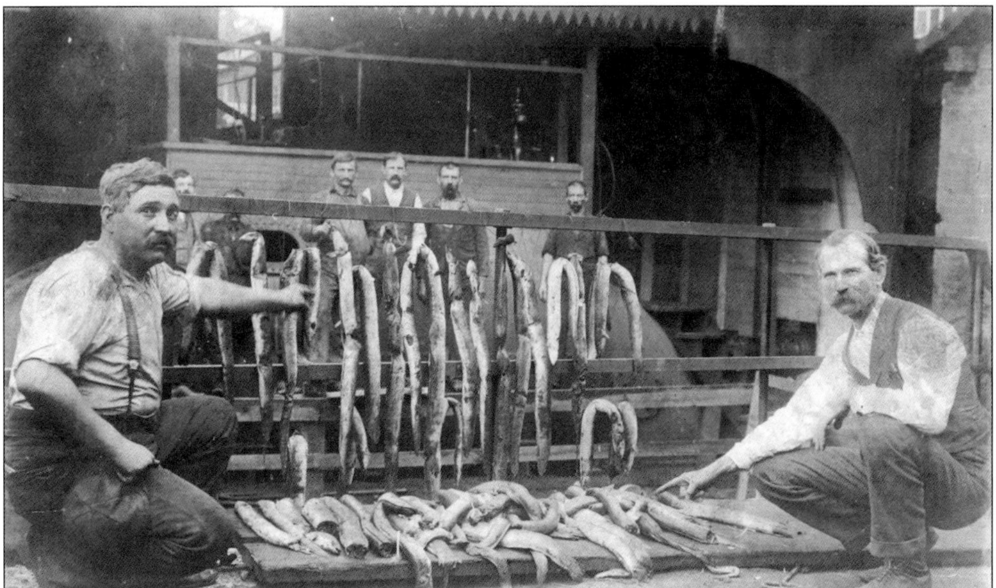

Waterpower could be unreliable for early cotton mills, especially during floods. Sometimes, more unusual occurrences could cause a mill to cease operations. In 1896, eels became caught in the waterwheel of the Trion Cotton Mill. Workers had to stop the wheel to remove the eels before they could resume work. (Courtesy Trion Public Library.)

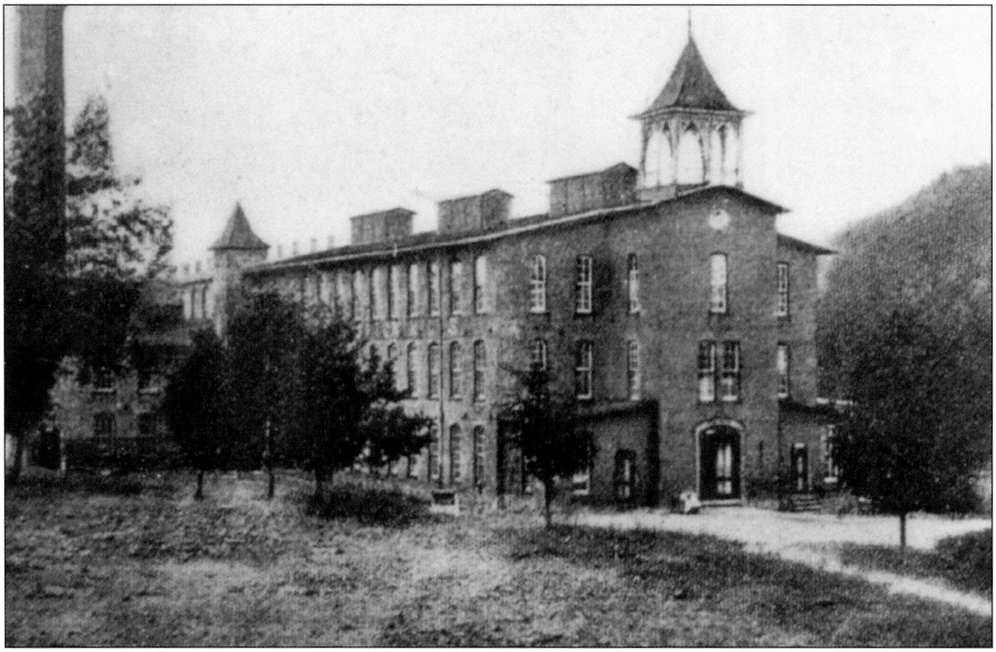

Crown Cotton Mill, the first large-scale cotton mill in this part of the state, opened in Dalton in 1884 and produced duck and osnaburgs. By 1910, the company employed 650 workers, many of whom lived in mill village housing. Employment at Crown Mill was a family affair. In its first few decades, an average of four family members within a household worked a job in the mill. (Courtesy Whitfield-Murray Historical Society.)

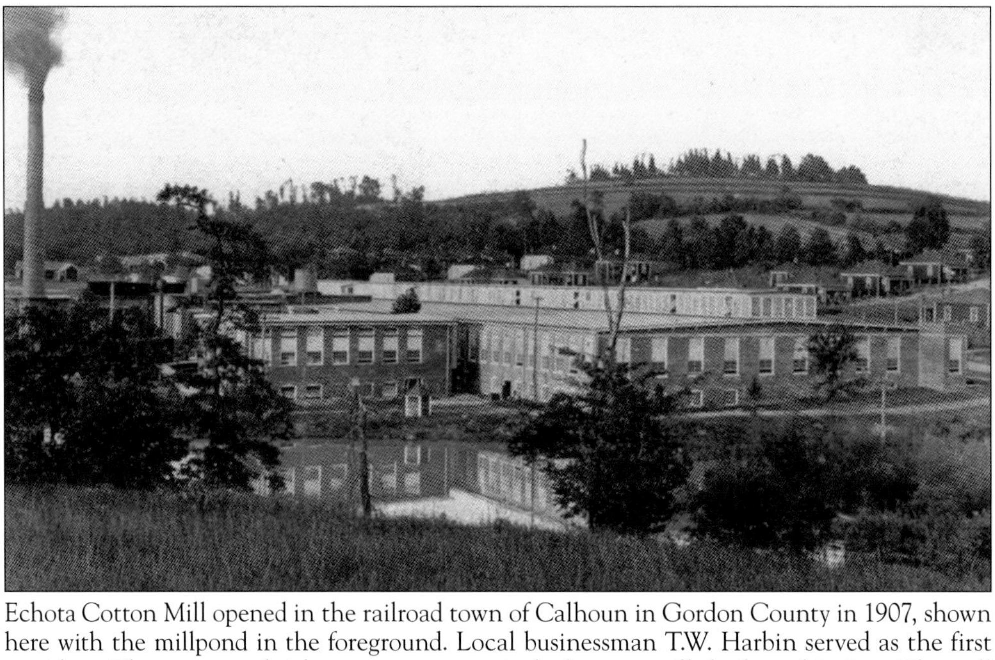

Echota Cotton Mill opened in the railroad town of Calhoun in Gordon County in 1907, shown here with the millpond in the foreground. Local businessman T.W. Harbin served as the first president. The two-story brick structure was typical of cotton mills built at this time. The mill produced sheetings in 1910, employing 65, but added coarse yarns and employed 110 by the early 1920s. (Courtesy Gordon County Historical Society.)

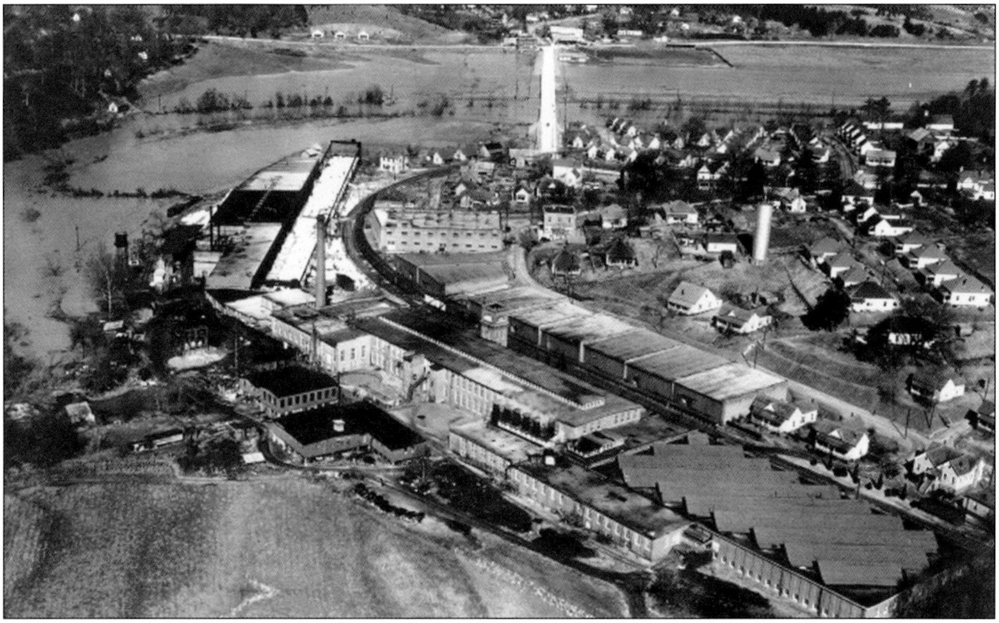

Established by local investors in 1899, Canton Cotton Mill began with a large brick mill along the Etowah River and railroad line. By 1910, the mill had shifted from producing cotton to denim, a material popular in men's work clothes at that time. In 1923–1924, the company added a three-story brick mill building and a new mill village. Canton Cotton Mills employed around 500 workers in the early 20th century. (Courtesy Cherokee County Historical Society.)

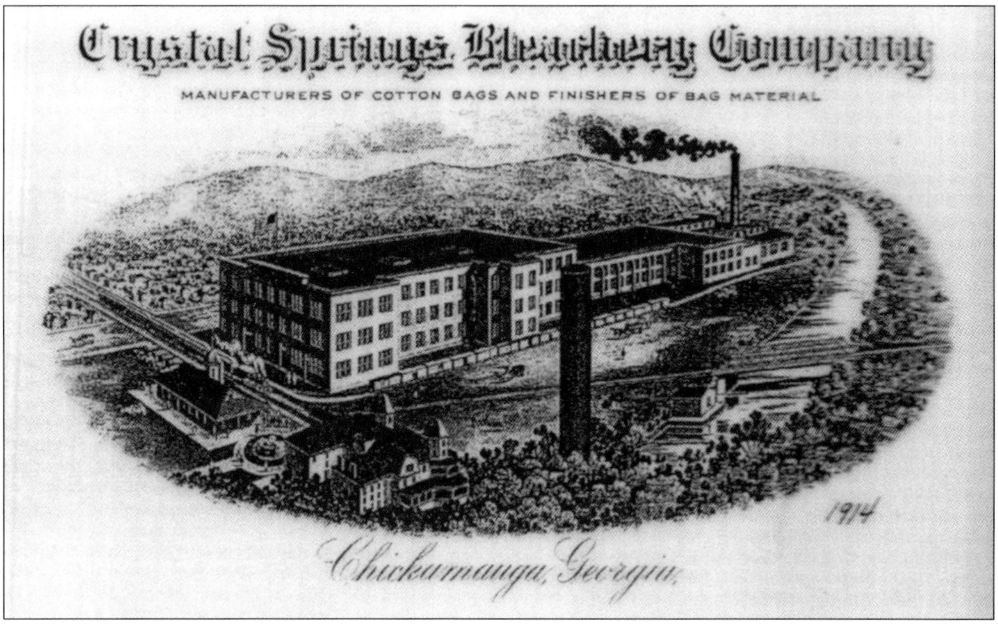

Daniel Ashley Jewell and W.L.L. Bowen built Crystal Springs Bleachery in Chickamauga in 1909, shown here in a 1914 illustration. The company produced and bleached bag goods. By the early 1920s, its 350 workers made over 100,000 yards each day. After employing over 1,000 people in the mid-1970s, Crystal Springs Print Works closed in 2013, and the mill was torn down in 2014. (Courtesy Chickamauga Public Library.)

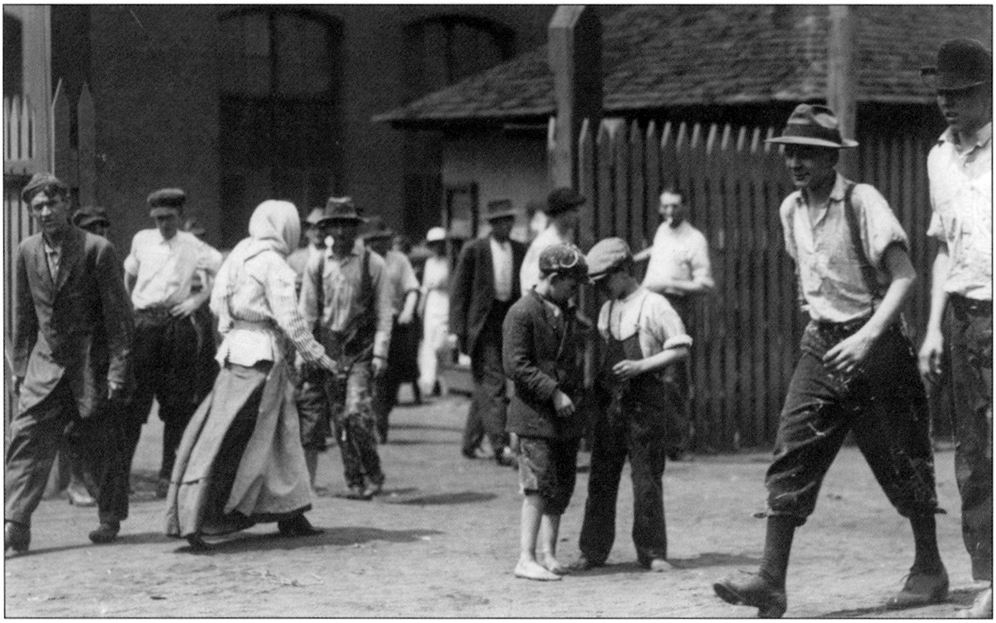

Photographer Lewis Hine recorded "noon hour" at the Massachusetts Mill in Lindale in 1913. He described this as the largest operation in Georgia, with well-built mills and houses and well-kept grounds. "Not a thing neglected, except the children," he lamented, noting that "dozens of children under 12 worked here. The wages of the children under 12 were not necessary if older members of the family did their part." (Courtesy LOC, LC-DIG-nclc-02753.)

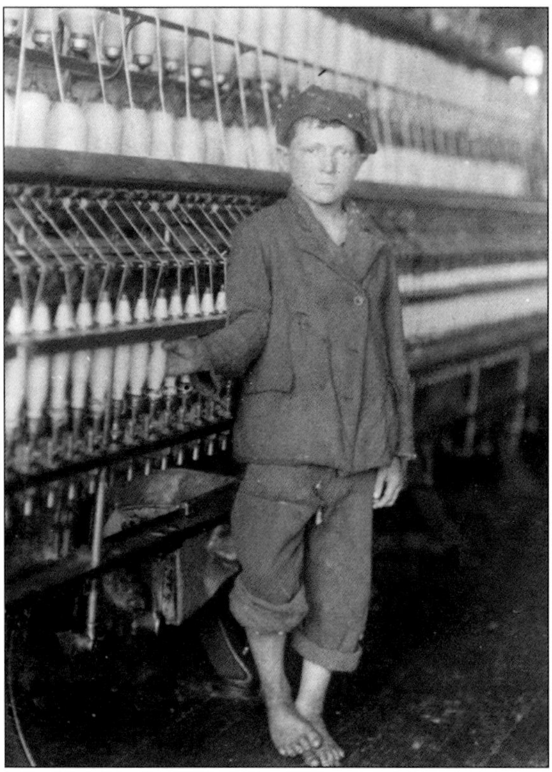

Ten-year-old Norman Hall worked as a doffer at the Massachusetts Mill in 1913. Doffers removed bobbins or spindles full with spun fiber and replaced them with empty ones. Hine described "tiny little chaps, sweeping, doffing, spinning." While the mill had added automatic banding machines, "no one has bothered much about mechanical sweepers and doffers as long as there remains so much human material within easy reach." (Courtesy LOC, LC-DIG-nclc-02789.)

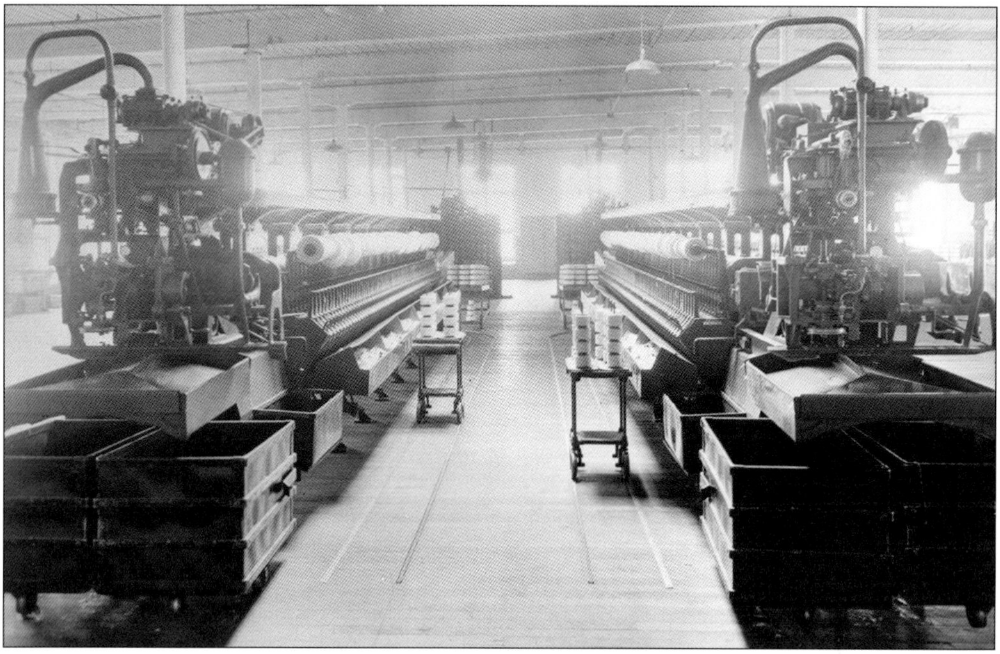

Crown Mill merged with Massachusetts-based West Boylston Manufacturing Company in 1925 to open Boylston-Crown Mill in southeast Dalton, contributing to the city's industrial boom of the 1920s. Crown planned to produce cotton fabric for tires and automobile interiors, and partnered with a northern firm to do so. By 1925, the mill operated 14,000 spindles. This photograph shows the spooler room in the 1920s. (Courtesy Georgia Archives, Vanishing Georgia Collection, wtf240.)

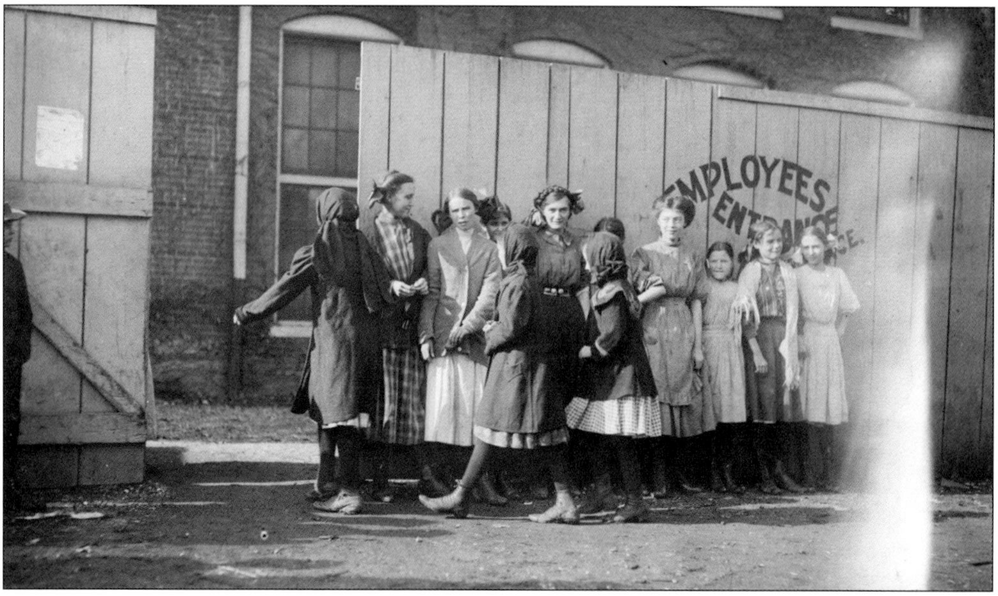

Hosiery mills appeared in this region by 1900. The Richmond Hosiery Mills in Rossville was the oldest and largest hosiery mill in northwest Georgia. Established in 1898 to produce socks for men, women, and "misses," it employed 400 in 1910 and 700 by 1922. This 1913 photograph shows several teenage girls who worked there visiting near the employee entrance while waiting for their shift to start. (Courtesy LOC, LC-DIG-nclc-01986.)

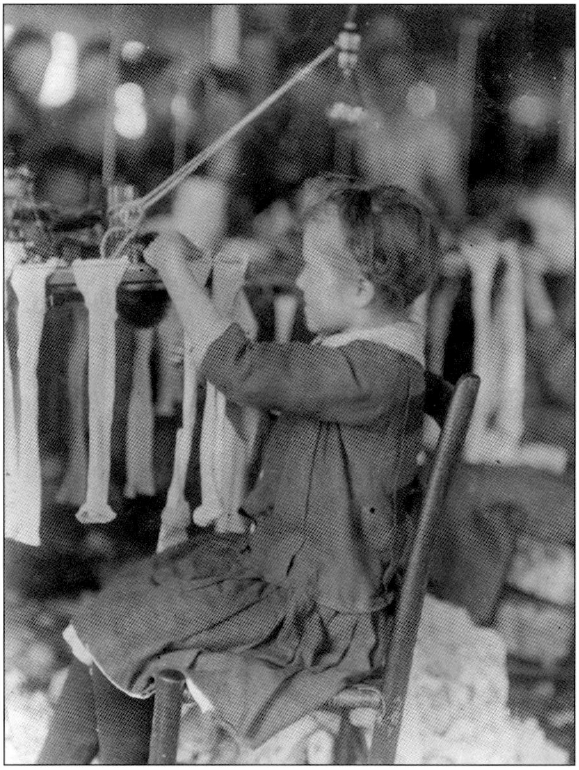

Photographer Lewis Hine documented this young girl working on a stocking at Cherokee Hosiery Mill in Rome in 1913. Established in 1910, this mill produced seamless hosiery on circular knitting machines. Hine described this company as "a small mill, with five workers apparently under 12 years of age. The youngest are turners and loopers." (Courtesy LOC, LC-DIG-nclc-02778.)

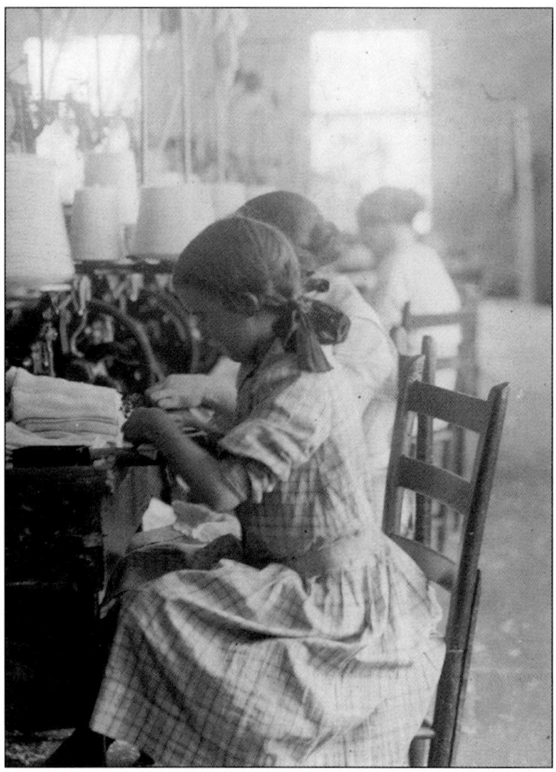

This girl worked as a "topper," sewing the elastic band around the top of the socks, at the Walker County Hosiery Mill in Lafayette in 1913. When visiting this mill, Lewis Hine spoke to a father who had a "large family all in the mill work." The father commented that his "two grown daughters each make about $20 a week in the hosiery mill here." (Courtesy LOC, LC-DIG-nclc-02765.)

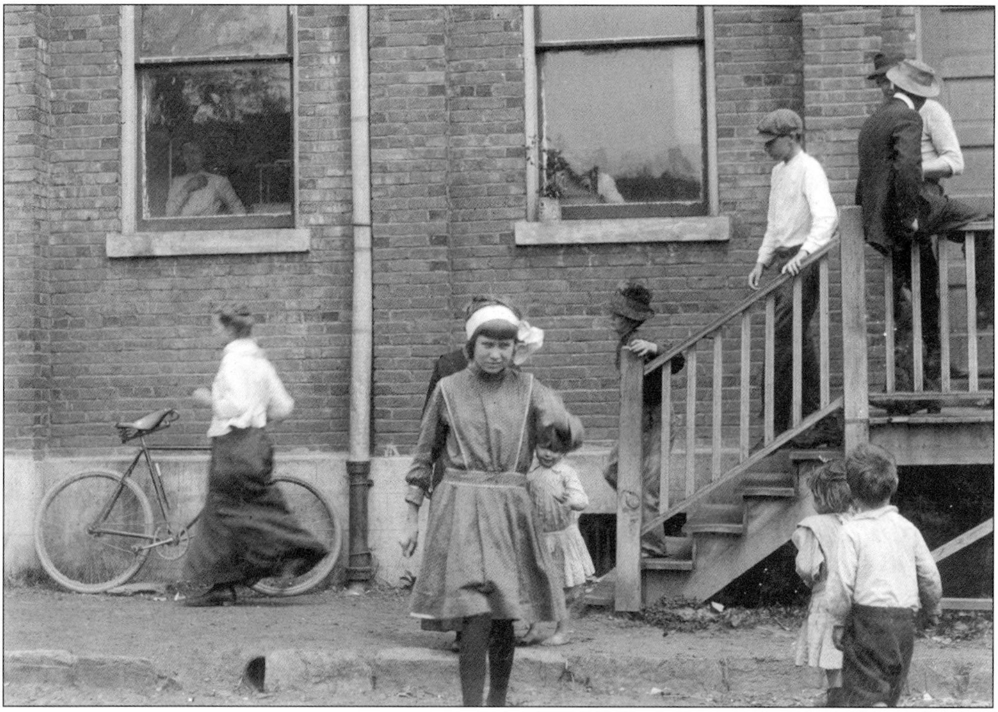

Note the wide range of ages in the children employed at the Rome Hosiery Mill in 1913. Lewis Hine described this as a medium-size, well-equipped mill, adding, "The workers are of the higher type than they are in the average cotton mills, and the wages are much higher for good workers." Employees in the Rome mills worked 11-hour shifts Monday through Friday and 5-hour shifts on Saturday. (Courtesy LOC, LC-DIG-nclc-02740.)

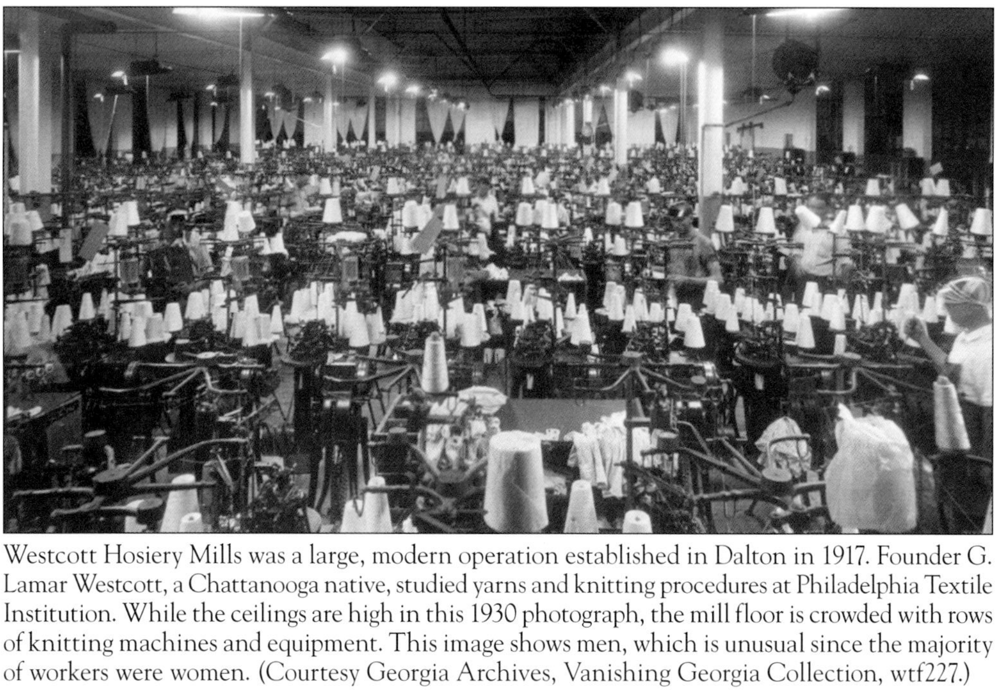

Westcott Hosiery Mills was a large, modern operation established in Dalton in 1917. Founder G. Lamar Westcott, a Chattanooga native, studied yarns and knitting procedures at Philadelphia Textile Institution. While the ceilings are high in this 1930 photograph, the mill floor is crowded with rows of knitting machines and equipment. This image shows men, which is unusual since the majority of workers were women. (Courtesy Georgia Archives, Vanishing Georgia Collection, wtf227.)

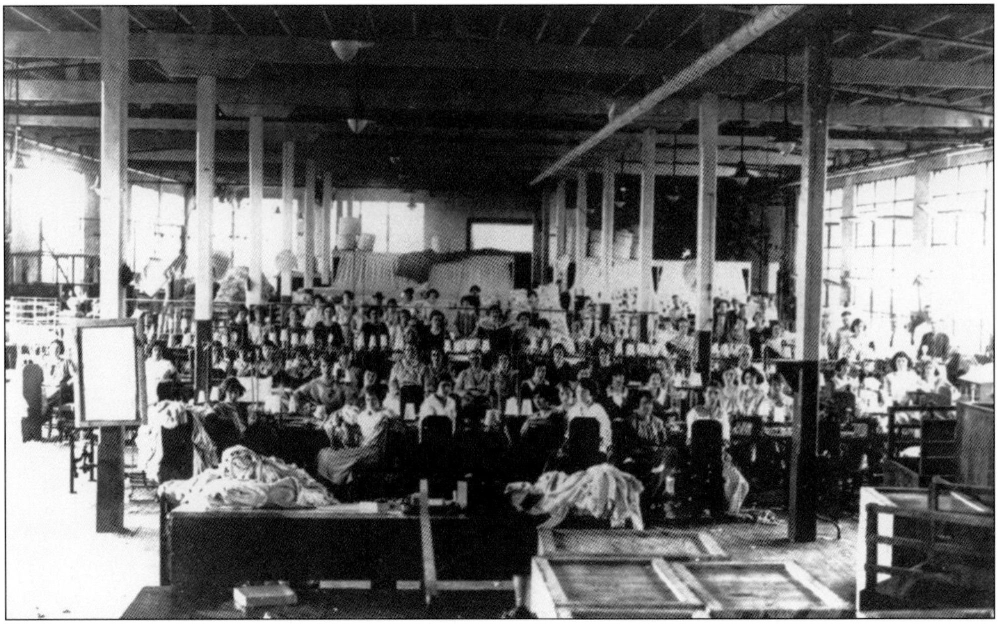

Most knitting mills in this region made hosiery, but Cartersville Mills, which opened in 1921, produced underwear and union suits for children and infants. In 1933, the mill became associated with A.S. Haight and Company in New York, which constructed additional buildings and added machinery. The name changed to EZ Mills in 1937. A primarily female workforce operates the knitting machines in this expansive interior. (Courtesy Bartow History Museum.)

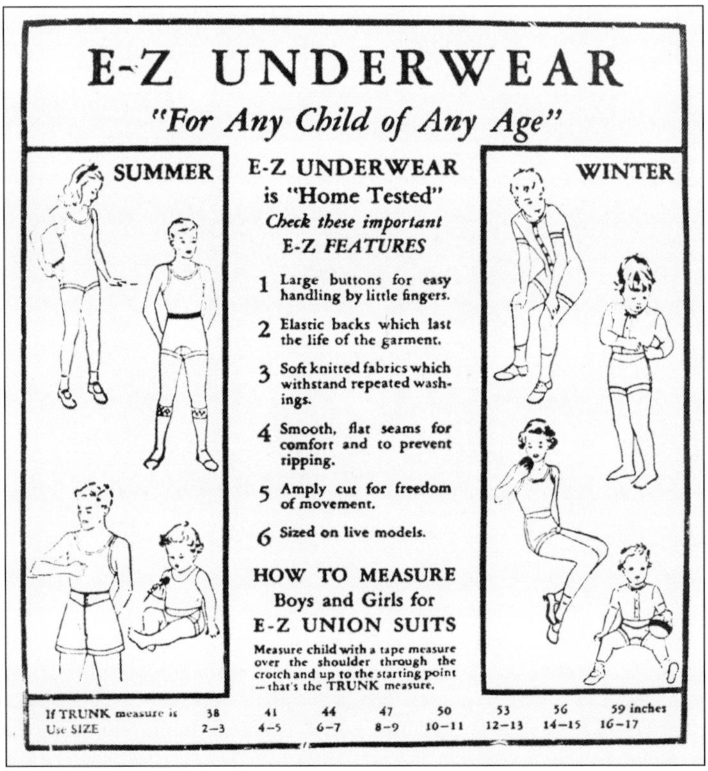

This 1940s advertisement shows the variety of underwear produced by EZ Mills in Cartersville. Note the use of "soft knitted fabrics" for "any child of any age." The union suit appears to be a company specialty. Popular in the late 1800s, the union suit became the standard undergarment for boys and working men in the early 20th century, but they were also worn by girls. (Courtesy Bartow History Museum.)

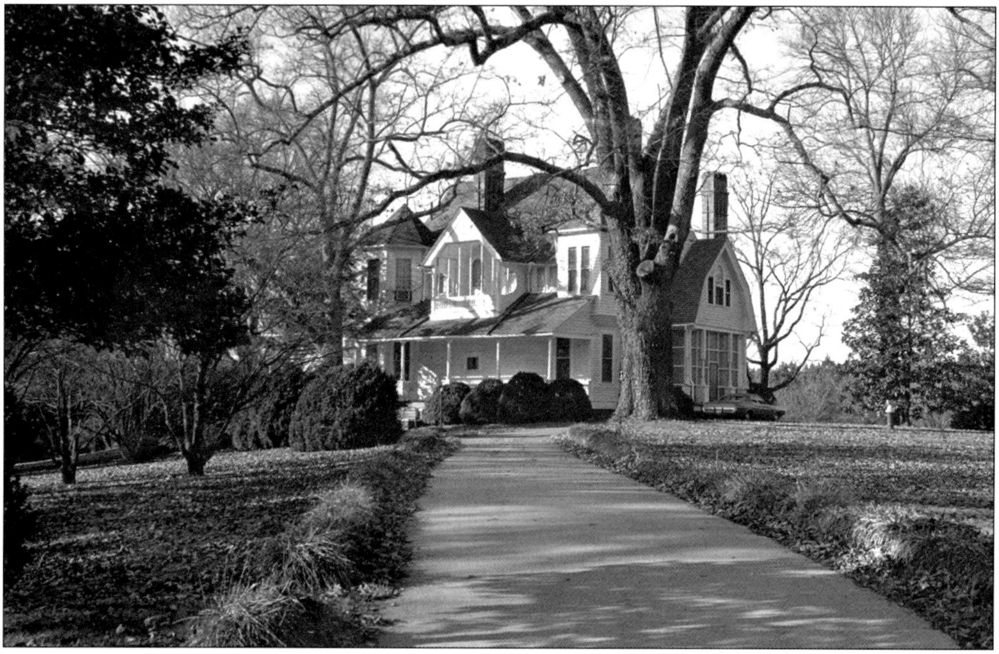

Company presidents and owners lived in stylish houses either on the edge of the mill village or in a fashionable town neighborhood. This photograph shows the ornate Queen Anne home for the vice president of the Trion Cotton Mill. These large, stylish houses illustrate the social hierarchy within the mill community when compared to the plain workers' homes. (Courtesy Trion Public Library.)

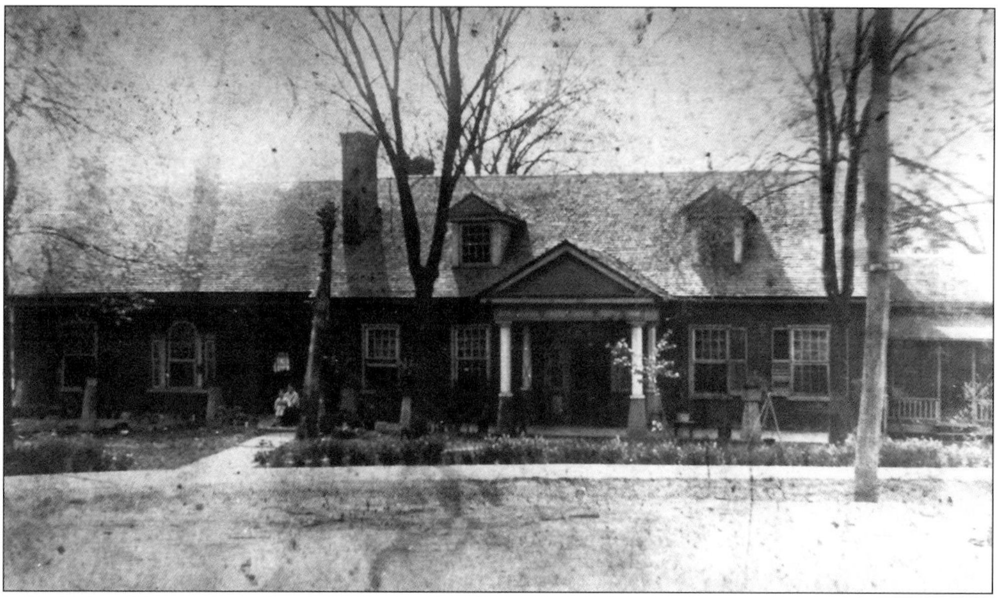

Frank Hamilton, superintendent and master mechanic of Crown Mills, lived here with his family between 1904 and 1983. This 1840 home, one of the oldest in Dalton, was located next to the mill. CrownAmerica remodeled the house for its office around 1986. In 1997, the Whitfield-Murray Historical Society acquired this home, and it now features exhibits and collections focusing on the region's textile industry, especially chenille. (Courtesy Whitfield-Murray Historical Society.)

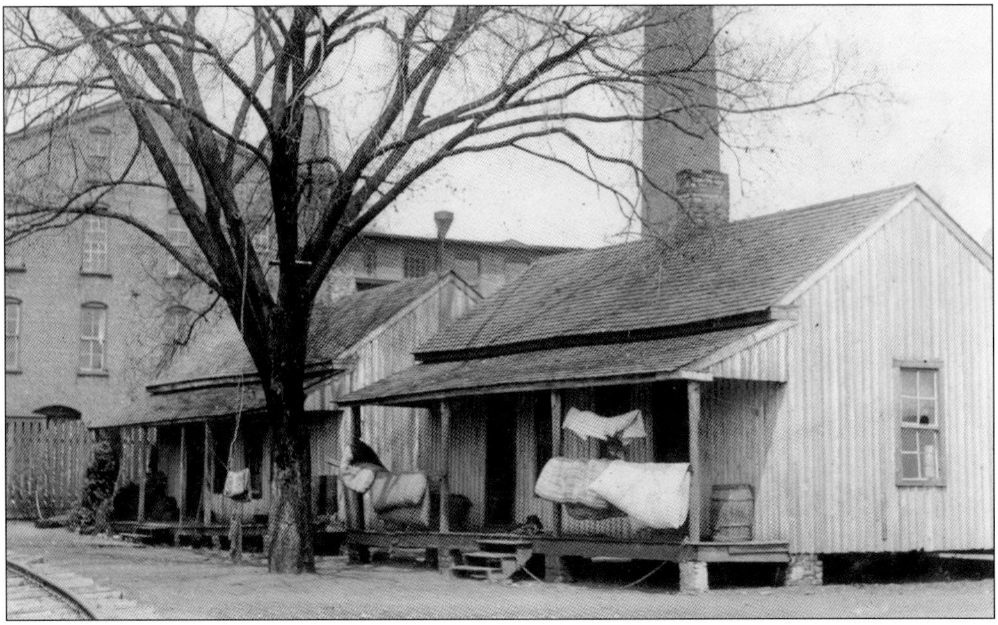

Lewis Hine documented these mill houses at the Floyd Cotton Mill in 1913. He described this as "a very small, run down mill" and the houses as "the worst of any mills there." Located adjacent to the mill building, the houses feature a familiar mill duplex plan with a central chimney, two front doors, a front porch, and a brick pier foundation. Note the bedding hanging on the front porch. (Courtesy LOC, LC-DIG-nclc-02772.)

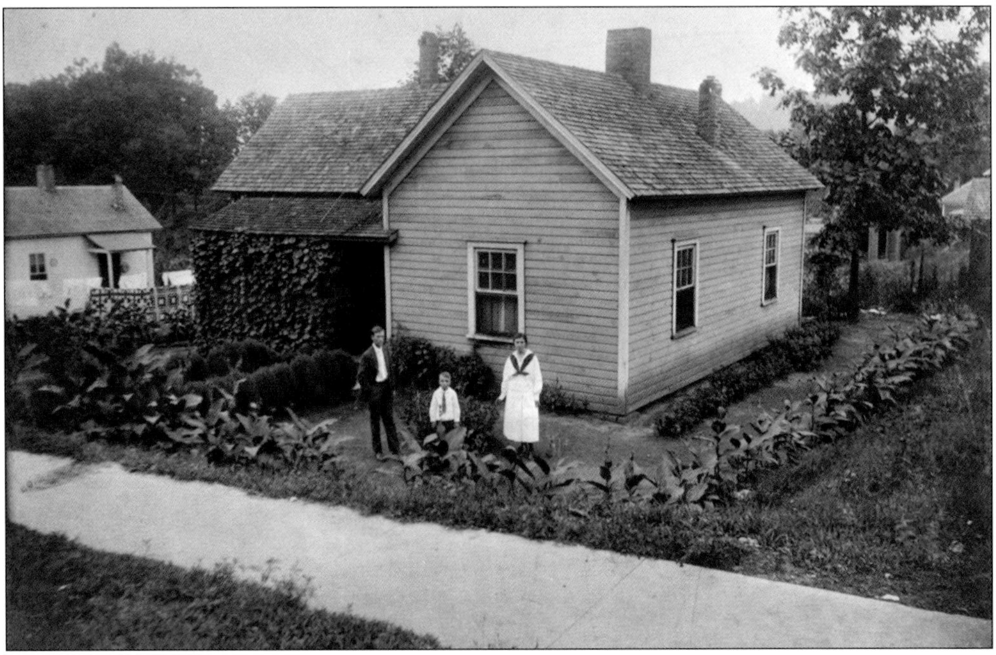

To encourage workers to maintain their homes in the mill village, companies sponsored improvement contests. This home on Chattanooga Avenue in Dalton won a 1919 Crown Cotton Mill contest for the most attractive yard and home. The family stands in front of an ornamental flower garden featuring lilies and boxwood. (Courtesy Georgia Archives, Vanishing Georgia Collection, wtf260.)

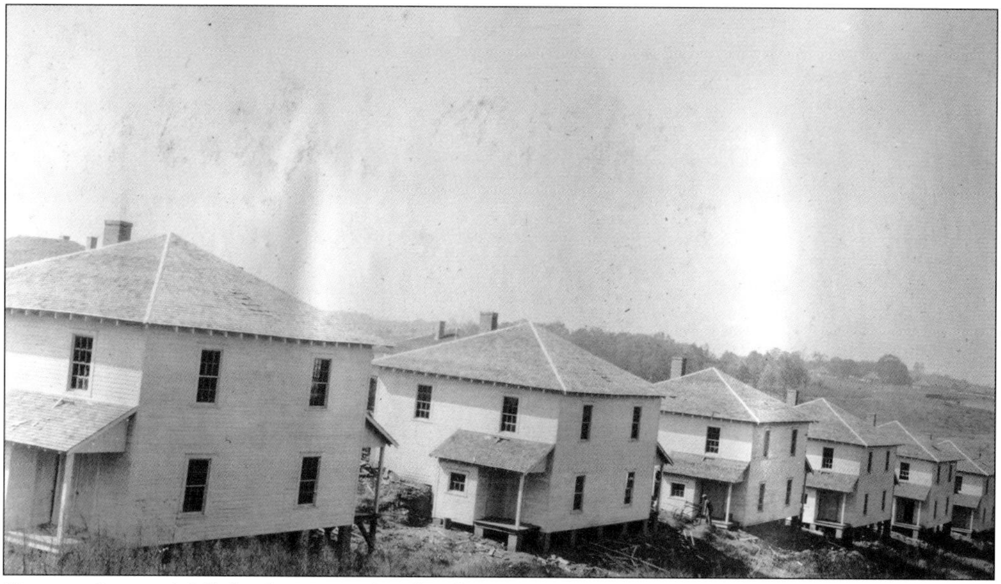

Canton Cotton Mills built a second mill village with around 150 new houses in late 1923 along with the construction of Mill No. 2. These two-story, pyramidal roof duplex houses were larger and more modern than traditional mill homes, and included food pantries, closets, painted walls, free water and electricity, and flush toilets. The mill village, shown here in 1943, also included two miles of paved roads. (Courtesy Cherokee County Historical Society.)

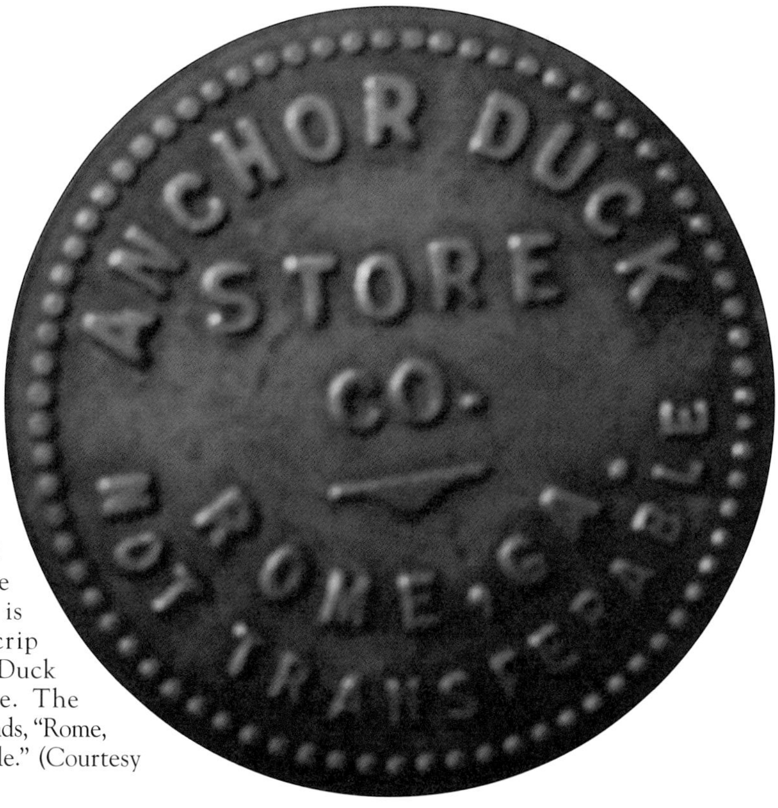

Many cotton mills paid their workers in scrip that could only be redeemed at the company store. Consequently, employees had to pay the often-inflated prices that the store offered. This coin is an example of scrip from the Anchor Duck Company in Rome. The bottom of the coin reads, "Rome, GA. Not Transferable." (Courtesy Leon Shiver.)

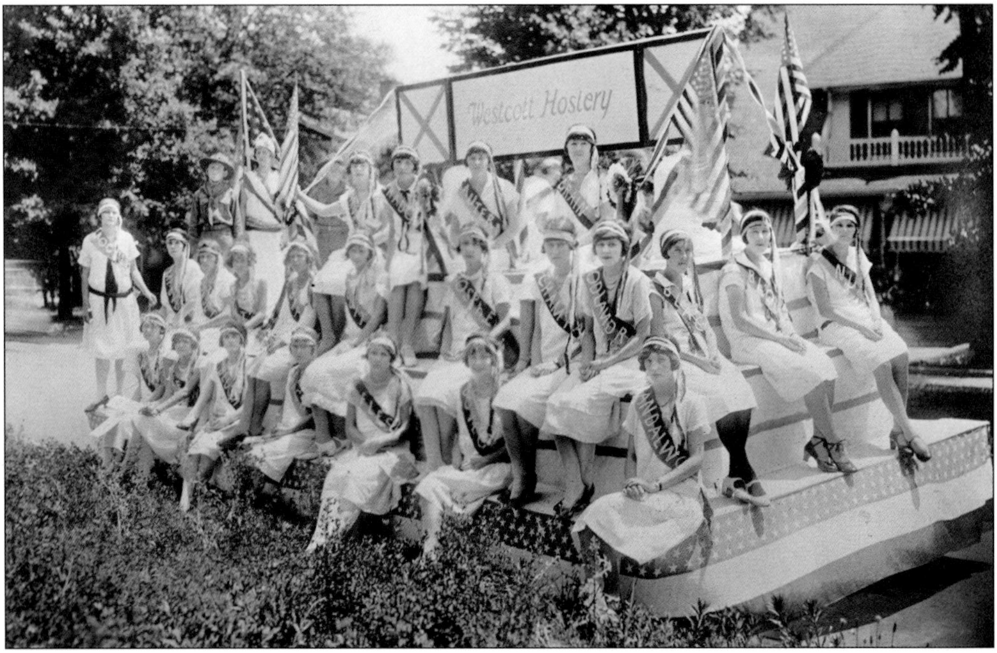

Mill companies often sponsored floats in community parades to showcase their goods. The women, probably employees, on this Westcott Hosiery Mill float in a Dalton parade are wearing products made at the mill. This photograph was taken in 1917, the year the company opened. (Courtesy Georgia Archives, Vanishing Georgia Collection, wtf253.)

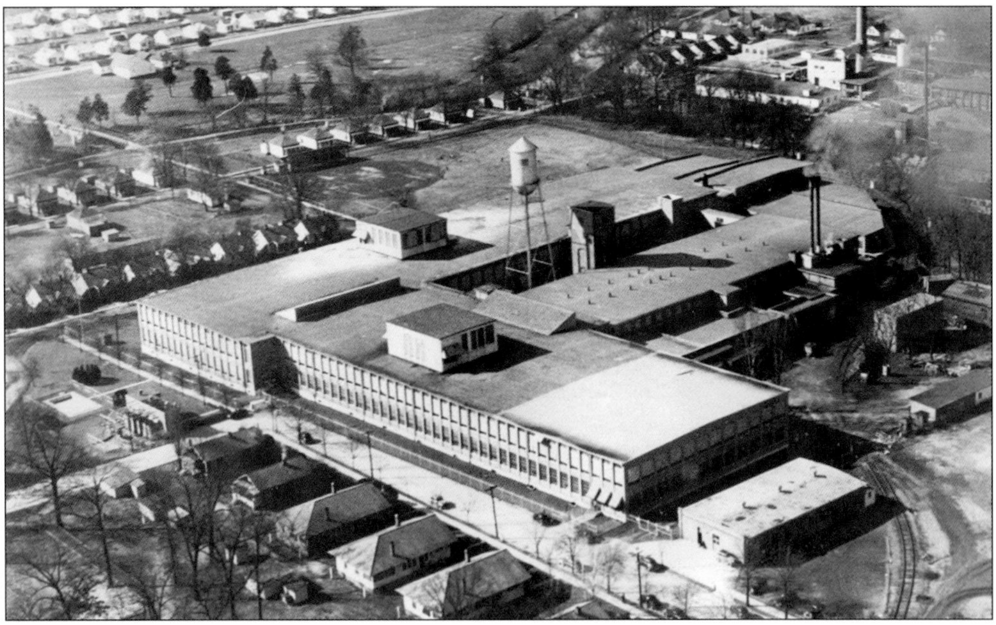

With the popularity of automobile travel in the 1920s, Goodyear Tire and Rubber Company expanded its operations into the South and across the world. In 1925, Goodyear purchased the Cedartown Cotton Manufacturing Company, its first mill in Georgia, to produce cotton cord and cloth for tires. The Polk County Historical Society in Cedartown has many photographs and artifacts from this company's history on display. (Courtesy Polk County Historical Society.)

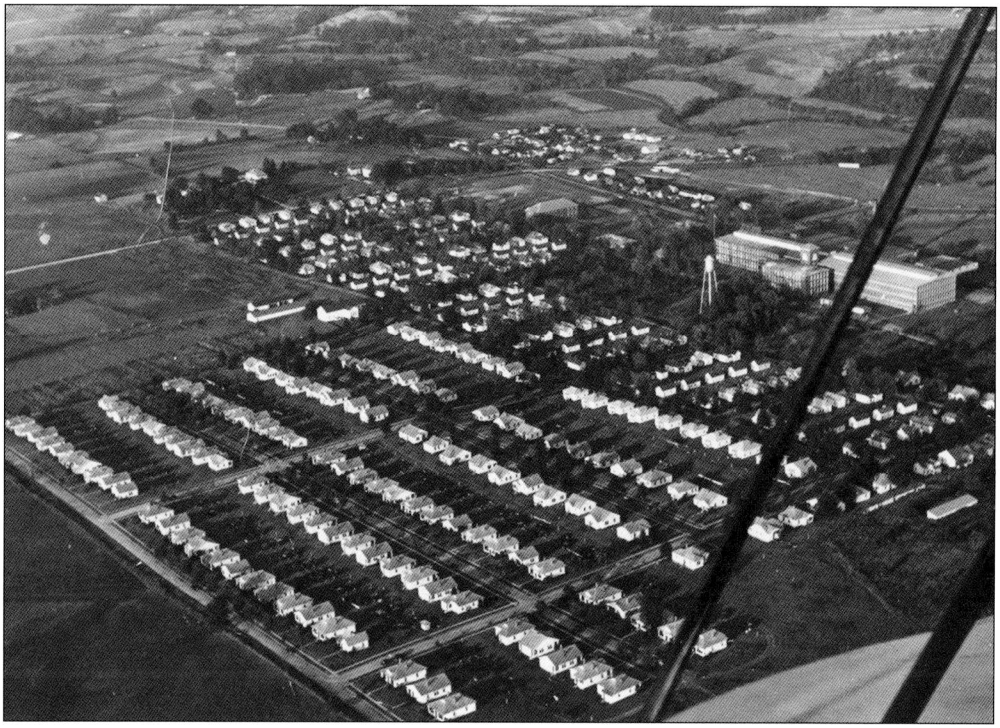

In 1928, Goodyear purchased the American Textile Company (ATCO) in Cartersville, a 1903 cotton mill and village, to produce cotton tire cord. Goodyear expanded the mill village to include almost 300 houses and added many amenities, including a park, garden space, scout troops, a band, and a baseball field. The exhibits at the Bartow History Museum in Cartersville highlight the impact of Goodyear on the community. (Courtesy Bartow History Museum.)

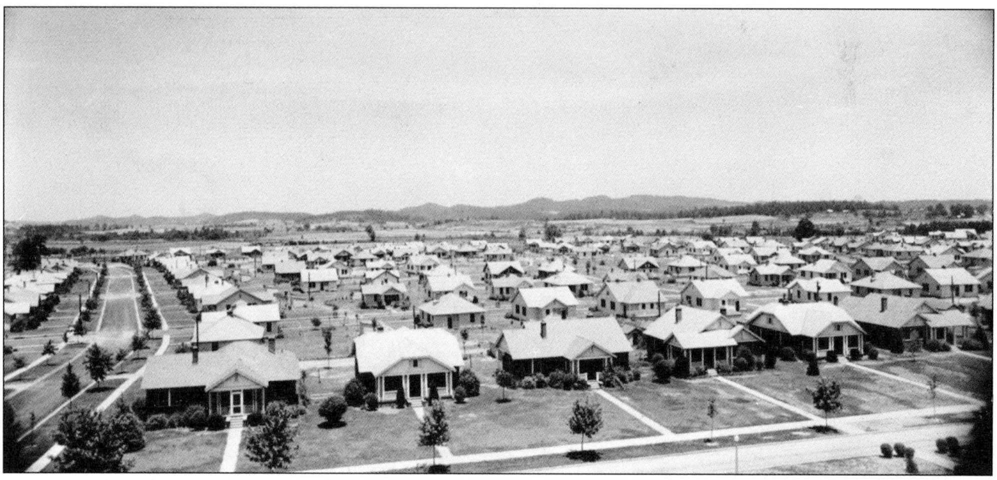

In 1929, Goodyear constructed a new cotton textile mill in Rockmart, the third it owned in this region. As with its other plants, Goodyear built a mill village for the workers. This 1930 photograph of the newly constructed homes shows the variety of modern house plans and styles built to attract workers. Goodyear built the brick houses in the front, called "Boss Row," for the managers. (Courtesy Georgia Archives, Vanishing Georgia Collection, plk 198-84.)

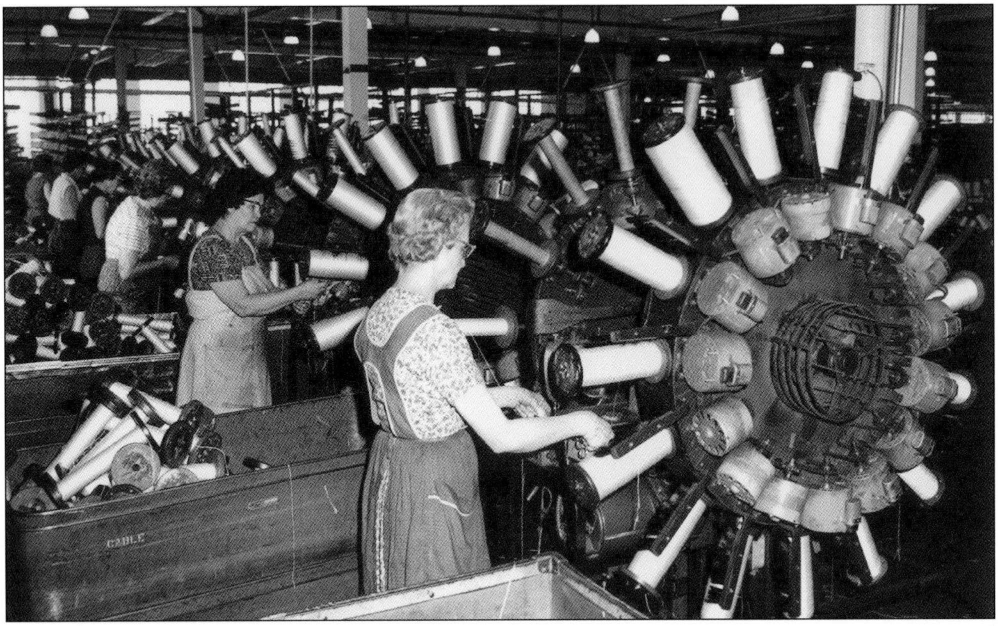

All three Goodyear plants operated as cotton textile mills, processing raw cotton into tire cord and fabric. Women filled many of the positions. These women in the spool room in the Cedartown mill are splicing together the cotton yarn on larger spools to send to the weaving room. Women wore aprons to hold their tools, including scissors, a small snipper, and a hook if they worked in the weaving room. (Courtesy Polk County Historical Society.)

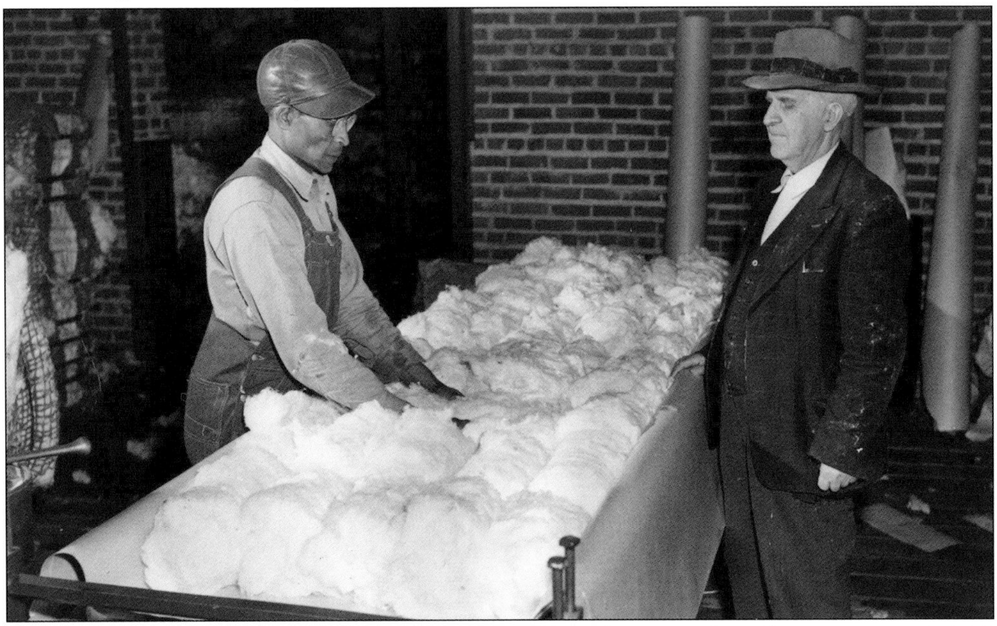

The number of African Americans employed in the southern textile mills never exceeded 4.5 percent between 1900 and 1960. In this 1943 company photograph, a black employee at the Cedartown Goodyear plant works in the picking room. Southern cotton mills, such as Goodyear, hired black workers only in the cotton house, opening room, and picker house or in janitorial positions. (Courtesy of Polk County Historical Society.)

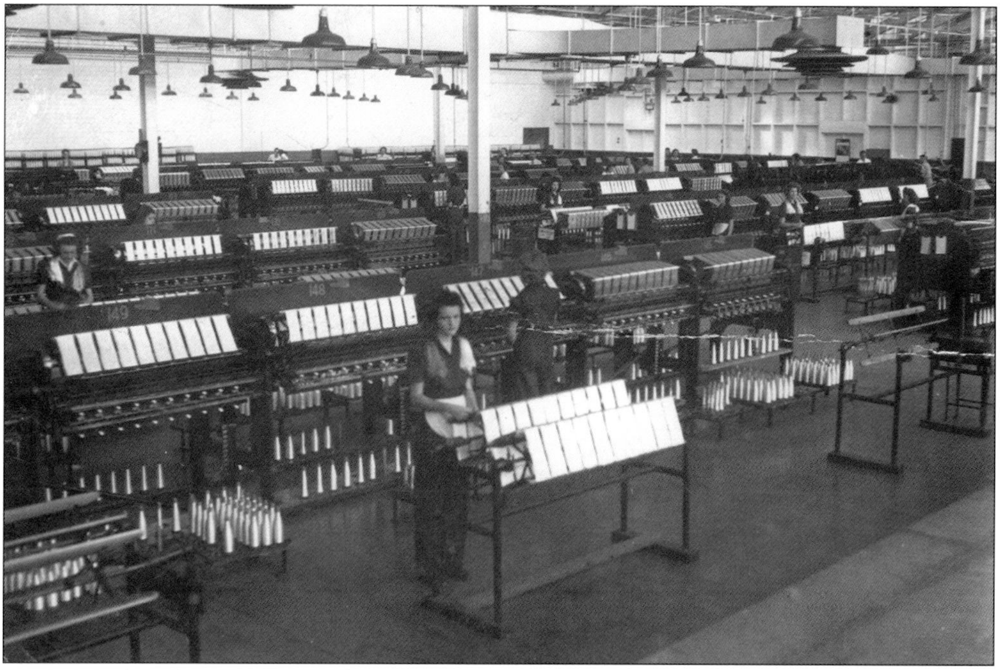

In 1930, Italian American manufacturer Chatillon Corporation of America opened a modern rayon plant in Rome, later acquired by Tubize and then Celanese. Rayon was the first synthetic fiber, developed as a replacement for the desirable but expensive silk. Commercial production of "artificial silk" started in the United States in 1910, and the acetate fiber was named rayon in 1924. Note the modern, clean interior of the skein room. (Courtesy Russ Harwell.)

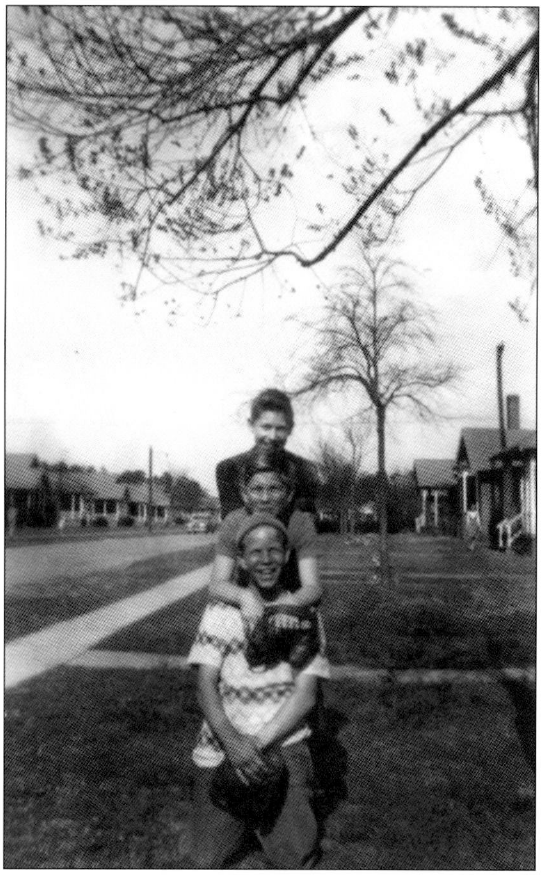

Three boys play in a yard of the Tubize mill village in the 1940s. The new Chatillon mill anticipated hiring 4,000 workers. The company had not intended to build a mill village, which was no longer fashionable, but owners quickly realized that they needed to provide housing to attract workers. Riverside Village eventually featured almost 500 single-family, brick-veneer homes in popular styles. (Courtesy Rome Area History Museum.)

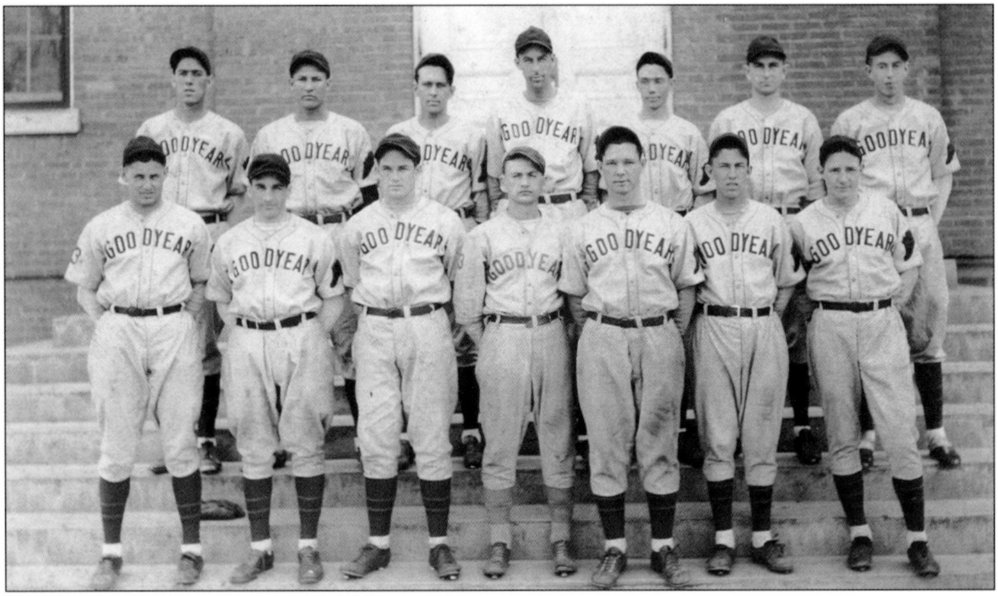

Baseball was a popular sport in southern mill communities in the early 20th century. In 1931, six mills created the Northwest Georgia Textile League, including the Tubize and Anchor Duck mills in Rome, Pepperell Mill in Lindale, and the three Goodyear plants. This photograph shows the ATCO team from the Goodyear plant in Cartersville. Slugger Rudy York became famous and went on to play in the major leagues. (Courtesy Bartow History Museum.)

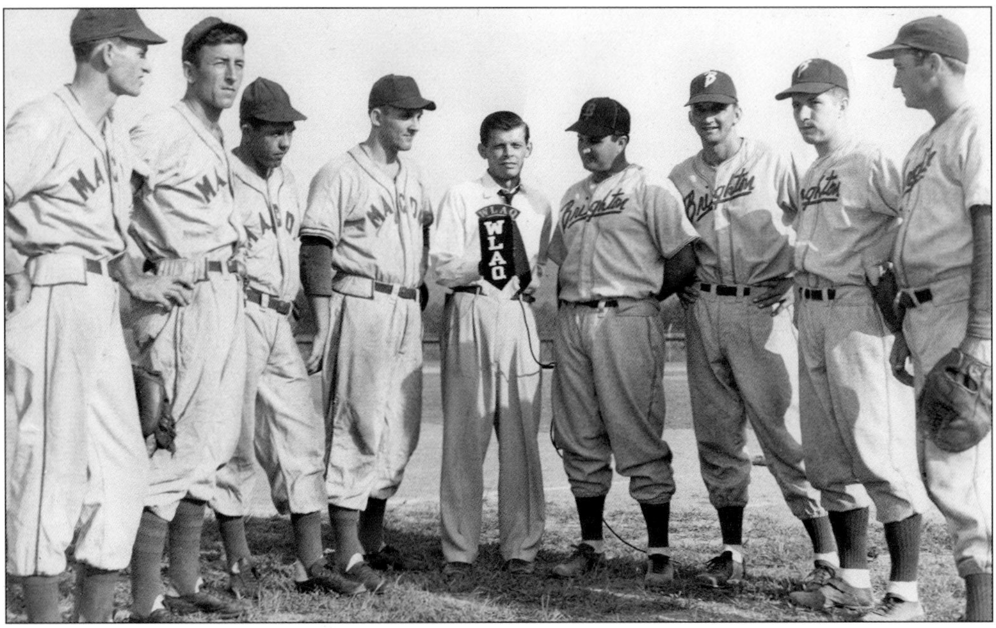

The Brighton Mills in Shannon joined the Northwest Georgia Textile League in 1932. Community members flocked to the games. Rivalries were fierce, including when Brighton supervisors unsuccessfully tried to lure Rudy York from the Cartersville Goodyear squad to play on their team. Announcer Lee Mowry from Rome radio station WLAQ broadcast the games. Many people preferred broadcasts of mill games to those of the major leagues. (Courtesy Watters District Council for Historic Preservation.)

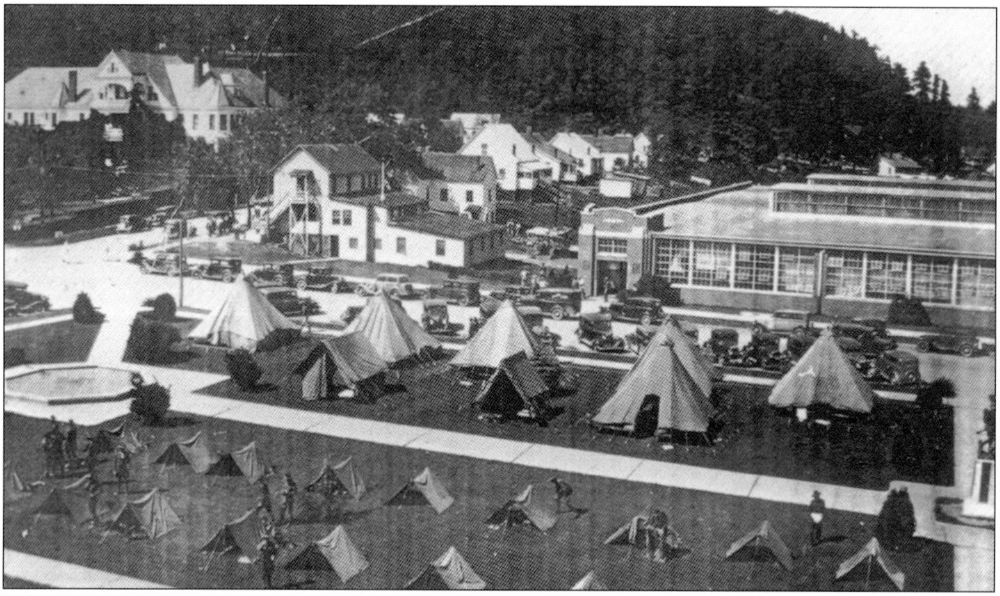

"Flying squadrons" of union organizers from Rome arrived at the Riegel Mill in Trion in August 1934 and encouraged members of a newly-established union to join the General Textile Strike. This photograph shows strikers camping in tents outside the mill. On September 5, after a deputy opened fire on two strikers, a fight ensued in the mill. A striker and deputy were killed and six others wounded. (Courtesy Trion Public Library.)

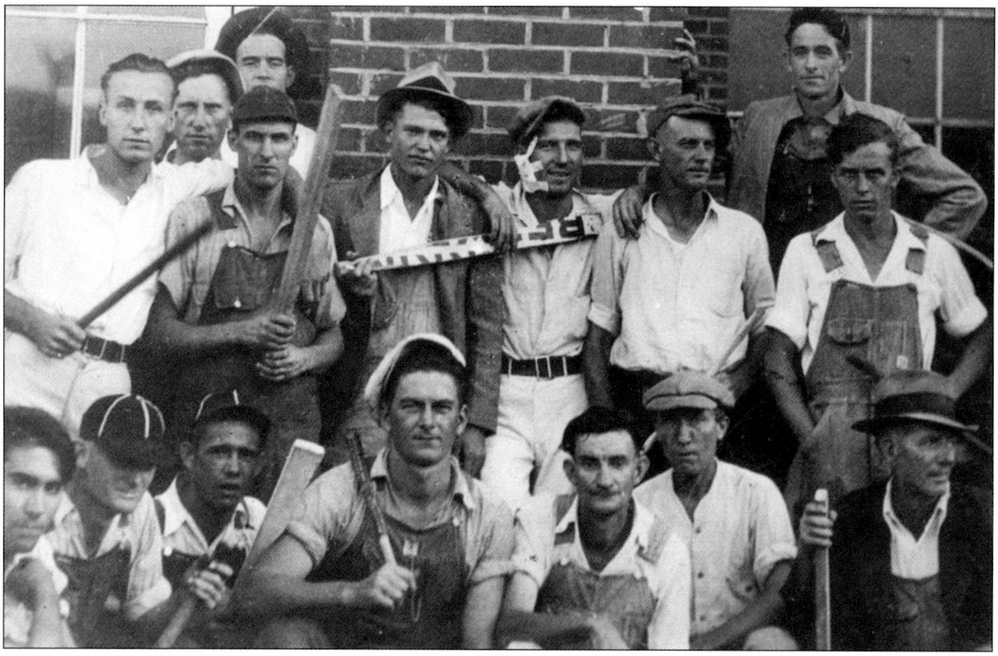

This photograph from the next day, September 6, shows strikers outside the mill with various weapons. The mill did not reopen until September 17, when National Guardsmen with machine guns stood behind cotton bales and prohibited strikers from entering the mill. Notice the man with the bandaged face in the second row, who may have been one of those wounded the previous day. (Courtesy Wayne State University.)

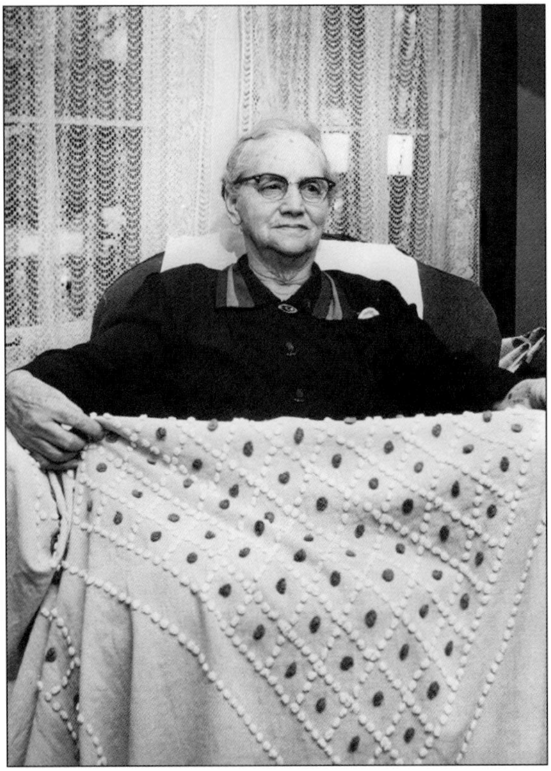

Catherine Evans Whitener, shown here around 1960, is credited with bringing the Southern Appalachian Craft Revival to the region at the turn of the 20th century. Whitener's interest in hand tufting began at age 15, when she admired a candlewick "counterpane" and tufted a bedspread of her own. She would soon develop a home business that led her to teach the craft to other women. (Courtesy Bandy Heritage Center for Northwest Georgia.)

Whitener began to stamp sheets for spread patterns and share them with other women as her own business grew. This painting, *The Hauler*, on display at the Hamilton House in Dalton, depicts the development of the candlewick handicraft industry in the northwest Georgia region. Here, a male hauler drops off craft materials to "candlewickers" on their front porch. (Courtesy Whitfield-Murray Historical Society and Gordon County Historical Society.)

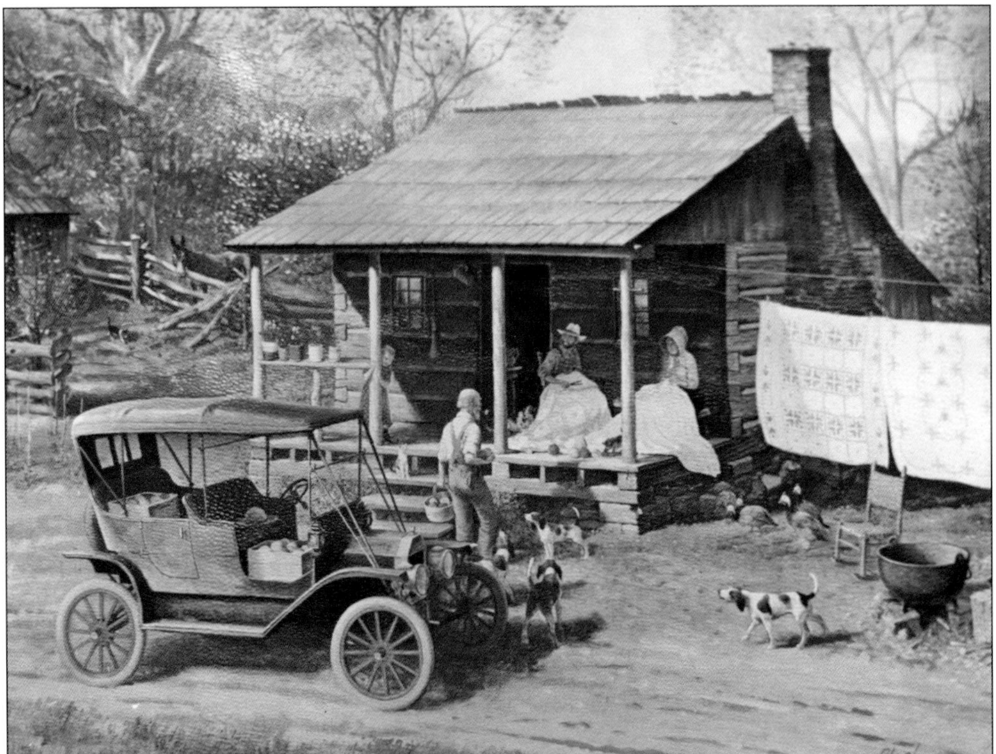

Ethel May Stiles in Ringgold demonstrates rubbing a chenille pattern onto fabric in 1934. A plain piece of unwashed cotton muslin was stretched over the pattern, then rubbed with a wooden block covered with lead. This process created black dots to identify locations for stitches. Later, Stiles, and sometimes her children, worked for B.J. Bandy's "spread house" in Dalton from her home. (Courtesy Georgia Archives, Vanishing Georgia Collection, cat006.)

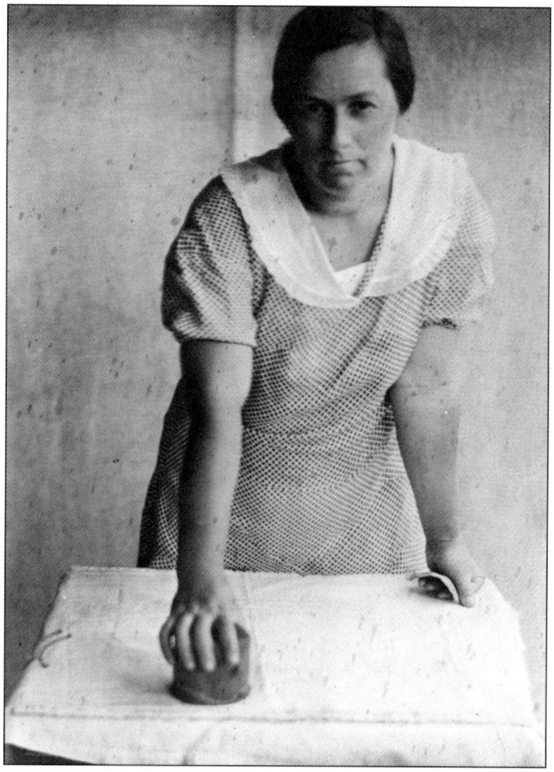

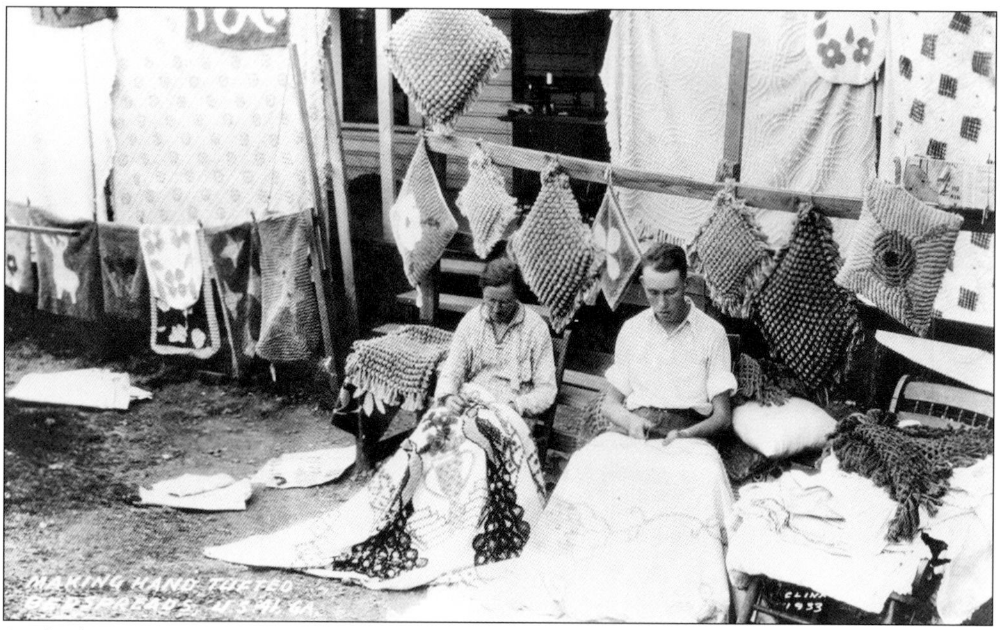

By the late 1920s, women made tufted bedspreads, rugs, and other garments in their homes and displayed them on clotheslines, or "spreadlines," along US Highway 41. Passersby would purchase the products as they traveled along this busy stretch of the Dixie Highway from Chattanooga to Atlanta. The road became known as Bedspread Boulevard by 1936 for the growing number of spreadlines. (Courtesy Georgia Archives, Vanishing Georgia Collection, brt122.)

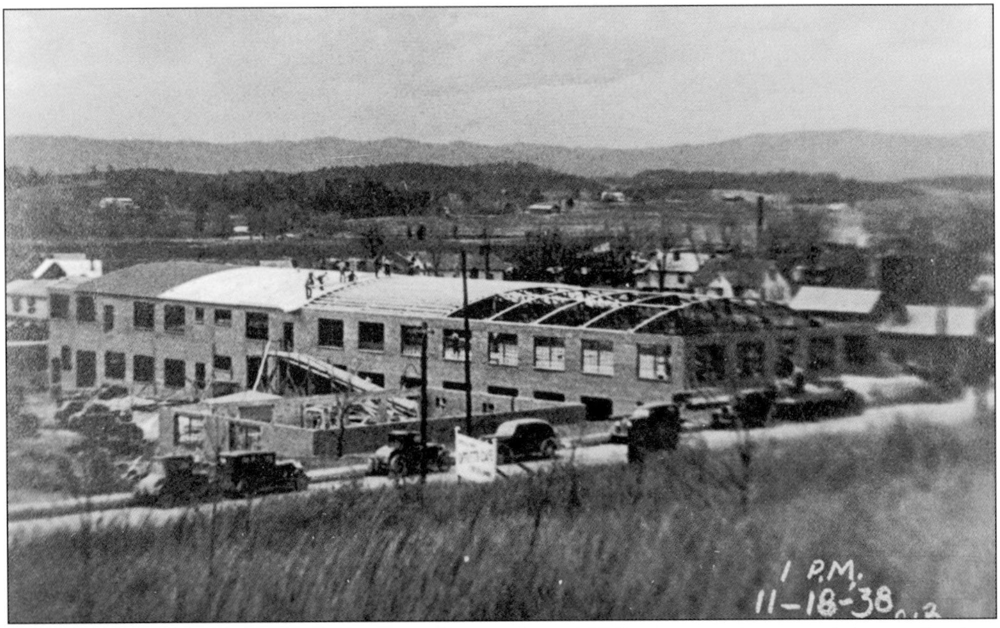

As chenille bedspreads became popular in the 1920s and 1930s, companies moved the production of spreads from homes and spread houses into small factories, such as Mount Alto Bedspread Company in Calhoun, shown under construction in this 1938 photograph. Later renamed Velvetone and Forrest Mills, this is thought to be one of the first modern tufting factories in the area. (Courtesy Gordon County Historical Society.)

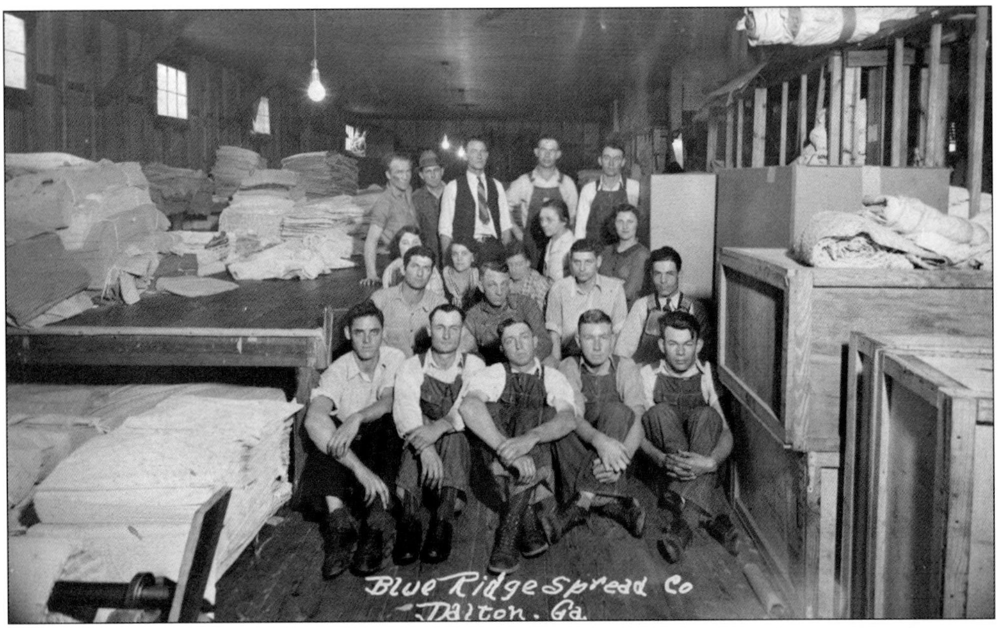

At first, candlewick and chenille tufted textiles were primarily a cottage industry of rural women in the Appalachia region. However, as women became successful, men started "hauling" businesses and spread houses. This 1950 photograph shows men working in the stamping department of the Blue Ridge Spread Company in Dalton. The stamped spreads would then be sent out for women to tuft in their homes. (Courtesy Georgia Archives, Vanishing Georgia Collection, wtf041.)

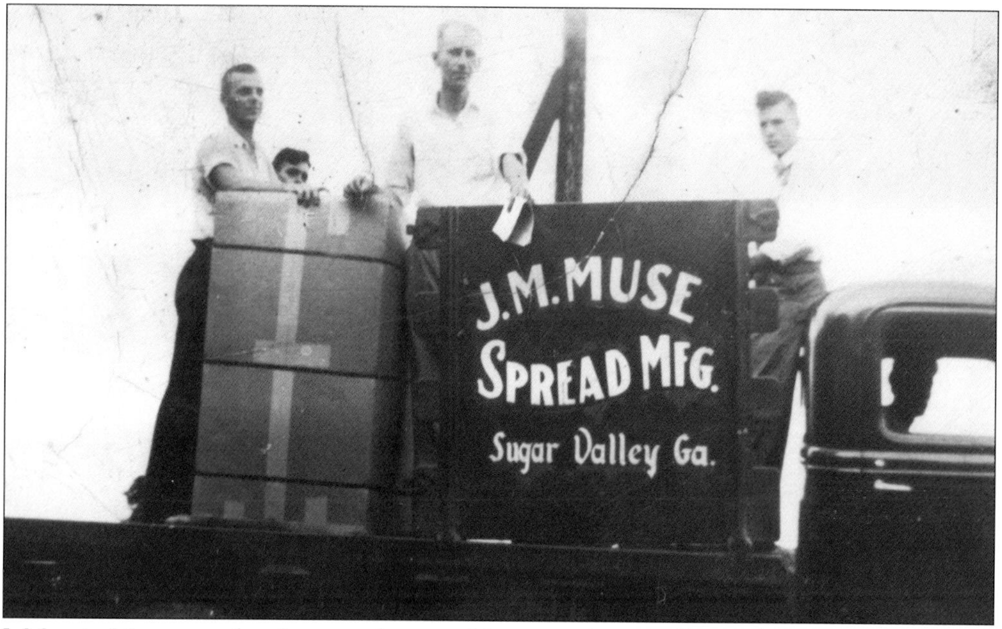

J. Marvin Muse owned and operated a spread house in Sugar Valley in the 1930s, as advertised on the truck seen in this 1940s photograph. One local resident recalls that families would "lay off the patterns" (stamp) and work them as they had time. "All of the work was paid in scrip," which "was only to be traded for items at Muse's General Store," according to the resident. (Courtesy Gordon County Historical Society.)

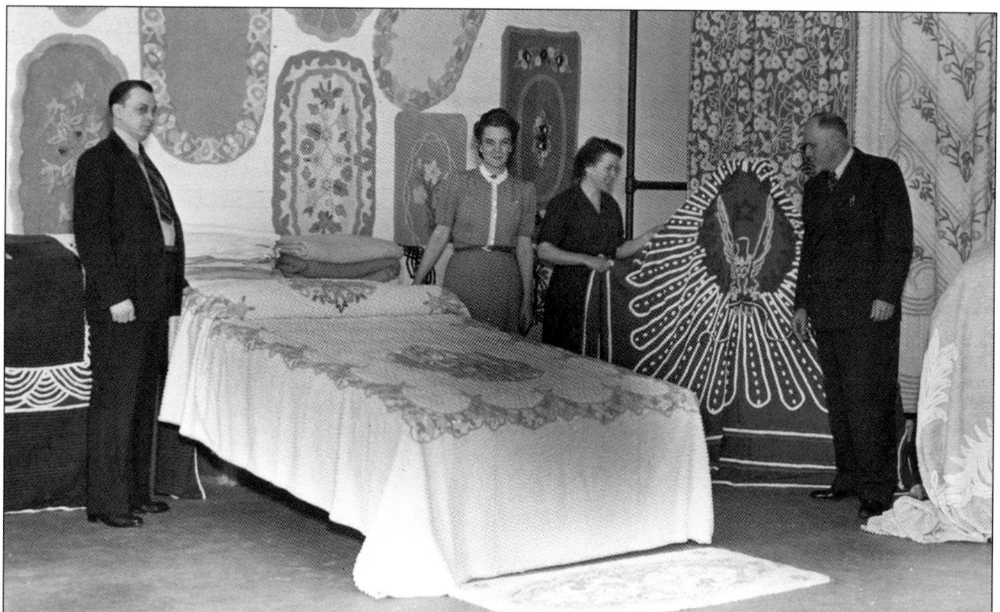

B.J. Bandy and his wife, Dicksie, entered the candlewick industry with Muse in the 1920s after Catherine Evans Whitener shared spread patterns with the couple. The Bandys went on to own and operate many other chenille businesses, including Bartow Textiles in Cartersville. In this c. 1945 photograph, B.J. Bandy (far right) entertains buyers in the Bartow Textiles showroom. (Courtesy Bartow History Museum.)

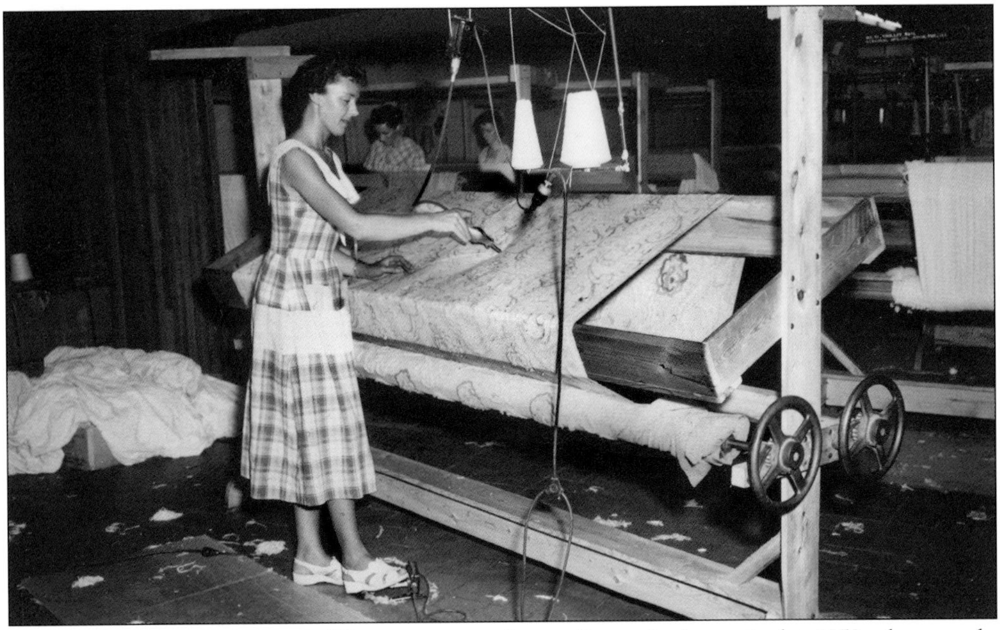

Hosiery manufacturer G. Lamar Westcott patented a needlepunch, shown in this 1950s photograph, which sped up the tufting process and produced more intricate designs than single-needle tufting machines. Westcott used the needlepunch to bring the production of tufted bedspreads into the Cabin Crafts factory he helped found in Dalton around 1931. This new tool revolutionized both the chenille and, later, carpet industries. (Courtesy Bandy Heritage Center for Northwest Georgia.)

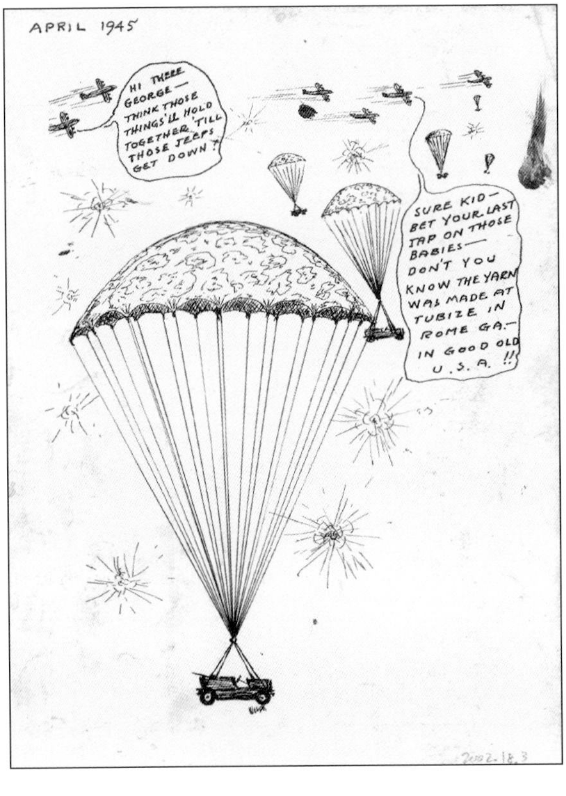

Textile mills across the region thrived with new military contracts during World War II. The Tubize company in Rome made parachute cloth and rope out of rayon. Paratroopers played an important role during the war. In 1940, the US military created its first parachute battalion and the first parachute school at Fort Benning. Displays for these Tubize products filled Rome store windows, advertising the company's contributions. (Courtesy Rome Area History Museum.)

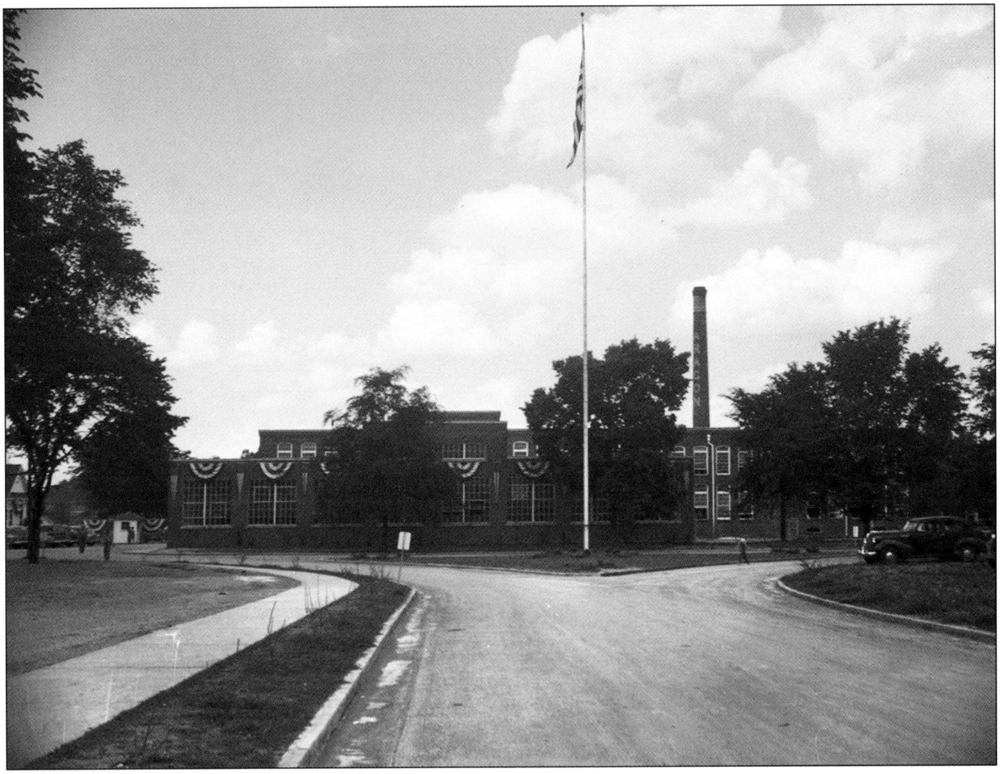

In 1943, Aragon Mills celebrated receiving the Army-Navy E-Award with patriotic buntings hanging from the front office building. The award recognized a company's continued production during wartime: making materials for the war effort, ensuring the quality and quantity of products, overcoming production obstacles, maintaining fair labor standards, training additional employees, and keeping good records for the health and safety of the workforce. (Courtesy Special Collections and Archives, Georgia State University Library.)

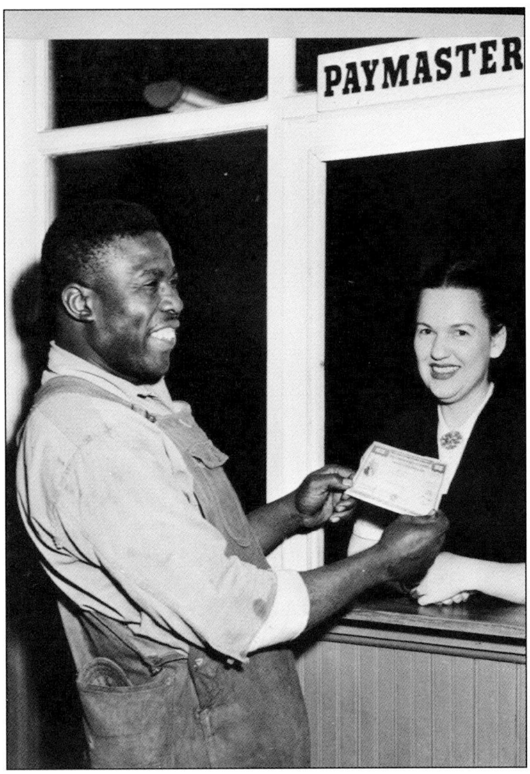

A black employee at the Cedartown Goodyear plant buys a war savings bond in 1943. African Americans benefited briefly from World War II. With critical labor shortages, black employees worked longer hours and sometimes received pay increases. Some companies hired African Americans to fill production lines, positions not previously available to them, but these jobs disappeared after the war. (Courtesy Georgia Archives, Vanishing Georgia Collection, plk136-84.)

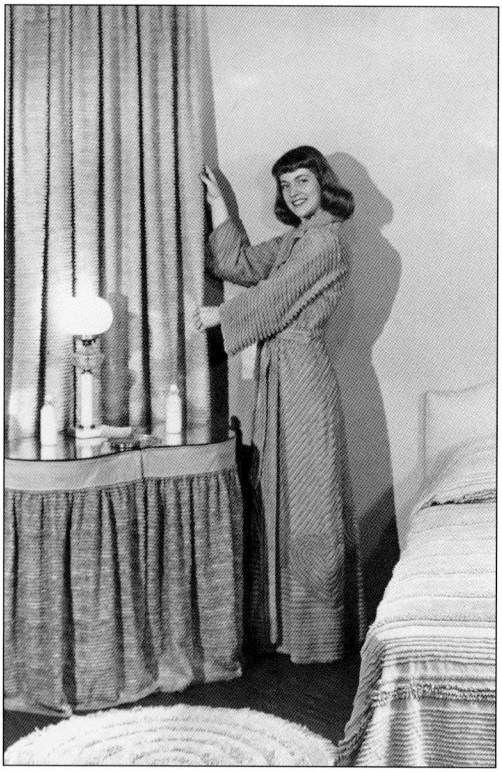

By the 1940s, tufting was no longer used simply for bedspreads or rugs. Chenille became fashionable throughout the household and in women's clothing, as seen in this c. 1960 advertisement test photograph. Chenille products were now sold across the country, creating a thriving industry in northwest Georgia until the 1960s and 1970s, when chenille ceased to be fashionable. Notice all the chenille products in this image. (Courtesy Bandy Heritage Center for Northwest Georgia.)

The popularity of the roadside chenille businesses and spreadlines declined between the 1940s and 1970s. As new technologies developed, tufted textiles continued to move from a home and spread house industry to factories. Here, a row of women machine tuft chenille bedspreads around 1960. This photograph was taken just six decades after Catherine Evans Whitener sold her first candlewick bedspread. (Courtesy Bandy Heritage Center for Northwest Georgia.)

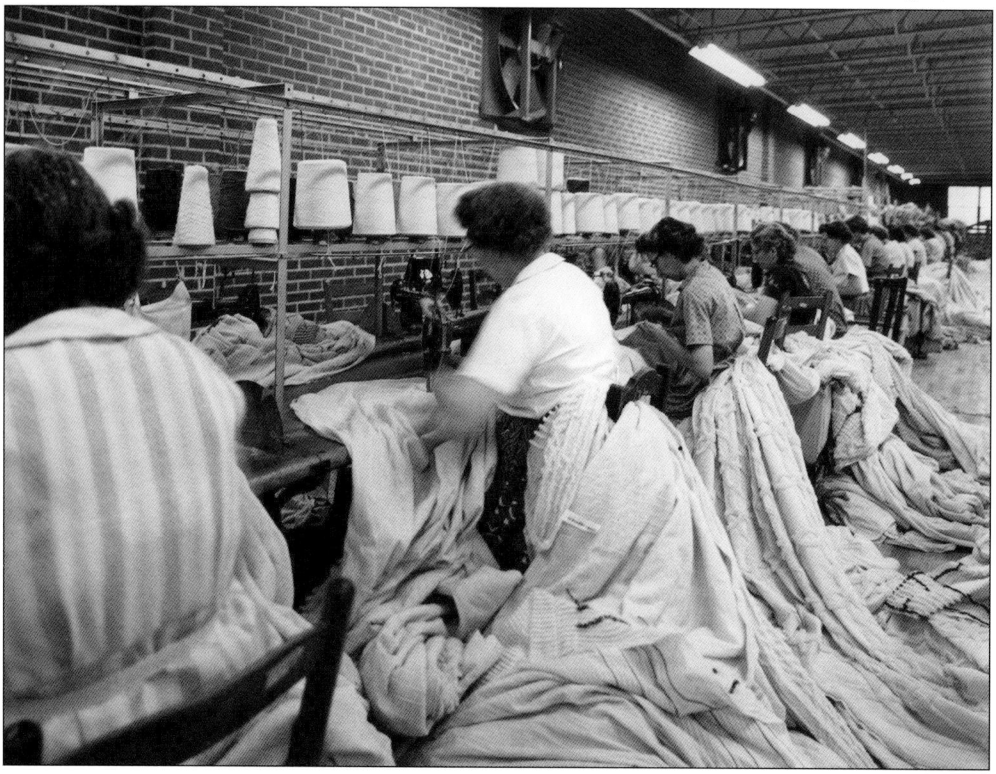

The rug in this photograph reads, "Home Means More with Carpet on the Floor." By the mid-20th century, the popularity of carpeted floor coverings began to shift one of the region's primary industries from chenille to carpet. The same technologies that spurred the development of chenille were used in the carpet industry that was established in northwest Georgia. Here, a carpet salesman discusses carpeting options with a customer around 1960. (Courtesy Bandy Heritage Center for Northwest Georgia.)

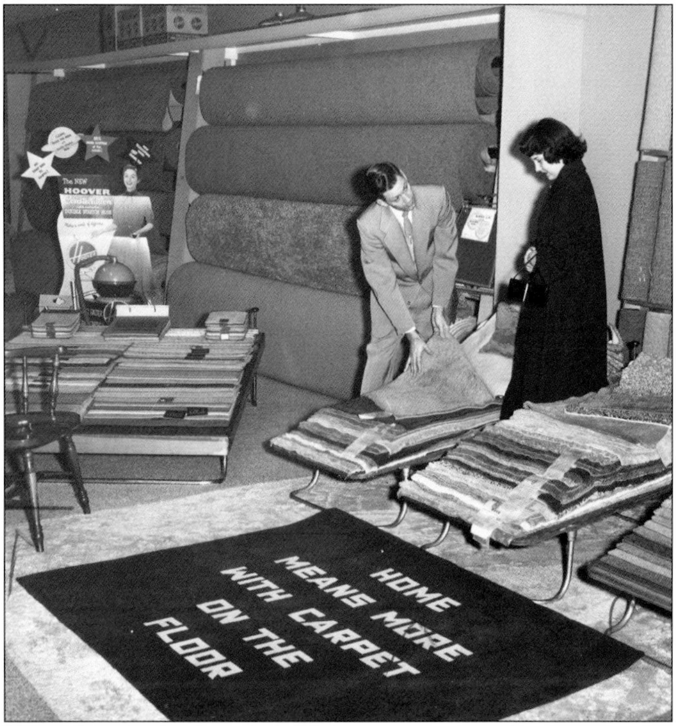

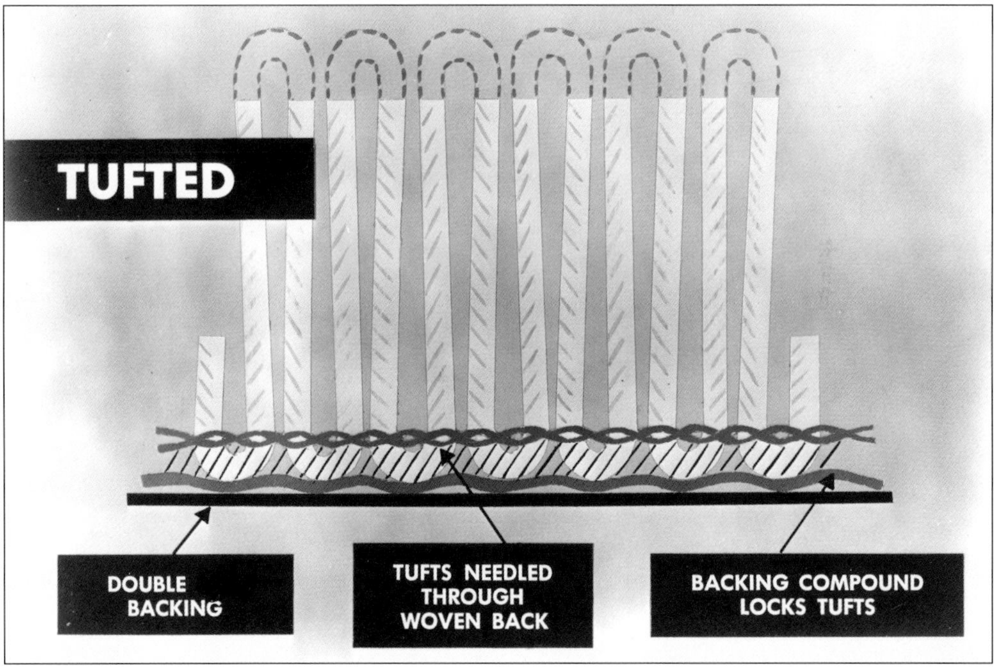

This diagram of tufted carpet depicts the similarities between candlewicking and machine-made carpets that were made in Dalton. The tufts were woven through the primary backing, and then the tufts were opened by shearing. This basic process is similar to candlewicking in that thread was woven through fabric and then cut open after a washing process, which created the soft tufts of thread. (Courtesy Bandy Heritage Center for Northwest Georgia.)

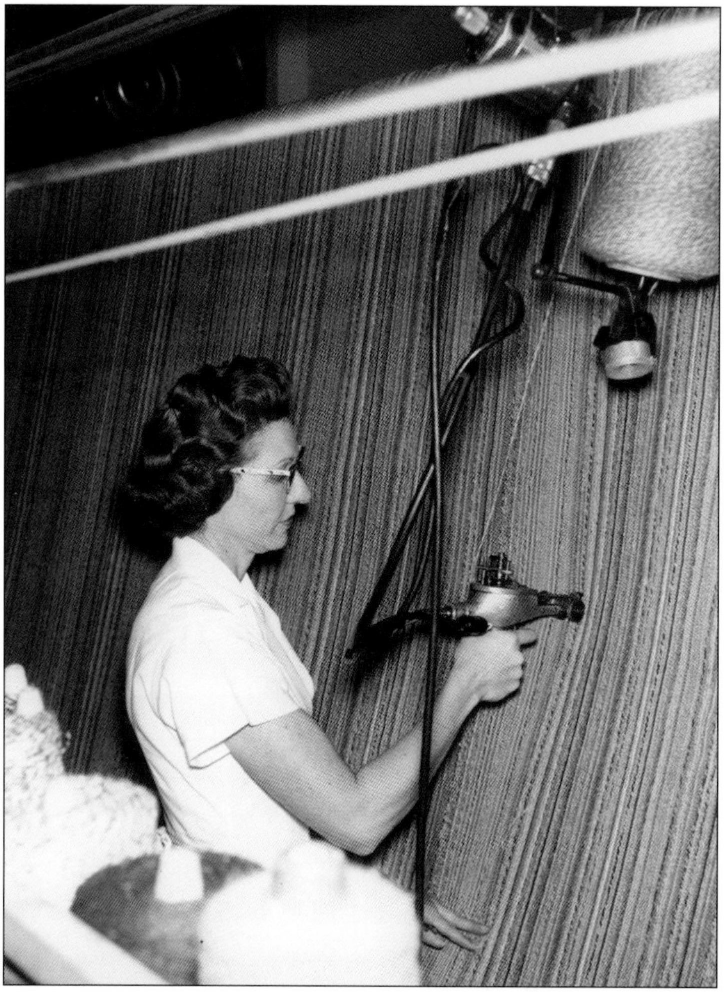

The needlepunch was used not only in chenille production, but also in carpet factories. In the c. 1960 photograph at left, a woman is using a needlepunch tool to correct imperfections in machine-tufted carpet, such as missing tufts or breaks in the tuft line. Similarly, the photograph below shows women smoothing the finish, or pile, of tufted carpet or correcting machine-made imperfections by hand, much like the worker using a needlepunch. (Both, courtesy Bandy Heritage Center for Northwest Georgia.)

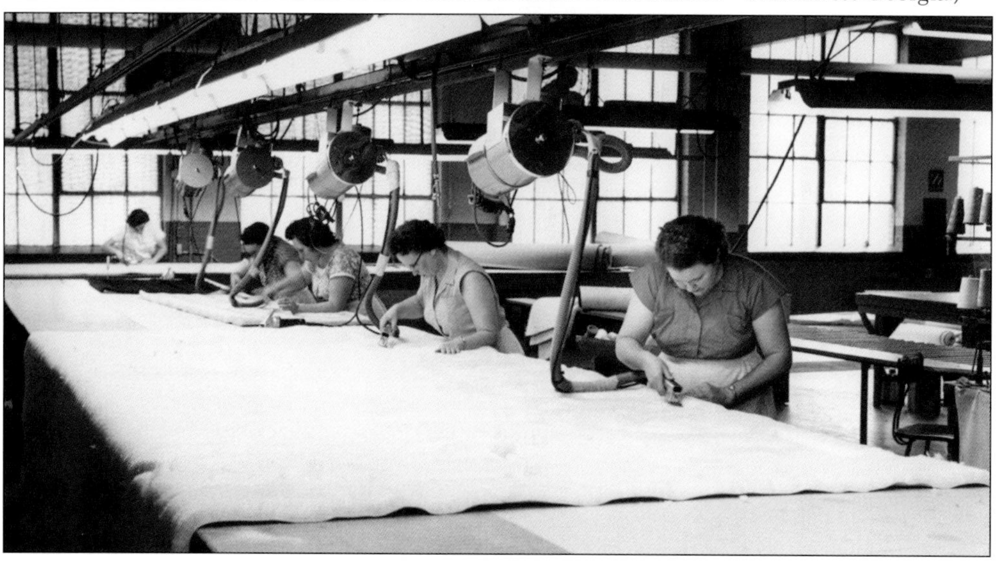

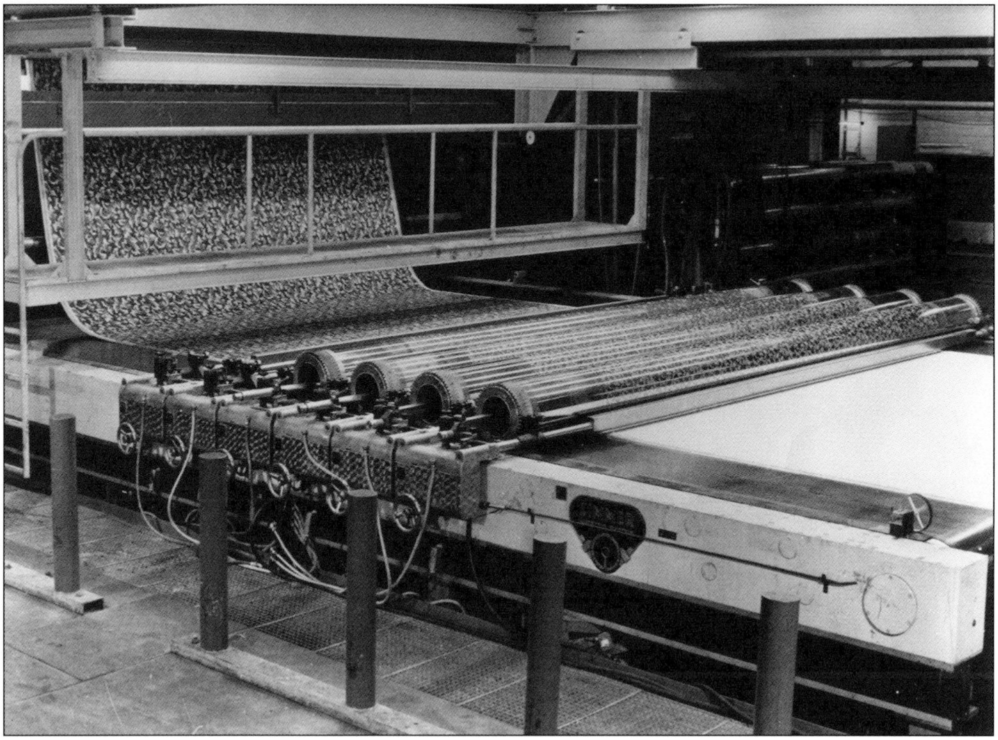

During the mid-20th century, and as the carpet industry grew, manufacturers in northwest Georgia began to incorporate new technologies that increased production and satisfied new trends. In this c. 1960 photograph, tufted carpet is being screenprinted with four different color applications. (Courtesy Bandy Heritage Center for Northwest Georgia.)

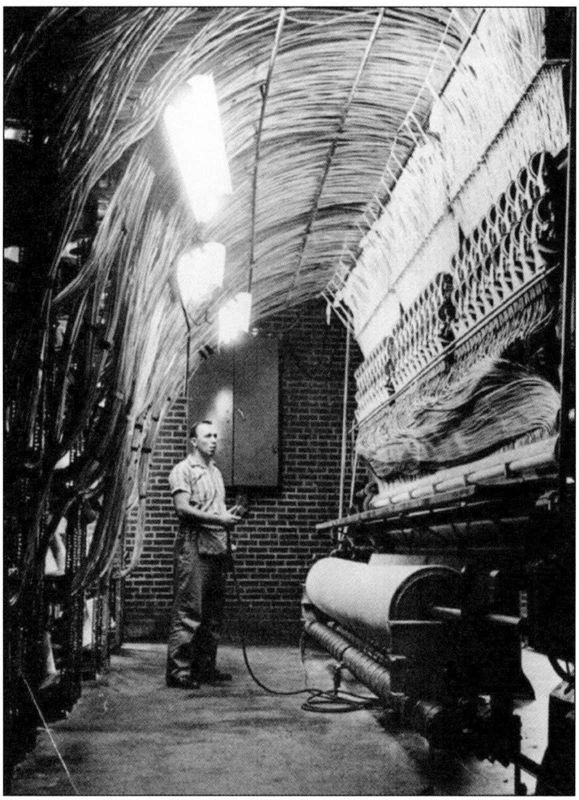

This image from Shaw Carpet Industry in 1964 shows the jet-air loom, a new machine that could thread the yarn at high speeds from the cones on the left through tubes. The jet-air loom kept the needles threaded and saved time by eliminating manual labor. By adopting modern technology, the carpet mills remained competitive after World War II. (Courtesy Shaw Industries.)

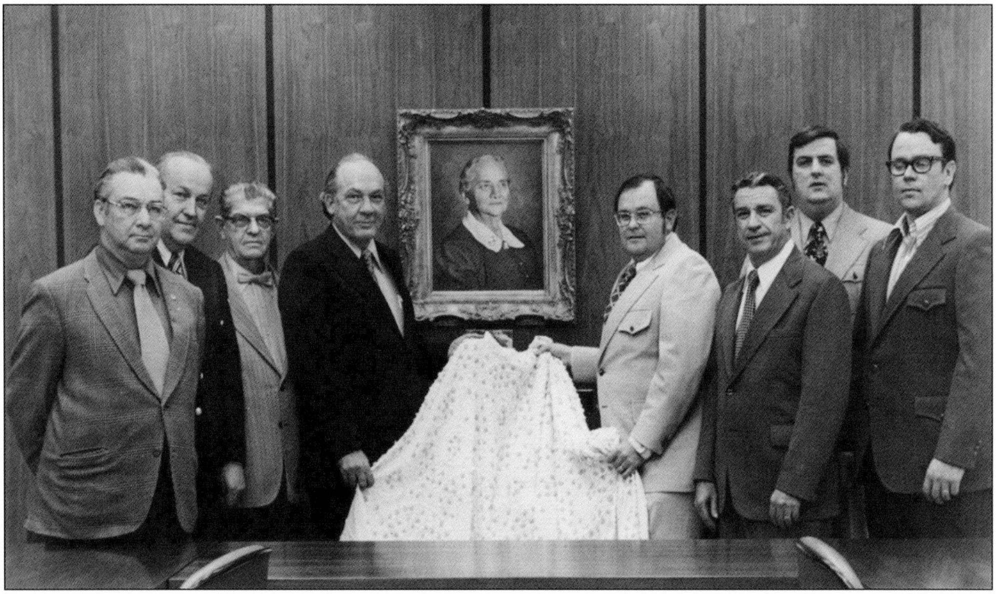

In 1971, the Carpet and Rug Institute (CRI) was founded in Dalton to serve the booming carpet industry in the region. In this photograph, inaugural members of the CRI's Bedspread Division, including Georgia Textile Corporation of Calhoun and Kuhlman Chenilles of Adairsville, hold a chenille bedspread as they stand in front of Catherine Evans Whitener's portrait. (Courtesy Bandy Heritage Center for Northwest Georgia.)

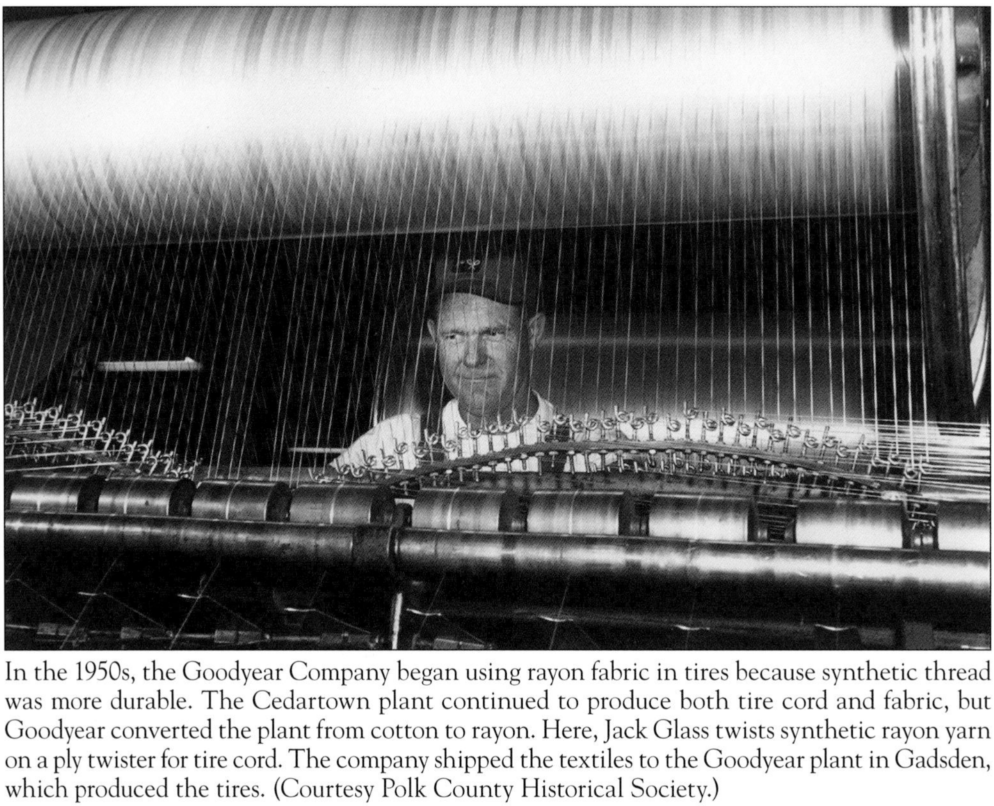

In the 1950s, the Goodyear Company began using rayon fabric in tires because synthetic thread was more durable. The Cedartown plant continued to produce both tire cord and fabric, but Goodyear converted the plant from cotton to rayon. Here, Jack Glass twists synthetic rayon yarn on a ply twister for tire cord. The company shipped the textiles to the Goodyear plant in Gadsden, which produced the tires. (Courtesy Polk County Historical Society.)

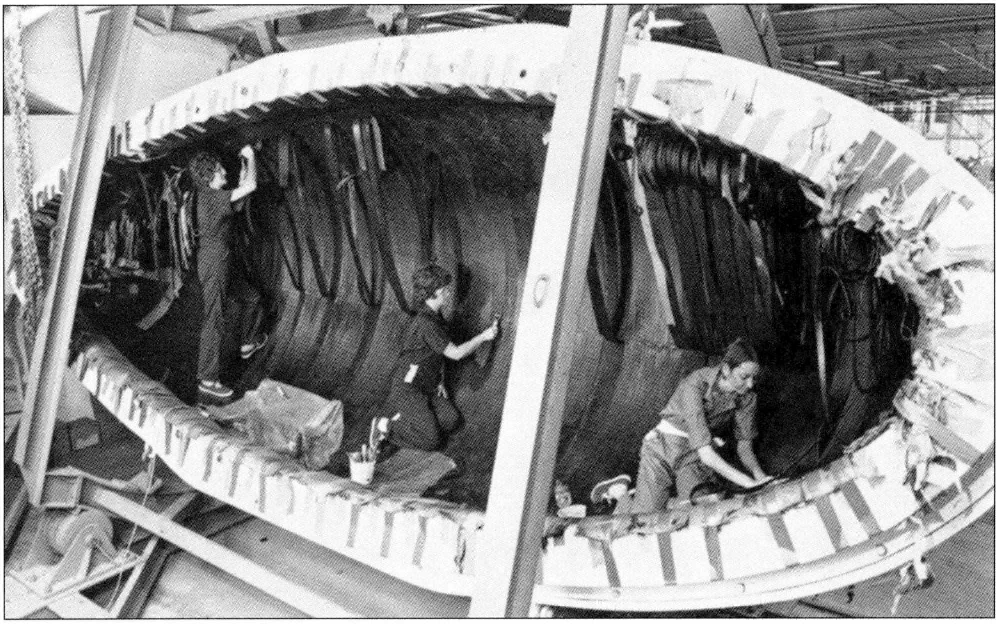

Goodyear converted its Rockmart plant entirely to rubber production in the early 1950s and removed all cotton operations. One of the first products employees made was this rubber life raft for the military. Later products included fuel cells, dunnage bags, oil containers, and even parade balloons and small parachutes for bombs. Although sold several times, the plant is still in operation as Meggitt Polymers and Composites. (Courtesy Rockmart Historical Museum.)

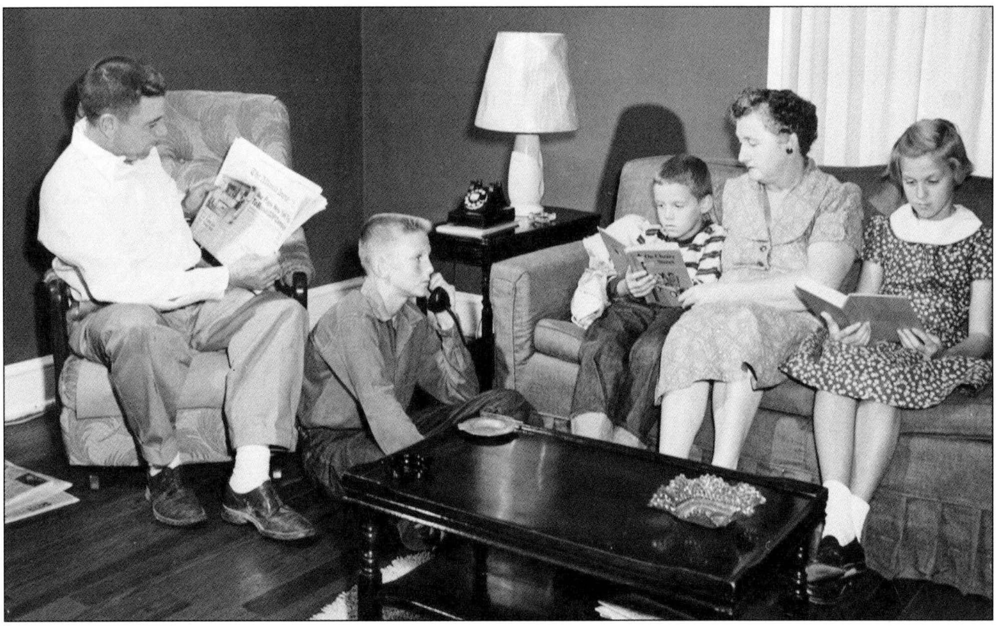

The Goodyear Company consistently promoted its plant and workforce as modern, compared to the traditional image of the mill family. This 1954 company photograph depicts a "typical Goodyear Mill family" living in one of the company homes in Rockmart. Note that most of the family members are reading and the son is talking on the phone in their up-to-date home. (Courtesy Georgia Archives, Vanishing Georgia Collection, plk178-84.)

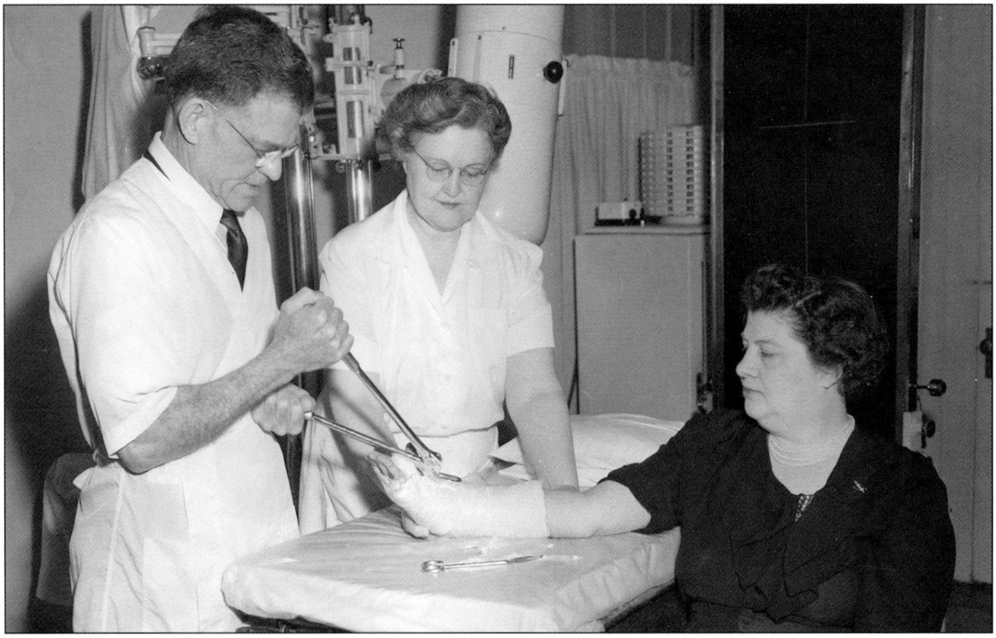

In the early to mid-20th century, some of the larger textile companies built medical clinics to serve their workers. In this 1943 photograph, a company doctor at the Goodyear clinic in Cedartown removes a cast from a female employee. The clinic also sponsored a blood drive that year and promoted health among employees. (Courtesy Polk County Historical Society.)

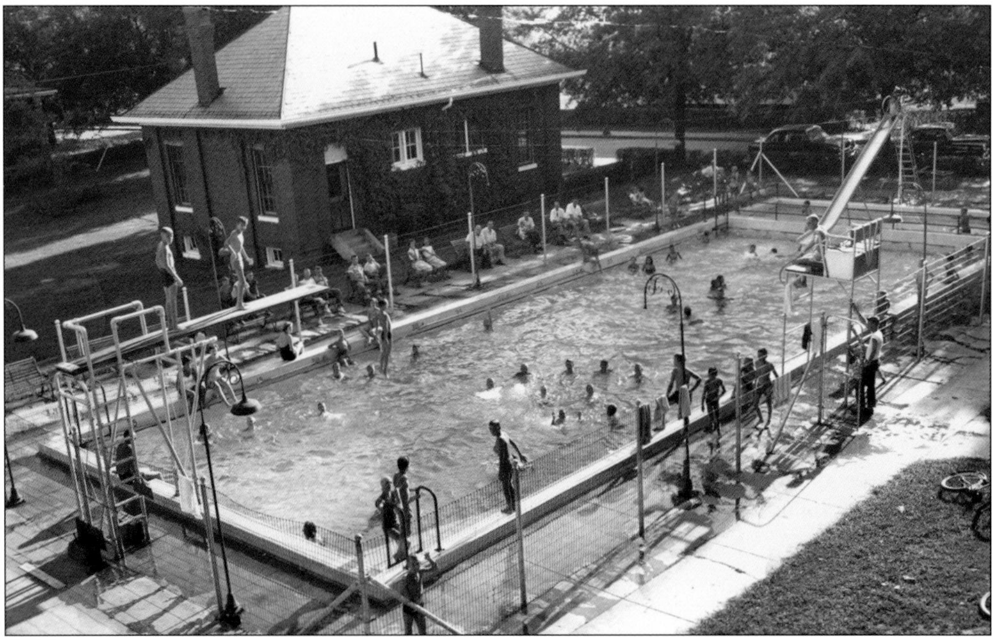

Goodyear and other large companies provided an array of recreational facilities for workers and their families. Here, employees and their families at the Cartersville plant enjoy the company pool during a hot summer day in the 1960s. The Cartersville company also provided ball fields, playgrounds, and parks, and sponsored athletic teams, volleyball games, and annual field days. (Courtesy Bartow History Museum.)

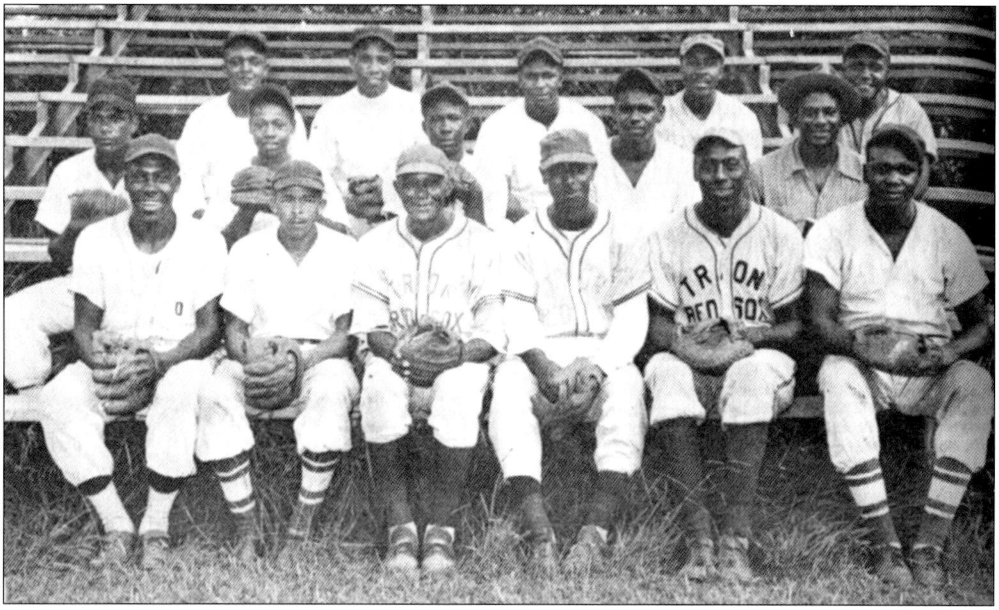

By the late 1930s and early 1940s, some textile companies sponsored African American baseball teams. The Trion Red Sox, shown here, earned an excellent record in 1952, with 21 wins and only five loses. African American teams played in separate leagues, but their games were a very popular source of entertainment in black communities during the Jim Crow era. Some team members went on to play in the Negro Leagues. (Courtesy Trion Public Library.)

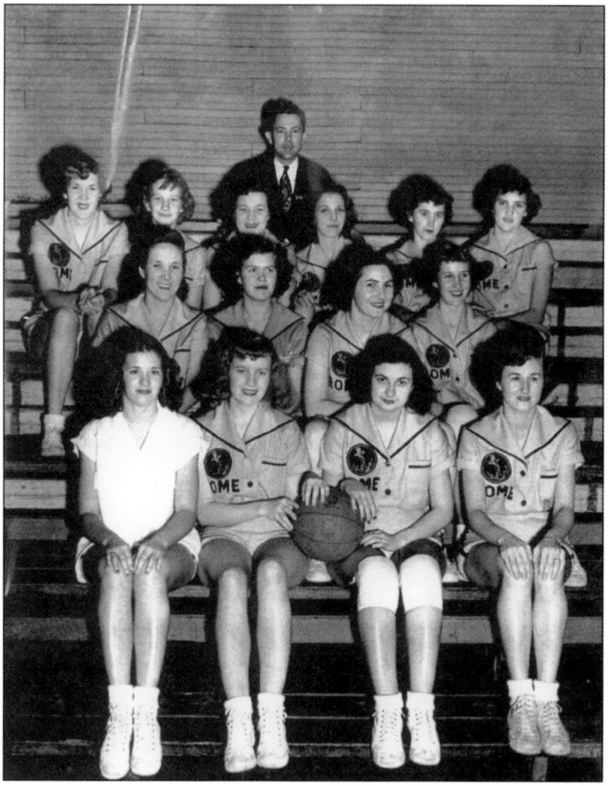

Southern textile companies began to sponsor women's teams in the 1920s and 1930s. This photograph features the women's basketball team from the Anchor Mill in Rome. Textile league teams were among the first opportunities for women to participate in organized sports, and basketball was by far the most popular in the mill communities. Southern textile leagues were influential in promoting basketball as a sport for women. (Courtesy Leon Shiver.)

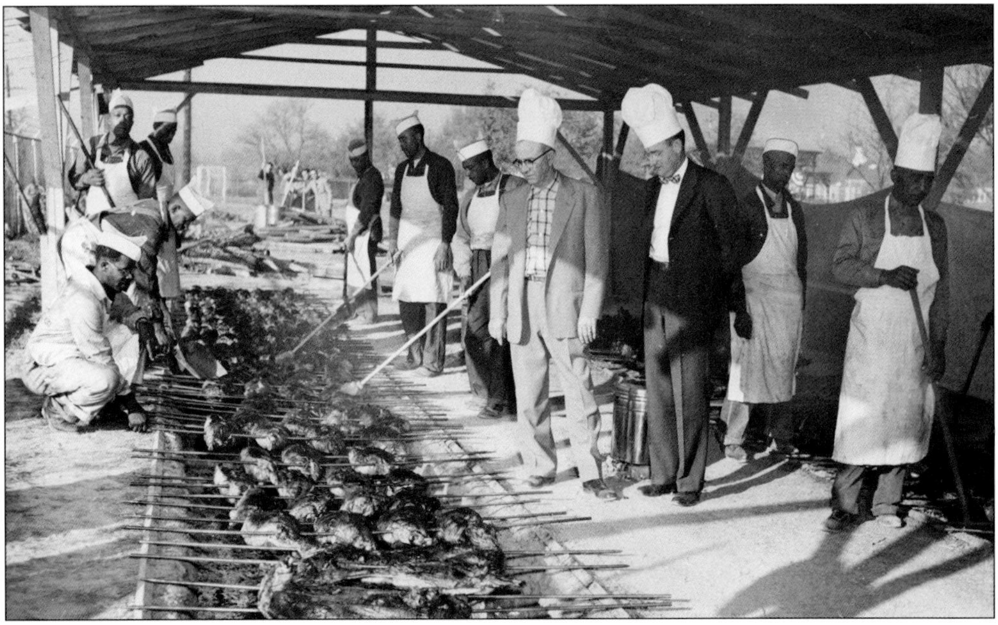

Many companies sponsored annual field days for their employees and families, and barbecue was a popular attraction. Here, company supervisors observe African American cooks preparing the meat over the pit at the Rockmart field day in 1950. In the Jim Crow era, African Americans worked the most menial jobs at the mill, but they could showcase their culinary skills at these events. (Courtesy Georgia Archives, Vanishing Georgia Collection, plk181-84.)

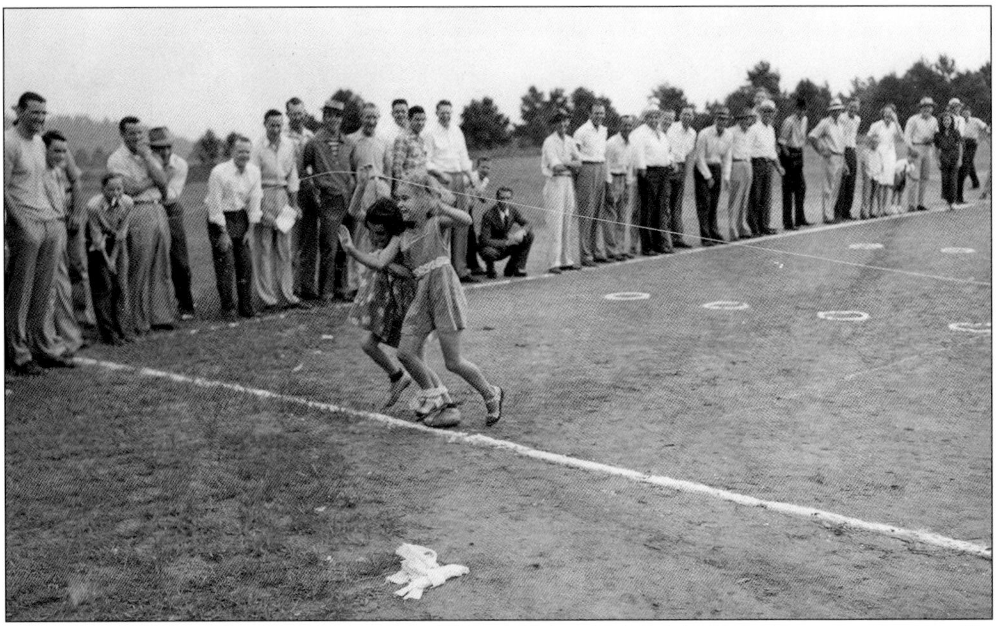

The Brighton Mills in Shannon organized this Fourth of July celebration for its employees. The event featured a parade, lunch, and activities for all members of the family, including this three-legged race for the children. These types of field day events brought the community together and promoted company pride. Note the parents proudly watching the races. (Courtesy Watters District Council for Historic Preservation.)

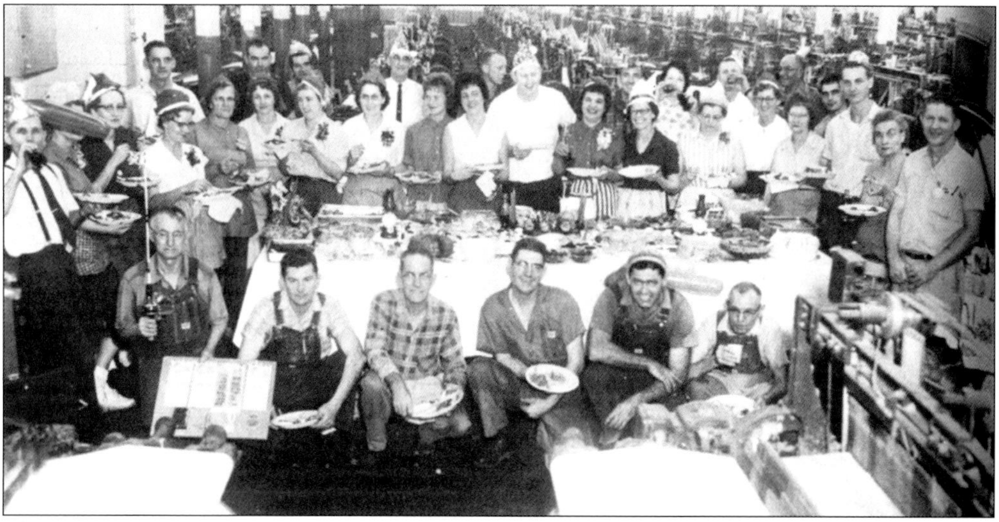

Christmas was an important time in southern mill villages, and companies sponsored celebrations for their employees. Here, the workers in the Riegel Mill weaving room in Trion enjoy a Christmas dinner on the mill floor in 1962. Workers brought in their favorite dishes to share and proudly displayed them for the photographer. Note the looms in the background. (Courtesy Trion Public Library.)

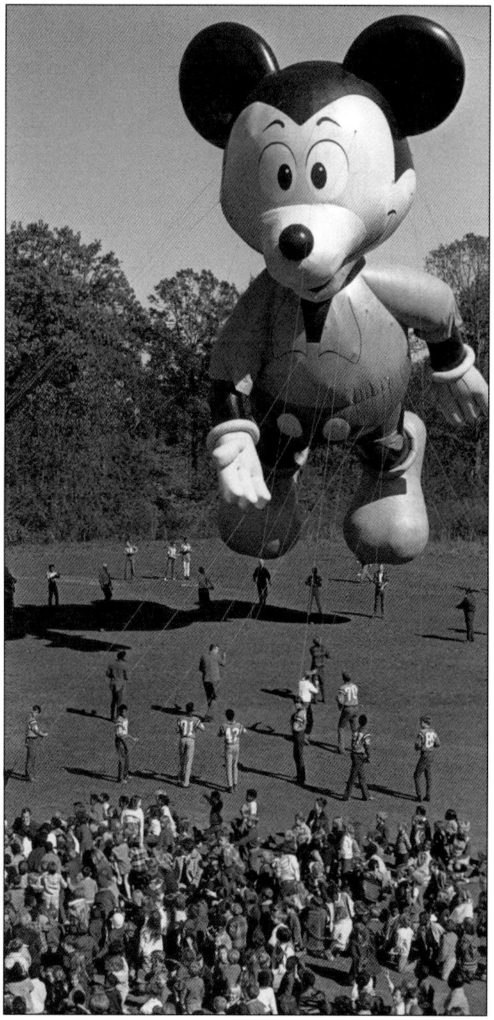

Goodyear employees and their families took great pride in the large rubber parade balloons produced at the Rockmart plant. Cedartown resident Linda Smith designed this Mickey Mouse balloon for the Macy's Thanksgiving Day Parade. The Rockmart plant employees made this and other balloons in the 1970s. (Courtesy Rockmart History Museum.)

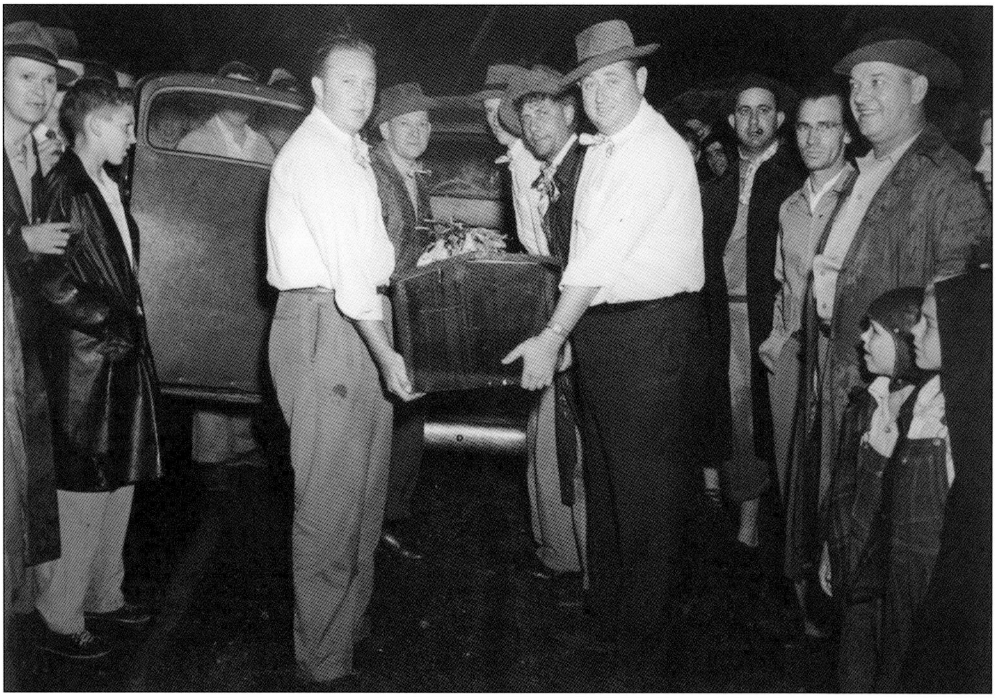

In 1946, the Congress of Industrial Organizations (CIO) began Operation Dixie to organize southern textile workers. Company owners countered that the union was communist. In 1947, Lindale workers who opposed the union held a funeral for the CIO in effigy, featuring a coffin, hearse, and gravestone, which read, "This is to signify that American citizens of Lindale, GA do not approve of the CIO and its communistic element." (Courtesy Daniel Scott Wilson.)

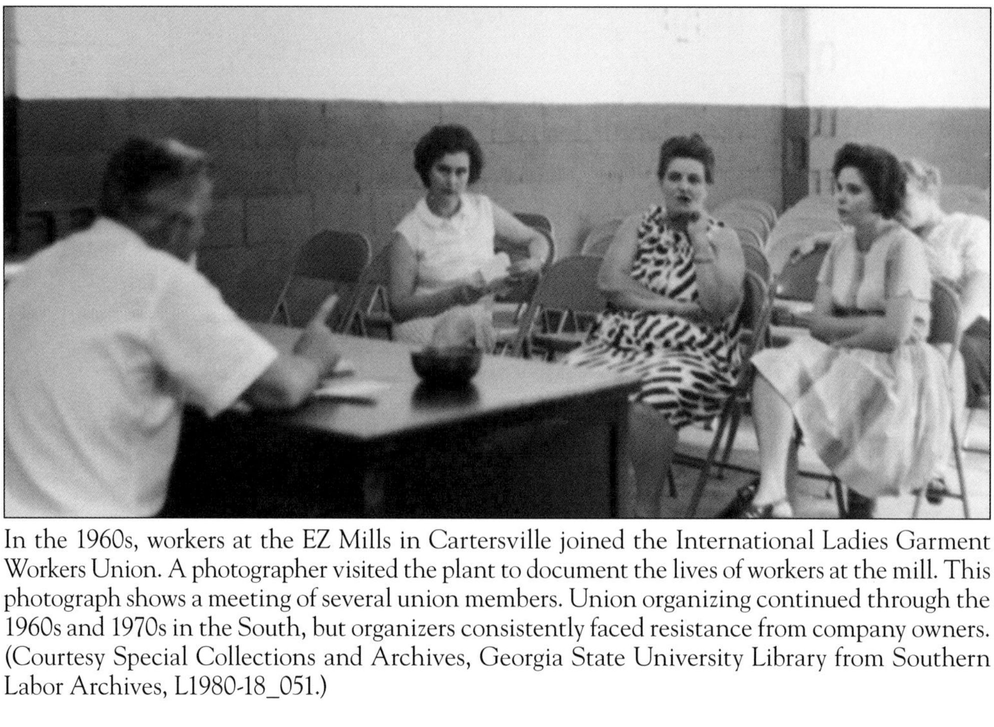

In the 1960s, workers at the EZ Mills in Cartersville joined the International Ladies Garment Workers Union. A photographer visited the plant to document the lives of workers at the mill. This photograph shows a meeting of several union members. Union organizing continued through the 1960s and 1970s in the South, but organizers consistently faced resistance from company owners. (Courtesy Special Collections and Archives, Georgia State University Library from Southern Labor Archives, L1980-18_051.)

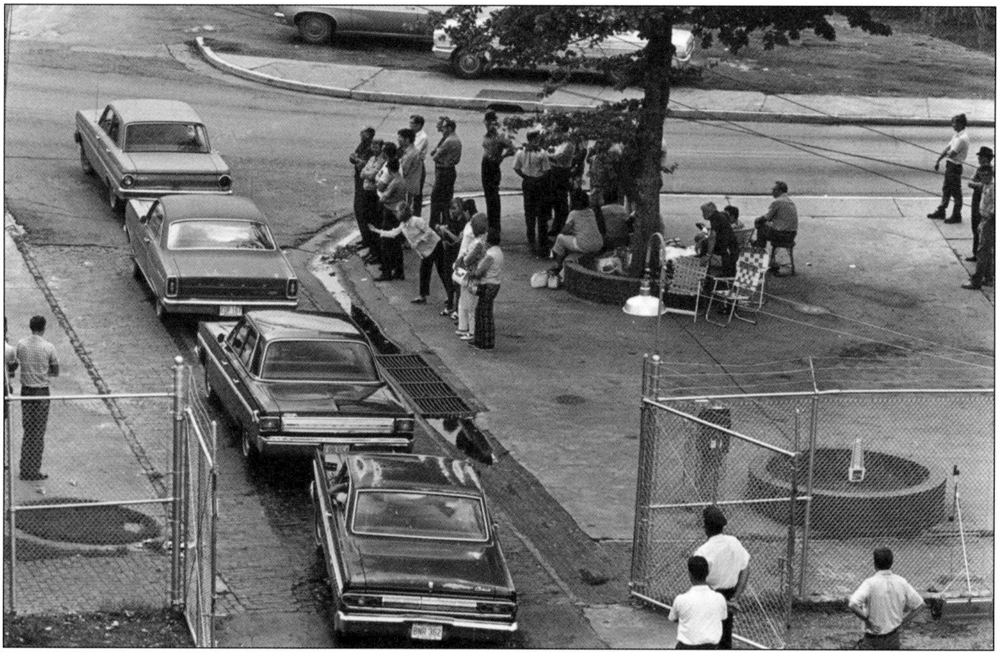

Striking workers with the Textile Union Workers of America (TUWA) line up at the main door of the WestPoint-Pepperell Company in Lindale in 1971 to keep employees from breaking the picket line. Supervisors carefully watched and identified the strikers through the company's surveillance system. WestPoint fought hard against all union efforts. (Courtesy Daniel Scott Wilson.)

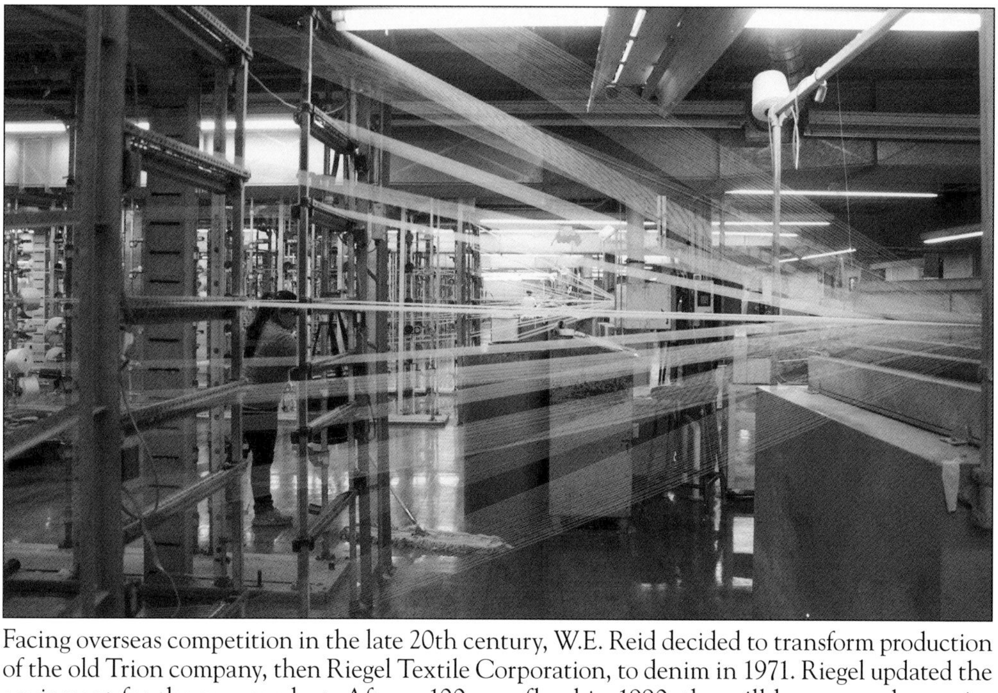

Facing overseas competition in the late 20th century, W.E. Reid decided to transform production of the old Trion company, then Riegel Textile Corporation, to denim in 1971. Riegel updated the equipment for the new product. After a 100-year flood in 1990, the mill began another major modernization campaign. Now Mount Vernon Mills, the company produces over a million yards of denim fabric daily. (Photograph by Kymberli Darling.)

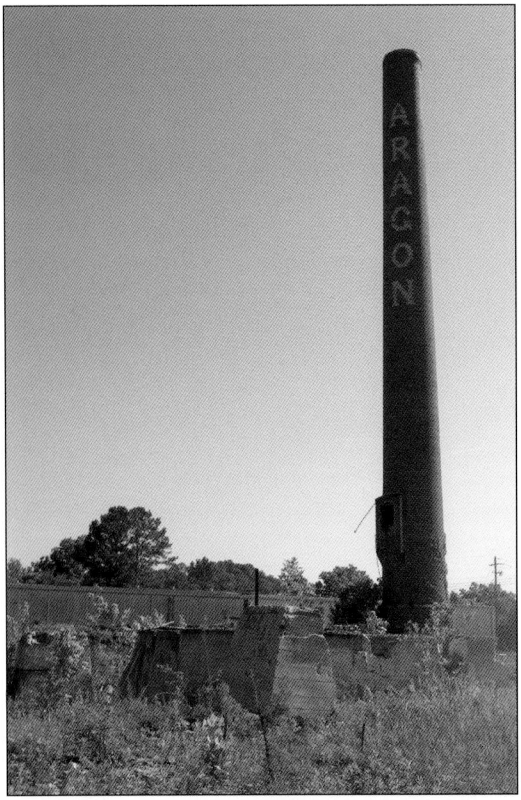

Aragon Mills opened in 1899 with New York investors, and established a close-knit mill village. After the mill closed in 1970, Si Khan, an activist and folk musician, wrote "Aragon Mills" about the closing and its impact on the community. "There's no smoke at all comin' out of the stack, for the mill has pulled out and they ain't comin' back," he sang. (Photograph by Janae Hightower.)

Benjamin Prater built a cotton gin, wool carder, grist mill, saw mill, and syrup mill in 1855. In 1977, the Prater's Mill Foundation acquired the cotton gin, dismantling and moving it to Varnell. Today, visitors to this historic site can see a cotton gin and an excellent collection of chenille products. This photograph shows the lint flue in the foreground, with the gin in the background. (Courtesy Ann McCleary.)

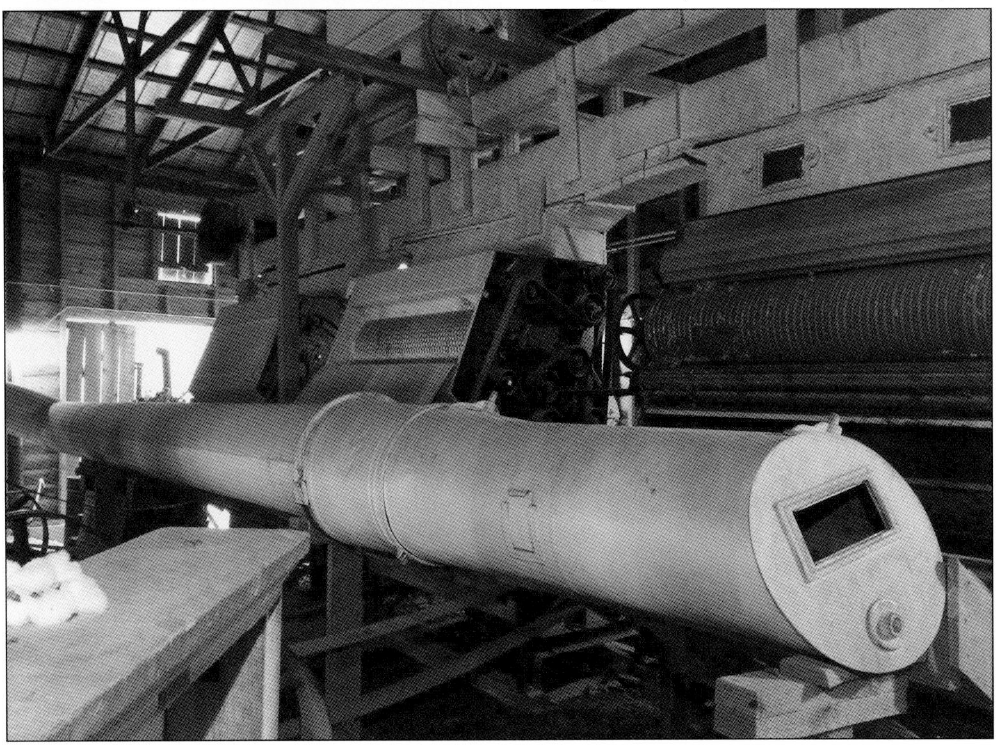

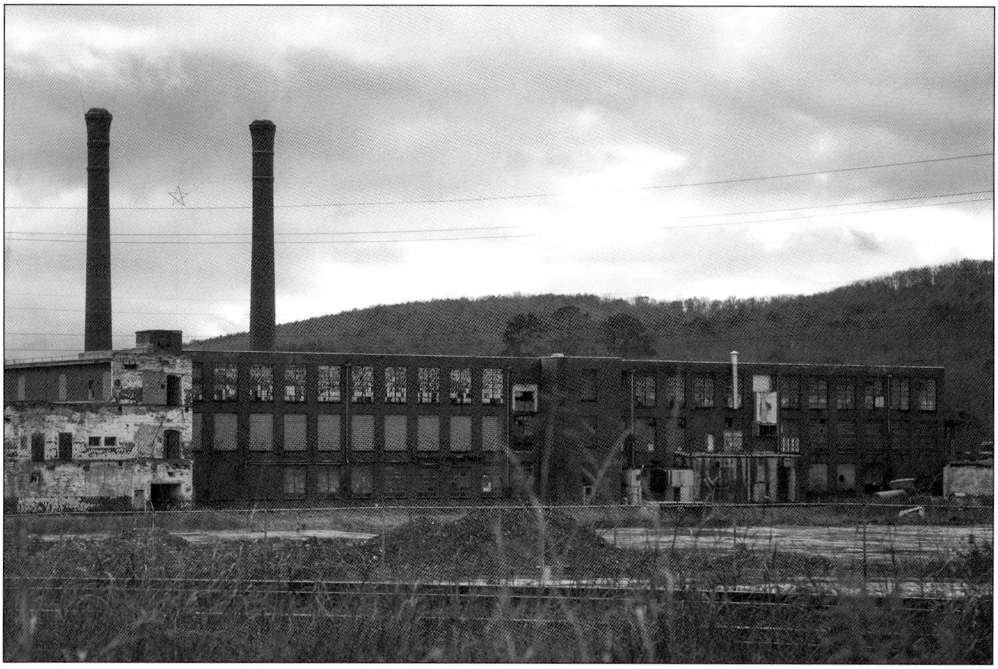

In 1933, several employees of Pepperell Manufacturing Company in Lindale made a wooden star, lined with lights, to hang between the mill's smokestacks at Christmas and inspire the workers during the Great Depression. The event became such an important part of the community Christmas celebration that residents continued the tradition even after the mill closed in 2001. This image shows the raising of the star in 2014. (Photograph by Patrick J. Elias.)

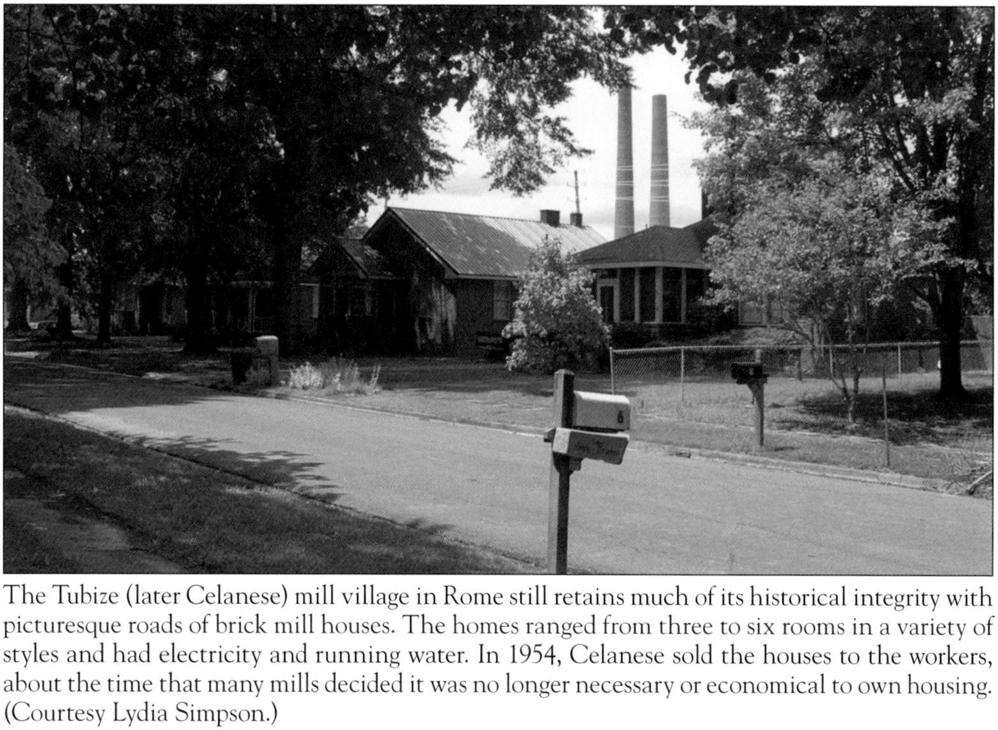

The Tubize (later Celanese) mill village in Rome still retains much of its historical integrity with picturesque roads of brick mill houses. The homes ranged from three to six rooms in a variety of styles and had electricity and running water. In 1954, Celanese sold the houses to the workers, about the time that many mills decided it was no longer necessary or economical to own housing. (Courtesy Lydia Simpson.)

Consistent with our mission to preserve history on a local level, this book was printed in South Carolina on American-made paper and manufactured entirely in the United States. Products carrying the accredited Forest Stewardship Council (FSC) label are printed on 100 percent FSC-certified paper.